A Practical Guide to Middle and Secondary Social Studies

A Practical Guide to Middle and Secondary Social Studies

Second Edition

JUNE R. CHAPIN

Notre Dame de Namur University

PEARSON

Boston ■ New York ■ San Francisco
Mexico City ■ Montreal ■ Toronto ■ London ■ Madrid ■ Munich ■ Paris
Hong Kong ■ Singapore ■ Tokyo ■ Cape Town ■ Sydney

Series Editor: Kelly Villella Canton
Series Editorial Assistant: Angela Pickard
Executive Marketing Manager: Krista Clark
Editorial-Production Service: Omegatype Typography, Inc.
Composition Buyer: Linda Cox
Manufacturing Buyer: Linda Morris
Electronic Composition: Omegatype Typography, Inc.
Photo Researcher: Omegatype Typography, Inc.
Cover Administrator: Kristina Mose-Libon

For related titles and support materials, visit our online catalog at www.ablongman.com.

Between the time web site information is gathered and published, some sites may have closed. Also, the transcription of URLs can result in typographical errors. The publisher would appreciate notification where these errors occur so that they may be corrected in subsequent editions.

Library of Congress Cataloging-in-Publication Data

Chapin, June R.
    A practical guide to middle and secondary social studies / June R. Chapin.—2nd ed.
      p. cm.
    Includes bibliographical references and index.
    ISBN 0-205-49243-6
    1. Social sciences—Study and teaching (Secondary) I. Title.
  H62.C358 2007
  300.71'2—dc22
                                                      2006043190

Printed in the United States of America

10 9 8 7 6 5 4 3 2 1   11 10 09 08 07 06

Photo credits appear on p. 269, which constitutes a continuation of the copyright page.

Brief Contents

Contents

Chapter 4   Active, Student-Centered Strategies   91

Chapter 6   Teaching History   154

Chapter 7   Teaching Geography, Economics, and the Behavioral Sciences   185

Chapter 8   Teaching Civic Education and Global Education   213

Preface

■ NEW TO THIS EDITION

The revisions in this new edition reflect important trends impacting the teaching of middle school and secondary social studies. The 2001 No Child Left Behind (NCLB) legislation mandated that all students have the right to learn. The teaching of social studies has changed and continues to change due to this increased accountability by the federal and state governments through standards and testing. Now, more attention is being given to achievement gaps of low-achieving students in a high accountability–focused environment. NCLB is forcing social studies teachers to focus more on the teaching of reading, especially vocabulary, because reading is related to social studies achievement. Along with the new essay incorporated into the SAT, writing is being emphasized more in many classrooms, as well. In addition, it is necessary to foster a workforce that values and rewards thinking skills, problem solving, creativity, and teamwork. More emphasis, therefore, is being given in this edition to reading, writing, and thinking skills in the social studies.

As a consequence, this edition presents new units, including three units showing different ways to teach the American Revolution. New lesson plans, new sample classroom episodes, controversial issues, resources, and web sites reflect the recent trends. Recent research is emphasized, and the whole text has been infused with attention to technology. Chapter 9 presents new material on wireless technology, WebQuests, handheld computers, tablet PCs, blogs, and computer security. Every chapter contains new material reflecting recent trends. In particular, more attention has been given to differentiated instruction, English language learners, primary sources, reading nonfiction, concepts, NCLB, gender issues, the Civic Mission of Schools, the teaching of religion, and globalization.

Concurrent with NCLB is mounting criticism of how both middle and secondary schools are to meet the needs of all students in a changing global economy. Dropout rates of African Americans and Latinos are getting more attention. Therefore, school reform and redesigning schools for a changing world at both the middle and high school levels will have an impact on the teaching of social studies.

In light of these trends, all the revisions in this text strive to teach social studies creatively and thoughtfully to better serve the needs of all students. Students *can* become engaged in learning in their social studies classrooms.

■ ORGANIZATION OF TEXT

Let us look at the organization of this text. The first chapter discusses the basic middle school and high school social studies curriculum. Then, for clarity, the next four chapters can be considered as a unit. Chapter 2 focuses on planning, Chapters 3 and 4 on instructional strategies, and Chapter 5 on assessment. In practice, all are interrelated. When you start to think of *what* content or skill you choose, you have to decide *how* you are going to teach it (methods) and then how you will *assess* what has been taught. The emphases on history, geography, economics, and civics are the main thrust of most states' social studies standards, and this text aims to help teachers in these important curriculum areas. Therefore, the next three chapters focus on the teaching of history; geography, economics, and the behavioral sciences; and civic and global education. Finally, Chapter 9 examines both technology and professional growth.

■ TO THE STUDENT

You, like most individuals preparing to become a middle or secondary social studies teacher, already believe that the major goal of social studies education is citizenship education. You recognize the importance of this goal and that *all* students must be prepared to interact with the increasing diversity of their communities and the nation, as well as with the complexity of global issues that are shaping the world. Although we are all unique individuals, we share the responsibility of helping to develop knowledgeable and responsible citizens who act on core values and beliefs. How to incorporate the best teaching practices and creative enthusiasm in the classroom is the main focus of this textbook. Lesson plans, units, and instructional resources listed throughout the text suggest activities you can try as you participate in the classroom. The small group and individual exercises integrated into all the chapters can help you more thoroughly explore the key issues the text introduces. The text encourages you to be a more active teacher rather than a passive one in the hope that the students in your classrooms will also be encouraged to play active rather than passive roles. At the end of each chapter, a controversial issue is summarized to expose you to current issues in education.

■ ACKNOWLEDGMENTS

Many thanks to the countless students and colleagues who have contributed to this text. I owe a great intellectual debt to all of them. Special praise to Ray McHugh, who has throughout many years always patiently and carefully critiqued my professional work. Our reviewers, in particular, served an important role in improving and updating this text for the second edition: Timothy Anderson, Nebraska Wesleyan University; Judy Butler, State University of West Georgia; James K. Daly, Seton Hall University; Ray Dusseau, Wisconsin Lutheran College; and Glenda Moss, Indiana University–Purdue University Fort Wayne.

June R. Chapin

A Practical Guide to Middle and Secondary Social Studies

Chapter 1

Middle and Secondary Social Studies

Before giving practical guidance in the teaching of social studies, this chapter discusses the underlying elements of the present social studies curriculum. The following topics are covered here:

- Why Become a Social Studies Teacher?
- What Should Be Taught? State Standards and No Child Left Behind
- What Is "Social Studies"? A Single-Subject Discipline?
- Why Should Social Studies Be Taught? Goals of Civic Education
- What Content Should Be Taught, and When?
- Should Values and Character Education Be Taught?

■ WHY BECOME A SOCIAL STUDIES TEACHER?

You have already enrolled in a class preparing you to become a social studies teacher. What factors influenced your decision? Jot down how some of the following were influential, and to what extent:

Had inspiring and interesting social studies teachers

Family member(s) was a teacher

Want to be of service to others

Like to read historical novels

Care about children/young people

Like the subject matter

Enjoy visiting historical sites and other travel

Received good grades in social studies courses

Interested in political issues

Member of student council or other organizations such as Model U.N.

Worked with youth groups such as those sponsored by churches

Always wanted to be a teacher and join an important profession

Desire to change or reform present system

Schedule of hours and summer vacation can permit family activities, travel, hobbies, and the like

SMALL GROUP WORK	**WHO SHOULD BE A SOCIAL STUDIES TEACHER?**
1.1	*Share your list with other members of the class. The list contains some characteristics of teachers in general as well as some more specific to social studies teachers. Yet we all know that teachers are diverse and come from varied backgrounds with many motives for wanting to teach. Every teacher is unique.*

After sharing your list, think about what criteria you think there should be for individuals who want to be a social studies teacher. Do you think there should be different standards for middle school social studies teachers? For high school social studies teachers? A common observation is that many middle school teachers lack subject matter competency, and that many high school teachers need to use better educational methods to motivate student learning.

Now compare your criteria with those required for the certification of social studies teachers by your state.

Certification

You, as a new teacher, now need to be a "highly qualified" teacher in the subject you teach. In an effort to support quality learning and instruction, one provision of the No Child Left Behind (NCLB) Act of 2001 requires that there be a qualified teacher in *each* content area that students are required to take. The more controversial element of the testing mandate of NCLB is discussed in Chapter 5.

Almost all teachers, 92 percent, have full, regular teaching certificates (Ingersoll, 2003). But experts identified a serious problem: Too many teachers were teaching "out of their subject field." At the middle school level, some teachers did not have enough educational units in the subject they were teaching. At the secondary level, about one-fifth of classes in math, science, English, and social studies was taught by teachers who lacked full teaching certificates in those subjects. Disadvantaged schools were more likely to have misassigned teachers, and these teachers were most likely to be concentrated in the lower-tracked classes.

The No Child Left Behind Act defines *qualified teachers* as those with a college degree, a teaching certificate, and competence in their subject. Competence in a subject is to be demonstrated by having a major, an advanced certificate, or passing a test in the subject. However, each state is charged with determining what constitutes a highly qualified teacher in the different subject areas and grade levels for that state. Each state defines how many units constitute a major and what is required for teacher certification. Not everyone is satisfied with these certification requirements. For example, conservatives (Stotsky, 2004) and a few teacher educators believe that many of our history teachers do not know enough history and therefore depend too much on textbooks.

About forty-two states require some form of teacher test. The main effort to improve teacher quality is through entry-level testing of basic skills such as reading and math. Over half of the states require high school teachers to pass a subject-knowledge test to receive a license. *The rationale for this is that knowledge of subject matter is essential for successful teaching.* The more a teacher knows and the more skill a teacher has, the more likely the students are to learn.

In addition, pedagogical (teaching methods) knowledge is tested in about half of the states. However, it is recognized that tests of content and pedagogical knowledge are incomplete measures for evaluating a teacher. Therefore, a student-teaching assignment or internship to prepare students to deal with the realities of the classroom is required in almost all states. "Out in the field," the human dimensions of the prospective teacher, such as caring and perseverance, are really assessed. Does the teacher exhibit positive personal interactions with students? Does the candidate command the attention and respect of students? Is the teacher enthusiastic? Can the beginning social studies teacher guide students' understanding and deepen their insights into the subject? These and other questions are the true test for successful teaching. Increasingly, states are requiring a more careful assessment of the student-teaching or internship experience.

Your Background as an Influence

Reflecting on your background and motivation is important as you start your social studies teaching career. This is because we all tend to model the teachers that we had. Your days as a student in social studies classes are influencing what you think a good social studies program is and what methods should be used to achieve social studies goals. Your life experiences, especially previous teachers, shape what you think should happen in the classroom. In addition, your social, economic, and political experiences and ideas affect your interpretation of what a teacher is and what the curriculum should look like. Your beliefs about human potential, ethics, and culture are also entwined with your teaching beliefs and practices (Figure 1.1). In turn, the students and the school in which you teach influence what and how you teach. Most teachers do not get their "dream class," Advanced Placement U.S. History, or the top section. Regardless of what type of class you teach, increasing the engagement of students in any classroom is essential and is discussed further in Chapters 3, 4, and 8.

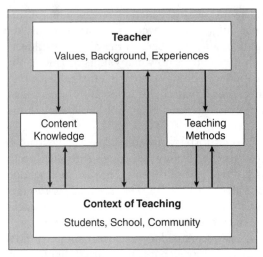

FIGURE I.I Influences on Teaching

WHAT DID YOU LIKE BEST?

What do you remember as being the best learning experiences you had in social studies classes? What were the most boring times? Is there much agreement in your group?

Even with the great diversity of widely different social studies teachers and classrooms plus your own experiences, you and your classmates probably remember learning experiences in which you were more actively involved, as in a mock trial, a debate, or participation in History Day. But these experiences typically did not happen every day. You may also remember doing boring worksheets. In the back of your mind, your previous teachers may connote what "normally" teaching social studies is supposed to be: standing in front of a class, imparting information, and getting students to read and to retain information from the textbook. These methods may have worked for you, as you now want to teach social studies. But for many students, the traditional style of teaching social studies is dull and uninteresting.

Mounting Criticism about Middle Schools and High Schools

In addition to some students' reaction to social studies, the public has had growing anxieties about what is happening to the achievement of all students in the public schools. There has been a loss of confidence and trust in many local school districts. The debates about charter schools, vouchers, and home schooling reflect serious concerns about how effective public schools are. Increasingly, parents want more choices for the types of school for their children. Others see the lack of financial support, unruly students, students who do not respect adults, gangs, and use of drugs as serious problems facing public schools. Social studies classes are also faulted for not producing more students who later become active, participating citizens who vote in local, state, and national elections or volunteer for civic affairs.

Middle-grade achievement is also being emphasized more. The widely acclaimed *Turning Points* of the Carnegie Council on Adolescent Development (Carnegie Corporation, 1989) reported a mismatch between the middle-grades structure and curriculum and the social, emotional, physical, and intellectual needs of young teens. Nevertheless, the message about social and emotional support had far more impact on educators than the corresponding message about the need to strengthen the academic subjects in the middle grades. *Turning Points 2000* (Jackson & Davis, 2000) directly confronted these critical questions for the middle school. Critics reject the idea that middle schoolers are developmentally unprepared for higher academic achievement. But defenders of the middle school are fearful that the major tenets of middle school philosophy will be cut as schools face the pressure of high-stakes assessments. In fact, some districts have abandoned middle schools, returning to the older K–8 design. They cite research (Offenberg, 2001) suggesting that eighth- and ninth-grade achievement was higher for students who attended K–8 schools than for those who attended middle schools serving similar communities. More research is needed on this issue of achievement in the middle schools versus the traditional K–8 model. More important than the form is what goes on inside the classroom.

Nevertheless, some middle schools are feeling the pressure from critics who are mounting an attack on the middle school movement. Middle school advocates believe that the idea of a separate school for students in this age group is a good idea. These advocates affirm that the core middle-grades practices such as a student-centered school, a clearly stated goal mission, a safe and orderly climate, a commitment to high standards, a rigorous curriculum coupled with personalized support, and interdisciplinary teacher teams and advisory programs can be implemented within the middle school format. Teams of teachers who share small groups of students (sometimes called "clusters" or "houses") and who stay with the same students for a longer period are strongly recommended. Smallness can create a personalized learning environment. There are also more calls for interdisciplinary teams to work for greater coherence across subject areas, courses, and grade levels, especially to improve reading, writing, and thinking in all content areas. In particular, reading is being stressed throughout the school day, partly due to testing requirements. A negative, however, is that although about three-fourths of all middle schools employ some form of team teaching, a much smaller percentage actually uses the teams effectively.

At first, the No Child Left Behind Act focused the public's attention on the elementary schools, with their required annual testing in the elementary grades. Although initially little attention was paid to the high school, now more scrutiny is being given to the challenges facing today's high schools. This has come about because of the increasingly diverse student body of high schoolers and the rapid changes in workforce and educational expectations. In particular, critics believed there is a mismatch between the skills needed for today's workforce and postsecondary education and what is taught in the high school.

Congress, governors, state education officials, and business leaders, as well as other groups, cite the Nation's Report Card (the National Assessment for Educational Progress), which indicates that at least 30 percent of high school students perform "Below Basic" on reading, math, and history. Furthermore, the achievement gaps between non-minority and Asian American students compared to minority students still exist. The high dropout rates of high school students (figures vary) increase the difficulty for these individuals to become productive workers and citizens. Even those who do graduate may not have the skills needed to succeed in the workforce and in postsecondary education. Many employers rate high school students' basic skills as only "fair" or "poor," while too many college students are required to take at least one remedial course in what they should have learned in high school during their college careers.

This critical viewpoint of high schools is probably best expressed by Microsoft chairman Bill Gates, who has stated that "America's high schools are obsolete." Associations and national foundations like the one supported by Bill and Melinda Gates are encouraging high schools to change. Gates and others believe that high schools must be redesigned as small schools, with classes that are rigorous and relevant to what all students need to know today. Change is needed in curriculum and instruction as well as in size. High schools have to be more challenging, interesting, and supportive of students.

Some high school students are also critical of their schools. They want fair policies equitably enforced, they want to get rid of "bad" teachers, and they want instruction that relates to "the real world." These students admire teachers who know their subject matter, have high standards, listen to students, provide individual attention, and have a sense of humor. In addition, student engagement studies report that about 40 to 60 percent of high school students are "chronically disengaged" from school (National Research Council, 2004). Only about 30 percent of high school students enrolled in college prep programs said that their schoolwork was meaningful (National Center for Education Statistics, 2004). Summarizing the various national conference concerns are the following high school reform ideas (Figure 1.2).

Currently, the most popular redesign features in implementing high school reform are the following: more support for meaningful, sustained relationships between teachers and students; high standards and performance-based assessment; and adaptive pedagogy. Although there is broad support for some of the reforms, other experts

FIGURE 1.2 Recommended High School Reforms

- Connect high school education to the world at large to prepare students for the world of work, higher education, and citizenship.
- Make college preparation the curriculum for all high school students.
- Improve professional development so that high school teachers have both content knowledge and pedagogical strategies to use in redesigned schools.
- All students, including English language learners, should read at or above grade level.
- Cut the high dropout rate, particularly in urban areas.
- Foster smaller, more personalized learning environments.
- Review state standards so that they are fewer in number and more flexible.

have pointed out the difficulties of bringing about the desired changes (Hammack, 2004). Realistically, change in the classroom depends first and foremost on what teachers are willing and able to do.

SMALL GROUP WORK	**REFORM THE HIGH SCHOOL?**
1.3	*Do you think that the high school needs to be reformed? Why or why not? Does it depend on the particular high school?*

■ WHAT SHOULD BE TAUGHT? STATE STANDARDS AND NO CHILD LEFT BEHIND

Troubled Times for Public Schools

The lack of confidence in public schools was illustrated by *A Nation at Risk,* published by the U.S. Department of Education (1983). This book was a critical factor in the **standards movement.** Standards are statements about what subject content should be taught. According to this document, a crisis existed in public education because there was a link between the economic competitiveness of our nation and our educational system. Economic advancement was seen as the nation's educational mission. According to this report, U.S. students were not prepared for adult work and responsibility due to watered-down content taught by poorly prepared teachers. Local school districts were failing to do the job of educating students. Yet not all agree that there is a crisis in education. Berliner and Biddle (1995) stated that the crisis has been "manufactured" to discredit public education and to serve various political ends.

Regardless of what is the reality, there is a *perception* of a crisis in U.S. education. Probably schools are better than they have been in the past. However, many students in urban schools cannot meet employers' expectations. In addition, the current system is not preparing many students for the demands of the new "Informational Economy," in which most workers will probably have several job changes, move to different locations, and be involved in social change. Therefore, better teaching is needed so that all students can learn from a more rigorous curriculum. This means the schools need to improve their curriculum.

In response to the mounting criticism of the public schools, in 1989 the governors of the states approved six national educational goals, which were later adopted in 1991 by President George H.W. Bush. The president, Congress, and state and local community leaders as well as business groups hoped that high academic standards based on national goals and their assessments for all students would be catalysts for reform and a stimulus for improving education. And some students, along with their parents, agreed that students were not being held to a high enough standard of performance, often due to grade inflation and low expectations for minority students.

National Social Studies Standards

In 1994, professional organizations published their social studies **standards,** what teachers are supposed to teach and students are expected to know (**content standards**) and be able to do (**performance standards**) at the end of a given time period. A performance standard measures how well a student's work meets the content standards. Often the performance standards have levels such as 4, 3, 2, 1 or Advanced, Proficient, Novice, and Basic. Standards with challenging curricula were expected to engage all students to perform at high levels. All students then would have access to higher-level knowledge and skills.

The National Council for the Social Studies (NCSS), the leading organization in the field, formulated ten broad curriculum themes/standards with five process (skill) standards (see Figure 1.3). In addition to the NCSS standards, organizations in four subject areas—history, geography, civics, and economics—also produced standards for their respective fields (see Chapters 6 to 8 for more discussion). Later in 1999, the American Psychological Association's standards for the high school psychology course were published.

The proposed first set of national history standards engendered a fierce national controversy, with critics concerned about what they regarded as an anti-Eurocentric bias and an emphasis on negative aspects of U.S. history (Chapter 6). These history standards were denounced by the U.S. Senate, and President Clinton's administration did not defend them. Furthermore, conservatives were worried about a national curriculum taking power away from the state and local governments. In turn, liberals were alarmed that the standards movement would hurt low-performing students, be culturally biased, have adverse effects on teaching and learning, stifle educators, and lead to further standardization. All these factors led to the states having control of formulating their own standards instead of all states having the same voluntary na-

FIGURE I.3 NCSS Curriculum Themes/Standards

Themes that are based on the major concepts of history and the social sciences:

- Culture (anthropology)
- Time, continuity, and change (history)
- People, places, and environment (geography)
- Individual development and identity (psychology)
- Individuals, groups, and institutions (sociology)
- Power, authority, and governance (political science)
- Production, distribution, and consumption (economics)

Themes that are broadly based and include many subject areas:

- Science, technology, and society
- Global connections
- Civic ideals and practice

Why would a president be supportive of NCLB?

tional standards. Even the federally mandated testing allowed the states to design and assess their own standards. Now almost all states have adopted standards for K–12 social studies, but not all states have statewide tests for social studies.

Impact of No Child Left Behind Act

By 2001, President George W. Bush and Congress were not satisfied with the progress the states had made. State standards were failing four subgroups of students: low income, minority, English language learners (ELLS or ELs), and students with disabilities (SWD). The goals of equity were not being met in educating these students, who had the right to learn. A bipartisan Congress then passed the most significant education reform act, No Child Left Behind (NCLB), in a quarter century. NCLB held all schools to measurable standards set by the individual states. NCLB mandated broader accountability, with required testing in reading, math, and science. Furthermore, if schools failed to achieve performance goals, they faced serious sanctions, including vouchers to parents for out-of-school programs and then eventually replacing the school staff or converting failing schools to charter schools. States had to establish *their own* annual tests aligned with *their own state standards*. This has resulted in great diversity among state standards and in what a given state considers to be proficient students.

The goals of NCLB are beyond reproach. NCLB also has brought a modicum of academic progress, especially for students who otherwise might receive little attention. However, by 2004 a revolt against NCLB was building up in some state legislatures, which were chafing under NCLB requirements. Legislatures were angry about the testing requirements, the large number of schools put on probation, and the cost of implementation. Although the public in 2005 strongly supported the federal law and did not want to see the goals diluted (Public Education Network, 2005), the respondents in this survey did not feel it was fair, when breaking down performance data for certain groups such as English language learners, that the whole school was labeled "in need of improvement." Furthermore, the respondents were concerned about children with disabilities not being able to pass unrealistic grade-level tests. The public also wanted more than only annual tests to measure student performance. As a result of these concerns, it was expected that the Department of Education will relax or change the interpretations of some of the mandates.

Supporters and Critics of Standards

The standards-based reform movement, with its assessment and accountability, generally had high support from the public. Parents especially want their children to have enough knowledge and skills to function in a technology-centered global economy. Standards also addressed the issue of discrepancy between Teacher A's and Teacher B's treatment of the same course in the same school, district, or state. Often the same courses taught by different teachers were wildly different in content and skills, depriving some students of equal access to education.

Standards can help both teachers and their students be clear about their purposes by developing explicit goals for learning. Students can find standards helpful when teachers spell out criteria for high-quality work, explain how the work will be assessed, and give examples of what the work looks like. Students then have a better idea of what to do and how to do it. When goals and expectations are very clear, more students can meet them. All the same, standards do not have the full support of all teachers. The most common teacher criticism is that standards force teachers to "teach to tests," resulting in rote learning. Teacher criticisms also include the following: not age appropriate (too difficult for the average student), too vague or too specific, too much content to cover, documents too long and filled with educational jargon, less attention to multicultural (Bohn & Sleeter, 2000) and global education, and too little attention to values such as caring. Teachers also felt that they as well as students had been left out of the loop in their district's decision-making process on the standards-based reform movement.

The standards movement engendered the most controversy on the issue of high-stakes testing (Chapter 5). But the vast majority of the public favored requiring students to pass statewide tests to graduate and ending "social promotion." The public felt that the only group to be exempt from a high school graduation test should be students in special education. However, some parents worried that if the standards were to be set too high, their children would not advance to the next grade, or might even be deprived of a high school diploma. Parents were not the only ones concerned. Typically, high-achieving schools were in mostly high-income areas, with lower scores in low-income, disadvantaged areas. Teachers in low-achieving schools felt themselves blamed for low scores and perceived that their efforts were not valued or appreciated.

A few critics thought that the standards were set too low and that high achievers were not properly challenged. They cited as evidence the fact that most states with graduation exams actually give them in the tenth grade, meaning that the tests really measure a tenth-grade education. In some states, the test's grade level is even lower than the tenth grade. In effect, some students pass their state graduation test but cannot pass their own state's college/university entrance test in English and math.

If too many students failed or were feared to fail the critical tests in a state, a backlash against the standards movement developed to ease or mitigate the consequences of having standards that were too high for students to pass. States provided other ways for students to be promoted or to graduate if they failed the tests. For example, although California law in 1998 banned social promotion, districts were given wide latitude to determine who was promoted, and the state-required reading test scores did not have to be used. The result was that with diluted local standards, few students were retained. Other states changed their graduation test requirement by also considering grades, classwork, and teacher evaluations rather than the test score alone. Minnesota shifted the state social studies assessment to the local district.

All test experts advocated using multiple measures and not just one test to decide who should pass or get a high school diploma. Again, experts regard both social promotion and retention as policies unlikely to bring about lasting gains in student achievement. Too often, low-achieving students continue to be low achievers after being promoted, and retained students do not catch up with their peers.

Impact of the Standards Movement

Will you and other teachers really change because of standards and testing? It may depend on the level of involvement and buy-in to the standards reform. Some teachers push for standards, whereas others resist them. Some teachers report that standards have increased their preparation time and decreased their enjoyment of teaching. Reform changes may exacerbate an already stressful job.

Will the standards-based reform succeed in raising student achievement? First, outcomes will vary greatly in different states and in different schools. Second, and most important, teachers are the primary agents of educational change. You, as a teacher, are the gatekeeper of the curriculum. You and other teachers choose both the content and how to prepare students for standards and testing. Some teachers may do drill-and-practice activities as an attempt to "teach to the test." But not all tests require mere content memorization, making drill-and-practice activities of limited usefulness. The best test preparation is a rich curriculum. All the standard reforms will fail unless the teacher understands and chooses classroom activities that enable students to achieve the standards.

However, teachers are unlikely to make standards a significant part of their classrooms if they lack subject matter proficiency such as in economics or geography, or do not have the professional skills necessary to implement effective lessons. Teachers need resources, support, and workshops to change their practice. To achieve success will require changes in curriculum, teacher preparation, classroom instruction, and assessment. A further problem is that, within a given school, teachers may be in different stages of implementating the standards. For these reasons, it may take years to really implement the standards.

Before you start the practical agenda for teaching social studies (Chapters 2 to 9), the rest of this chapter will focus on the following: (1) The debate of a social studies versus a single-discipline approach; (2) Why should social studies be taught? (3) What content should be taught, and when? and (4) Should values and character education be taught?

ON YOUR OWN	YOUR STATE SOCIAL STUDIES STANDARDS
1.1	*Secure a copy of your state social studies standards. Most are available on the Internet. Search by using your state's name followed by Department of Education (Ohio Department of Education) or Department of Public Instruction (Wisconsin Department of Public Instruction). In a few cases, the title may be different, as in Minnesota Department of Children, Families, and Learning.*
	What are the strong points of your state social studies standards? Do you see any negative aspects of the state standards? Do you think your state social studies standards promote better education for all students?

■ WHAT IS "SOCIAL STUDIES"? A SINGLE-SUBJECT DISCIPLINE?

The Social Studies Approach

The standards-based reform movement, as applied to the social studies, raised the question of what knowledge and skills are most important. What are the sources of subject matter for the social studies? Not everyone approves of the **social studies ap-**

proach. This issue can be illustrated by the use of names and titles. If someone were to ask what you do or what you will teach, how would you reply? Would you say, "I am a social studies teacher," or would you say, "I am a history teacher," or, "I am an economics teacher"? Also examine the title of the curriculum framework for your state. Is it similar to the title *Instructional Goals and Objectives for West Virginia Schools Social Studies,* or is it more like *California History-Social Sciences Framework*? These different names and titles underscore a long-standing debate in the field between two approaches, the social studies approach and the single-discipline approach.

The National Council for the Social Studies, the prime leader in the field, in 1992 adopted the following formal definition of the social studies.

> Social studies is the integrated study of the social sciences and humanities to promote civic competence. Within the school program, social studies provides coordinated, systematic study drawing upon such disciplines as anthropology, archaeology, economics, geography, history, law, philosophy, political science, psychology, religion, and sociology, as well as appropriate content from the humanities, mathematics, and natural sciences. The primary purpose of social studies is to help young people develop the ability to make informed and reasoned decisions for the public good as citizens of a culturally diverse, democratic society in an interdependent world.

According to this definition, social studies is an **integrated, multidisciplinary area of learning,** not a single discipline. It includes content from history, geography, economics, political science, and the behavioral sciences (psychology, anthropology, and sociology). Therefore, social studies proponents believe that it is best to study a topic such as the American Revolution or the Industrial Revolution from the perspective of many academic disciplines. Looking at social, economic, and political factors can better explain why the American Revolution occurred in 1776, as well as the many other revolutions that have taken place throughout the world. Focusing on technology, science and inventions, location of labor and resources, world markets, and the role of the entrepreneur can better clarify why the Industrial Revolution first started in England and then later spread to many other nations and is still going on today in the world.

For adherents of the social studies approach, one single discipline often cannot do the complete job of illustrating major concepts or issues. According to the advocates of the social studies approach, it is often necessary to use multiple academic disciplines to understand the content. This social studies approach is felt to be better able to analyze present social, economic, and political issues faced by an increasingly global society. Therefore, history should not be the exclusive framework for instruction. Instead, in many cases, starting with today's problems ranging from social security to global peace requires an interdisciplinary approach instead of a single-discipline approach. In particular, these advocates feel that the single-discipline approach neglects the behavioral sciences of anthropology, psychology, and sociology and the social studies approach does a better job of accommodating all of the disciplines. A basic problem for teachers using the social studies approach is securing adequate materials and resources for various topics.

Single-Discipline Approach

In contrast, proponents of a **single-discipline approach** believe it is essential that students learn the important content and methods of research (structure of the discipline) used by the scholars in the field. Some, but not all, of the critics of the social studies approach are scholars who wish to emphasize their respective subjects as the heart of the social studies curriculum. Their criticisms about the need to improve teaching and learning in respective subject areas are supported by data from the National Assessment of Educational Progress (NAEP), the Nation's Report Card, and other tests of what students apparently do not know. This is especially true at the high school level.

Some critics of the social studies approach believe that the teaching of history has been so diluted that students no longer learn "history." These advocates generally believe that history should be the dominant and overriding discipline. To support their point of view, Diane Ravitch and Chester Finn (1987) cite research about students' appalling lack of knowledge of important historical figures or events, such as when the Civil War occurred. Ravitch has been one of the chief proponents of the standards movement. Ravitch and others are concerned about the de-emphasis of history, literature, and other academic subjects. They may call what is being taught "social studies slush." As for more recent examples of lack of students' knowledge, on a National Assessment of Educational Progress U.S. history test item, only 41 percent of all eighth graders knew that "The Lend-Lease Act, the Yalta Conference, and the dropping of the atomic bomb on Hiroshima are all associated with the Second World War" (Beatty, Reese, Persky, & Carr, 1996). For twelfth graders, only 41 percent correctly marked that "The Monroe Doctrine was intended to discourage European involvement in the Americas."

Geographers also maintain that their subject is not being taught well and that U.S. students are practically geographically illiterate. For example, in a NAEP geography test item, only 51 percent of eighth graders could answer "Under which of the following circumstances would you be most likely to find snow in equatorial regions?" Correct answer: "In areas at high elevations" (Persky, Reese, O'Sullivan, Lazer, Moore, & Shakrani, 1996).

The NAEP 1998 Civics Report Card for the Nation reported that, at the fourth-, eighth-, and twelfth-grade levels, about 30 percent of all students lacked even the most essential knowledge of the political system or the role citizens play in it (Lukas, Weiss, Campbell, Mazzeo, & Lazer, 1999). This was a serious and discouraging finding. Civics was again tested in 2006. Economics was tested in 2006 at the twelfth grade and world history will be tested at the twelfth grade in 2010. One can assume that the results of students' understanding and skills in these two areas also will indicate a need for improvement. The National Council on Economic Education's (1999) survey on economic literacy showed that only 57 percent of adults and 48 percent of high school students had mastered even the most basic economic concepts. These discouraging findings point out the essential need for improvement in the teaching of the social studies.

Growing Support for the Single-Discipline Approach

States faced the differences between the social studies approach and the single-discipline approach as they formulated their own state standards for the social studies. Concerned by what they saw as serious deficiencies in student learning, more states chose to list separate standards for history, geography, economics, and civics, often drawing on the national standards already produced by the four academic organizations. To avoid controversy associated with the detailed first set of national history standards, many states' standards were deliberately very broad. In some cases, this necessitated the staff at the local school level to design a more detailed **curriculum**—the plans, methods, and materials to be used to implement the standards.

As a result of state standards, at the present time there may be more emphasis on a single-discipline approach than there was formerly, because there are separate state standards for history, geography, civics, and economics. Some teachers in these states now may feel they should focus more on teaching single subjects to meet their state standards. Historically, however, middle school teachers have usually felt a little more support for crossing disciplines and subject areas than have secondary teachers.

Advanced Placement Examinations

The Advanced Placement examinations in single subjects probably influence secondary social studies teachers to think in terms of a single discipline. In 2005, more than two million AP examinations were taken by more than one million U.S. high school students. This is more than double the number who took them ten years ago. U.S. History is the most popular AP course. A detailed guide for AP U.S. history exam coverage that has been prepared by historians and secondary history teachers is available on the Internet: www.collegeboard.org/ap. The purpose of this guide is to provide an outline for students and their teachers of the breadth of information, skills, and assignments found in corresponding college courses. Starting in 2007, schools need approval by the College Board (CollegeBoard.com) to be labeled as Advanced Placement. This means using a text from a list of preapproved college-level textbooks and other requirements. As a result of these AP requirements, AP social studies teachers may also give more time to writing so that their students will be familiar with answering essay questions.

Besides U.S. history, AP exams are also offered in economics (with a choice of macroeconomics or microeconomics), government and politics (with a choice of U.S. government and politics or comparative government and politics), human geography, psychology, European history, and world history. Other areas, such as sociology, are expected to eventually have an AP examination. Despite the controversy over tracking and giving differentiated curriculum to students, **access** for all students to AP courses in their schools is increasing because of concerns of equity. It is felt that students in all schools serving mainly low-income and rural students should have the same opportunity to take AP courses as students in more affluent communities. The goal is for all 24,000 secondary schools nationwide to offer AP courses. Therefore, directly and indirectly, the influence of AP courses, with their single-discipline perspective, will probably grow, especially if administrators see AP courses as a way to bring more rigor to the curriculum.

Most parents and college admission officers as well as school administrators applaud the growth of Advanced Placement examinations. Nevertheless, a few teachers believe that instead of giving high-achieving students a taste of college, AP encourages teaching to a test instead of eliciting creative thinking. The quality of AP courses also is an issue, especially if students do not actually take the AP exam. Is the AP course then just window dressing for college applications?

What Is in a Name?

In real practice, there is a considerable overlap between the social studies approach and the single-discipline approach. Both models have as their main goal the development of informed, responsible, and active citizens. Both approaches emphasize history. Equal time is not given to the other social sciences. Even in the social studies approach, history is typically used as the organizing framework for instruction.

Both approaches stress that improvement can be made in the teaching of social studies. Therefore, what actually goes on in the classroom is probably more important than the label given to the class—History, Social Studies, Core, Integrated Curriculum, and the like. However, for convenience, this text will generally use the term *social studies* except in specific discussions of subject areas.

■ WHY SHOULD SOCIAL STUDIES BE TAUGHT? GOALS OF CIVIC EDUCATION

Goals

Let us reinforce the idea that the main purpose, mission, or rationale for teaching social studies is civic education or, as it is often called, *citizenship education*. *Civic education* appears to be the preferred term used now, although both terms are used interchangeably. Almost everyone agrees that the central mission of the schools is to enculturate the youth in a social and political democracy.

To achieve civic education, there are four major goals. **Goals** are broad statements of desired outcomes. In education, they provide the pillars for setting up learning experiences. A goal is not reached in a day or even a year. Goals are long-term ideals or values that are determined socially. Examples of goals are the following:

- Lifelong learning
- Literate individuals
- Critical thinking

- Healthy and fit individuals
- Care and compassion

Here are four important social studies goals:

1. To acquire **knowledge** from history, the social sciences, and related areas
2. To develop **skills** to think and to process information
3. To develop appropriate democratic **values, beliefs,** and **dispositions**
4. To have opportunities for **civic participation**

These goals are not separate but instead are intertwined. As students acquire knowledge, there may be emotional attitudes attached, such as a high positive value given to the U.S. Constitution and the importance of adult voting. In a negative example, students can be taught skills such as how to use the Internet for getting information on public issues, but never choose to use the Internet for the purpose of increasing their knowledge and understanding. In this case, they have been taught something but do not value it enough to engage in this practice. Community participation or service learning may increase both knowledge about the local community and the skills needed to address problems in the community. All these examples show the connections between knowledge, skills, values, and civic participation. It is important to remember that teachers are not teaching just "facts"; they want to win over their students' hearts and minds to democratic values and citizenship.

Different Approaches

The difficulty with the goals of civic education for the social studies is that, although of practically no one disagrees with the goals, there can be many different interpretations of what is civic or citizenship education. The goal statements are very broad. Some experts would define citizenship in a multidimensional sense, with a great emphasis on global citizenship and human rights. Others would advocate a stronger commitment to diversity and multicultural education. Some experts want more emphasis on inquiry. Others see the development of students' tolerance and ability to think and to discuss as of prime importance. Still others support a more subject-oriented focus. Look at the different approaches to civic education that are outlined in Table 1.1.

You can easily see the many differences of these citizenship approaches. Each has strengths and weaknesses, although advocates of each position would disagree on their relative merits. One area of concern shared by all of these models is **indoctrination.** Every nation or social group brings up its children to reflect its own values and culture. Citizenship education has among its goals that students adopt the values of their society, such as respect for others, justice, freedom, and democracy. These are regarded as the basic values of our society and are not debatable. All the civic education models hope that the schools will be inspired to do their best to instill in students a commitment to democratic values, and the citizenship transmission model best illustrates this approach. This leads to the question of whether teachers include too much or too little affirmation of American values and policies.

TABLE 1.1 Different Approaches to Civic/Citizenship Education

Approach	Goals of Civic Education
Citizenship transmission	Students are taught knowledge and values as a framework for making decisions.
Social science/history	Students master social science/history knowledge and methods of the field.
Reflective inquiry	Students use knowledge and thinking to make decisions and to solve problems.
Personal development	Students develop a positive self-concept and a strong sense of personal efficacy.
Social criticism/reform/ critical pedagogy	Students develop understanding and skills needed to critique and transform society; often a focus on injustice/ inequality.

Note: See Robert D. Barr, James L. Barth, and S. Samuel Shermis, *Defining the Social Studies,* Bulletin 51 (Washington, DC: National Council for the Social Studies, 1977) for the first three approaches.

Indoctrination is the shaping of minds by providing information without permitting the individual to question or examine the information being transmitted. Indoctrination sets out to instill or internalize certain values in students or to change the values of students so they more nearly reflect certain desired values. Here you can easily see a dilemma between indoctrinating students in shared democratic commitments and encouraging critical thinking. The schools have the job to instill democratic values in their students. Yet to indoctrinate a "correct" answer to an issue puts us on shaky ground. Most social studies experts believe it is the job of the teacher to help students think about the issues, to arrive at good conclusions on their own, but not to dictate right answers.

Learning the structure of the discipline with its major concepts and methods—the social science/history approach—is now more popular and is evident in more state standards. But this approach has been criticized for not socializing youth into the political system. The reflective inquiry models promise a great deal but have been difficult to implement in a consistent manner across the social studies curriculum, especially if teachers are concerned about covering sufficient content. The personal development approach, with its emphasis on improving the self-concepts of students, has been generally accepted at the middle school level but is being criticized for not putting enough emphasis on academic achievement. After reviewing the five evaluations of citizenship approaches given in the last few paragraphs, it is worthwhile to form your own evaluation, perhaps based on a combination of elements from the different models.

However, although most social studies teachers, school boards, and state legislatures see citizenship education as the main goal for social studies courses, the public, according to a Phi Delta Kappa/Gallup Poll, overwhelmingly (around 60 percent) believes that it is more important for the schools to prepare students for college or work than for effective citizenship (Rose & Gallup, 2000). From the majority point of view, the purpose of education is less to educate citizens than to provide students with educational credentials to help them get better jobs. This viewpoint is the one we also hear from government and business leaders who are worried about the economic consequences of inadequate education. This can be called the human capital model, in which schooling is seen largely as a handmaiden to economic development and individual economic opportunity. This situation illustrates a significant difference between the public and educators.

■ WHAT CONTENT SHOULD BE TAUGHT, AND WHEN?

Tradition and Present Placement

You can see that the four main goals of citizenship education and the definition of the social studies are so broad (some would say "loose") that widely different content and skills could be taught for each grade level. But this ignores the importance of tradition. Early in the twentieth century, the recommendations of the National Education Association's (1916) Committee of 1916 set the stage for the social studies content being taught throughout the United States.

What is the current status of placement of content in courses? How much is being retained of the historic 1916 pattern? Table 1.2 shows the 1916 recommendations in the middle column. The right column combines current students' reports to NAEP of their courses and the results of studies using analyses of transcripts, reported research, and state recommendations. The earlier elementary grades are included in the current column to show the repeating pattern of courses in U.S. history and world history/cultures.

Please remember that this is not a universal pattern of social studies courses taught in the United States, because there are different state and local requirements. In a NAEP survey of U.S. history courses when eighth-grade students were asked if they were currently taking a U.S. history course, 83 percent said yes and 17 percent said no. For the U.S. history course in grade 11, 79 percent of the students said they were taking such a course and 18 percent stated they were not. But regardless of when students take the course, an analysis of transcripts indicates that in 1994, 95 percent of high school graduates had taken one year of U.S. history. The second most popular one-year high school social studies course was world history, with about 60 percent of students having completed a one-year course. This figure would have been even higher if it had included courses in world cultures or area studies. Clearly, history courses dominate the social studies curriculum.

At the secondary level, the biggest change appears to be the shift from teaching civics and government courses in ninth grade, as was recommended in 1916, to teaching it in the twelfth grade. Less certain is what is happening at the sixth-, seventh-, and tenth-grade levels on world history/world cultures, as European history has been replaced by a more global history. Currently, a chronological approach in world history is replacing a relatively recent emphasis on world cultures. For example, in California the sixth grade covers ancient civilizations to around the Fall of Rome, the seventh-grade curriculum continues from that period to 1500, and the tenth-grade sequence concentrates on the modern period starting after 1500 A.D. Not all state curricula follow this division of time periods, but it is not atypical.

TABLE 1.2 Social Studies Grade Topics

Grade	1916 Recommendations	Current Scope and Sequence
4	—	State history, geographic regions
5	—	U.S. history with focus on earlier period, geography
6	—	World history, geography, less emphasis on world cultures
7	Geography/European history	World history, geography, with emphasis on world chronological approach
8	American history	U.S. history, focus on nineteenth century
9	Civics	Civics, increasingly taken by seniors (50 percent)
10	European history	World/global history, emphasis more on chronological than regional or cultural approach
11	American history	U.S. history, emphasis on twentieth and twenty-first centuries
12	Problems of democracy— social, economic, and political	Civics, economics; electives psychology and sociology (Niemi & Smith, 2000)

Note: Grades 4–6 were not covered in the 1916 document.

Textbooks

States with large populations, such as California, Texas, and New York, influence the entire nation's curriculum because of the role of textbook marketing. National publishers want as wide an audience as possible for their textbooks, and a prime consideration is the curriculum frameworks of the larger states. The process of designing and publishing textbooks is more expensive each year, partly due to the increasing amount of supplementary materials ranging from technology to student tests and workbooks that teachers now want with a textbook. Therefore, publishers are reluctant to deviate from the traditional and widely used patterns. Although the major publishers may publish a version of a state history for a given state, their norm is usually the national market. This results in continuity in topic placement in the social studies and reinforces a national curriculum even though state and local control exist. Textbooks make change difficult, although textbook committees try to make decisions based on what is best for their students.

Textbooks are a major determinant of what content is taught at each grade level. We have, in some sense, many of the same curriculum titles that we started with many decades ago. Some observers have called the social studies curriculum a "frozen curriculum" that is not adapting and claim that at the present rate of change, the landscape will not change much in the near future. If true, this raises the question of whether we have a curriculum that teaches what students really need to know today. Other experts maintain that curriculum is never static and changes do occur, such as the incorporation of multicultural education into the curriculum, although the titles of the courses remain the same.

SMALL GROUP WORK	**OBSOLETE CURRICULUM?**
1.4	*Does the present social studies curriculum logically connect subjects taught at the different grade levels? Is it a good idea to teach U.S. history at the fifth, eighth, and eleventh grades? This sequence is a holdover from a time when most students completed only eighth grade, at most. Before students left school, school boards felt it was a good idea for them to have a final U.S. history course.*

■ SHOULD VALUES AND CHARACTER EDUCATION BE TAUGHT?

Values

The broad values that teachers believe are important for students to learn have not changed in recent years. They include democracy, honesty, freedom of speech, courtesy, tolerance, and freedom of worship. Second, teachers and the general public agree that the home has the primary responsibility for developing children's values but that the school still has an important role to play. Third, there may be differences in how teachers and students view such issues as cheating on a test, not telling the truth, or misbehaving in class.

You have already seen that one of the goals of citizenship education is the teaching of traditional values. As with the different perspectives on citizenship education, there are also different approaches to the teaching of **values,** although there is overlap between the two. In the elementary and middle school, **character and moral education** programs may be in place. The purpose is to teach students to identify "good values" (such as citizenship, honesty, respect for others, kindness, cooperation with others) and put these values into practice. Such programs are part of a movement to socialize the nation's youth and try to correct and help young people who are harming themselves and others. Instances of school violence are often cited as evidence that schools need to do more with character education. However, character education is broad in scope and the term describes many programs: moral education, caring community, ethic/moral philosophy, violence prevention, and the like.

There is a link between good character and good citizenship. One criticism is that the schools' values are strongly influenced by the schools' interest in maintaining order, emphasizing effort, and fostering a sense of identification of students with their schools. Generally, a school does not interpret a good student citizen as one who questions the school's rules. For example, the following are some rules that many students would like to address:

- School lunch policy
- Teachers and classes

Should character education be stressed more in social studies classes?

- School bathrooms
- Parking issues
- Alcohol and other drugs
- Dress codes
- School sports

All the same, whether character education should be taught explicitly in the school curriculum is a thorny issue. Character education programs are less likely to be formally found at the high school level, partly because typically there are no specific courses in which it can be taught. However, this does not mean that the high schools are not trying to teach values to their students. For example, elimination of sexual harassment and school violence is a high priority of secondary schools. It is felt that students need instruction as a way to promote making school a safe learning environment free of harassment or violence.

You may have studied these different approaches for teaching values in your educational psychology course. However, regardless of what approach is used for teaching values, everyone agrees that the teacher is a **role model.** Your own behavior can show the proper way to act. Your students are observing you. They note what you do and say. (They are particularly concerned that you treat them fairly!) Your own values are shown by your behavior. (See Sample Classroom Episode).

There is no such thing as a values-free classroom, because everything you do as a teacher reflects your values. Your rules for the class and the school's rules are teaching values as well as commonly accepted behaviors such as cleanliness, promptness,

SAMPLE CLASSROOM EPISODE

LOOKING AT A TEACHER'S VALUES AND STUDENTS' VALUES

Exhausted, Judi Valdes looked over what happened during her first day of teaching. There had been no physical threats directed at her! In the back of her mind, that had always been a vague worry. Judi was glad to be teaching at Oakville High School in a working-class suburb. She knew she was hired only because she could teach economics. The other social studies teachers did not have the background or desire to teach the senior, one-semester economics course after the previous teacher had retired. That was the only reason that she, a new teacher, was teaching seniors.

After making some changes to an old questionnaire she had found, Judi gave an anonymous questionnaire to her students on the first day. She told the classes she wanted information on how many hours they worked so that the homework load would be equitable, and that the other information she requested would help her to better tailor the course to their needs. Judi carefully avoided asking any personal questions about their views on marriage, having children, and drug abuse. Nevertheless, she did ask if they thought various values such as honesty are "Very Important."

All three of her economics classes cooperated well with filling out the questionnaire, and Judi thought they appeared to be frank in their responses. However, tabulating their responses brought her some surprises. About 90 percent thought "success in work" and about 50 percent thought "having lots of money" was very important. She felt better finding that 85 percent thought "having strong friendships" was very important. Especially upsetting to her was that only 12 percent thought that "working to correct social and economic inequalities" was very important.

And look at how much money the students think they will make by the time they are age 30! Almost everyone thinks they will make over $50,000 a year. That certainly is not realistic. And the hours they presently work! At least half of the students work up to twenty hours a week and a few work more than that. Would projects requiring outside school work really be successful?

What should be the next steps? First, Judi thought that the economics course should have a heavy emphasis on correcting social and economic inequalities. Yet it looked like her values and her students' values were at cross-purposes. Should she proceed with her plans? Second, should she try to give her students a more realistic view about their possible future incomes, or would that only discourage them? Third, on a practical level, how much homework, along with a semester project, should she assign in light of many students' heavy outside work schedules?

If you were in the same position as Judi, what decisions would you make on these three questions?

TABLE 1.3 Different Approaches to Values Education

Approach	Purpose	Methods
Indoctrination	Values of students change in desired direction.	Variety of methods, selective data provided
Moral development (Kohlberg)	Students develop higher set of values; just community.	Moral dilemmas, small group discussion, teacher in devil's advocate role
Multicultural education (Banks)	Cross-cultural development; cultural heritage.	Variety of methods, experience diversity, reflection, role playing, participation in consciousness-raising groups, community inquiry
Global education, Peace education	Cross-cultural development by viewing world from global perspectives; foster attitudes that will support world peace.	Variety of methods, attention to values, reflective learning, moral dilemmas
Values clarification (Simon et al.)	Students become aware of their own values.	Variety of methods, self-analysis exercises
Analysis	Students use logical thinking to decide values issues.	Rational discussion, research, critical thinking
Caring (Noddings)	Care for self, care for others, altruism.	Modeling, dialogue, practice, confirmation, self-esteem
Social action	Students have opportunities for social action based on their values.	Projects in schools and in the community

Note: Difficulties arise when trying to place certain programs, such as substance abuse approaches like those of the Drug Abuse Resistance Education (D.A.R.E.) program, which stress self-esteem and drug-free behavior. Some people consider these programs to be "indoctrination," whereas others put them in the "analysis" approach because they may use medical research as a data source. There are similar classification problems with many of the value approaches.

honesty, and so forth. "Respect others." "If you are absent for a test, you must make it up at lunchtime within two days of returning to class." "In small group work, everyone needs to contribute." Values, however, may also be taught in a manner more subtle than direct teaching or telling students about the rules. There also may be a "hidden curriculum" based on a teacher's unexamined assumptions and biases, with the result (for example) that popular kids get more favorable attention or ELLs students are ignored.

Notice that the various approaches to values education, shown in Table 1.3, are generally not unique in their methodology; the Methods column often includes "variety of methods." Yet value approaches are not without controversy. Whereas almost everyone supports broad general values such as democracy, freedom of the individual, caring, all citizens should vote, and the like, parents want the school to support their values and they may object if they think a teacher is downgrading, questioning, or dismissive of their cherished values. Whether teachers should try to keep their own personal values out of the classrooms is another issue (Chapter 8).

Let us look at some potential problem areas in values education. As interpreted by educators, the moral development approach of Kohlberg (1966) aims to stimulate and foster more complex reasoning patterns based on a higher set of values. Some, but not all, of the multicultural and global education approaches also aim to move students to a higher and more complex level of values (Hanvey, 1975). These approaches are often based on four to six developmental stages. In general, these approaches find that individuals in the ethnocentric or first stage of any of the models are more hesitant and less open. Those at the higher stages are more interested in learning about and respecting other cultures and human rights.

The multicultural and global education approaches to values education are based on a belief that it is not enough to teach only content—although content is basic—about ethnic and racial groups or global issues. Individuals need to move to an important commitment to combat racism, all forms of prejudice, and discrimination, and develop into adults who accept individual differences. This commitment, according to Banks (1994), is typically created through the development of appropriate understanding, attitudes, and social action skills (Chapter 8). Some of these approaches have raised questions as to *whose* perspective is being taken as the norm. Carol Gilligan (1982), for example, has criticized Kohlberg for omitting a feminine perspective.

Approaches such as the caring approach of Noddings (2005) may also wish to reform the school, reconstruct society, or take some action. But not all community members will appreciate a classroom that examines discrimination in the community or labor conditions of the workers who make the clothing we buy. Parents, students, and the community may see the teacher as a political advocate for a viewpoint that is not their own. Students might complain about being brainwashed and claim that to get good grades, they must parrot back the teacher's views. However, the most criticism has probably been directed toward Sidney Simon (Simon, Howe, & Kirschenbaum, 1972) and his colleagues with their values clarification approach. This is a nonjudgmental approach, as students are encouraged to develop their own values, even if those include using drugs or other socially disapproved values.

Do any of these values education approaches work? The research evidence is not clear, as it is difficult to measure where students were at one point in time and what their values are at a later point in time after a certain program has been implemented. Do you measure what students actually do or what they say? Use data about dropout rates and fewer disciplinary referrals? You can see the problems in evaluating the effectiveness of these various approaches. Unfortunately, too often there is a reliance on ideology instead of a solid research base. However, many of the approaches might be effective for some students under certain conditions.

Nevertheless, it is important to think about your own values as you become a teacher. Your values will influence your planning and teaching, based on what you consider important for students to learn. Your values will affect how you teach controversial issues. They will also affect how you treat your students and your grading system.

ON YOUR OWN	YOUR VALUE APPROACH
1.2	*Of the various value approaches found in Table 1.3, which one(s) would you feel most comfortable teaching? Which ones might be more effective?*

LARGE CLASS DISCUSSION	CONTROVERSIAL ISSUE
	What requirements should there be to become a certified social studies teacher? More testing? Alternative certification? More academic courses in history?

■ SUMMARY

It is important to examine why you want to become a social studies teacher, because your background and values affect what you consider to be a good social studies program. Advocates of NCLB and state standards in the social studies want students to achieve higher academic proficiency and citizenship goals. Teachers ultimately make decisions about whether and how to teach the standards. There is a continuing debate between those who want a social studies approach or a single-discipline approach. There is also disagreement on approaches to citizenship education and the teaching of values. Tradition and textbooks help to explain the grade placement of social studies courses. You, as a social studies teacher, face the challenge of teaching diverse students the necessary knowledge, skills, and values to become contributing members of various communities ranging from the local to the global. **Improvement can be made to the teaching of social studies.**

■ REFERENCES ■

Banks, J. (1994). *Multiethnic education: Theory and practice.* Boston: Allyn and Bacon.

Beatty, A. S., Reese, C. M., Persky, H. R., & Carr, P. (1996). *NAEP 1994 U.S. history report card* (pp. 111, 119). Washington, DC: U.S. Department of Education, National Center for Education Statistics.

Berliner, D. C., & Biddle, B. (1995). *The manufactured crisis.* Reading, MA: Addison-Wesley.

Bohn, A. P., & Sleeter, C. E. (2000). Multicultural education and the standards movement: A report from the field. *Phi Delta Kappan, 82*, 156–159.

Carnegie Corporation. (1989). *Turning points: Preparing American youth for the 21st century*. New York: Longman.

Gilligan, C. (1982). *In a different voice: Psychological theory*. Cambridge, MA: Harvard University Press.

Hammack, F. M. (Ed।) (2004). *The comprehensive high school today*. New York: Teachers College Press.

Hanvey, R. (1975). *An attainable global perspective*. New York: Center for War/Peace Studies.

Ingersoll, R. M. (2003). *Out-of-field teaching and the limits of teacher policy*. Seattle: Center for the Study of Teaching and Policy, University of Washington.

Jackson, A. W., & Davis, G. A. (2000). *Turning points 2000: Educating adolescents in the 21st century*. New York: Teachers College Press.

Kohlberg, L. (1966). Moral education in the schools: A developmental view. *School Review, 74*, 1–30.

Lukas, A. D., Weiss, A., Campbell, J. R., Mazzeo, J., & Lazer, S. (1999). *NAEP 1998 civics report card for the nation* (NCES Report 2000–457). Washington, DC: U.S Department of Education. National Center for Education Statistics.

National Center for Education Statistics. (2004). *The condition of education*. Retrieved from www.nces.ed.gov/programs/coe.

National Council for the Social Studies, Task Force. (1991). *A vision of powerful teaching and learning in the social studies: Building social understanding and civic efficacy*. Washington, DC: Position Statement of the Task Force on Standards for Teachers and Learning in Social Studies; also included in *Social Education, 57*, 215.

National Council for the Social Studies, Task Force. (1992) *A vision of powerful teaching and learning in the social studies: Building social understanding and civic efficacy*. Position Statement of the Task Force on Standards for Teachers and Learning in Social Studies; also included in *Expectations of excellence: Curriculum standards for social studies*, (1994, p. vii). Washington, DC.

National Council for the Social Studies, Task Force. (1994). *Expectations of excellence: Curriculum standards for social studies*, Bulletin 89 (p. 3). Washington, DC: National Council for the Social Studies.

National Council on Economic Education. (1999). *Results of the survey of economic literacy*. Available at http://www.nationalcouncil.org/cel/index.htm.

National Education Association. (1916). *Report of the committee on the social studies of the commission on the reorganization of secondary education of the NEA—The social studies in secondary education: A six year program adopted both to the 6-3-3 and 8-4 plan of organization* (p. 12). Washington, DC: Government Printing Office.

National Research Council Committee on Increasing High School Students' Engagement and Motivation to Learn. (2004). *Engaging schools: Fostering high school students' motivation to learn*. Washington, DC: National Academies Press.

Niemi, R. G., & Smith, J. (2000). *Enrollments in high school government classes: Are we short-changing both citizenship and political science training*. Unpublished paper, University of Rochester. (See especially the work of Richard G. Niemi at the University of Rochester: niemi@mail.rochester.edu.)

Noddings, N. (2005). *The challenge to care in the schools* (2nd ed.). New York: Teachers College Press.

Offenberg, R. M. (2001). The efficacy of Philadelphia's K-to-8 schools compared to middle grades schools. *The Middle School Journal, 32*(4), 23–29.

Persky, H. R., Reese, C. M., O'Sullivan, C. Y., Lazer, S., Moore, J., & Shakrani, S. (1996). *NAEP 1994 geography report card* (p. 10). Washington, DC: U.S. Department of Education, National Center for Education Statistics.

Public Education Network, Lynn Olsen. (2005). Retrieved from www.edweek.org/ew/articles/2005/03/16/27pen.h24.html. January 18, 2006.

Ravitch, D., & Finn, C. (1987). *What do our 17-year-olds know?* New York: Harper & Row, 1987. (Also see Diane Ravitch, 1995, *National standards in American education: A citizen' guide*. Washington, DC: Brooking Institute.)

Rose, L. C., & Gallup. (2000). The 32nd annual Phi Delta Kappa/Gallup poll of the public's attitudes toward the public schools. *Phi Delta Kappan, 82*, 48.

Simon, S. B., Howe, L. W., & Kirschenbaum, H. (1972). *Values clarification*. New York: Hart Publishing.

Stotsky, S. (2004). *The Stealth curriculum: Manipulating America's history teachers*. Washington, DC: Thomas B. Fordham Foundation.

U.S. Department of Education. (1983). *A nation at risk: The imperative for education reform*. Prepared by the National Commission in Education. Washington, DC: Government Printing Office.

■ SUGGESTED READINGS ■

The history of social studies and of the men and women who influenced social studies is an interesting topic. See, for example, Saxe, D. W. (1991). *Social studies in schools: A history of the early years.* New York: State University of New York Press, and Hertzberg, H. W. (1981). *Social studies reform 1880–1989.* Boulder, CO: Social Science Education Consortium (project SPAN). More recently, Evans, R. W. (2003). *The social studies wars: What should we teach the children?* New York: Teachers College Press, outlines the history of attacks on social studies.

■ PROFESSIONAL JOURNALS ■

Professional journals are helpful for providing information regarding curriculum and best practices. The most important and widely circulated journal in the field of social studies is *Social Education,* the journal of the National Council for the Social Studies.

The second most popular general social studies journal is *The Social Studies.* More specialized journals such as *The History Teacher* and the *Journal of Economic Education* are helpful. Also valuable are the state social studies journals published in many states, such as California and New York.

■ WEB SITES ■

Character Education Partnership
www.character.org
Most important resource on character education, maintained by Character Education Partnership. This site gives the eleven principles of effective character education plus other resources.

Education Week
www.edweek.org
Top weekly stories and other features about educational issues.

ERIC
www.eric.ed.gov
World's largest source of education information with more than one million abstracts of documents and journal articles on educational research and practice.

National Council for the Social Studies
www.ncss.org
Site of the most important organization in the field of social studies, the National Council for the Social Studies. Material on its associated groups, conferences, workshops, standards, and resources.

National Middle School Association
www.nmsa.org
Primary middle school organization.

Public Education Network
www.publiceducation.org
Along with other educational issues, see the many reports on speaking out on No Child Left Behind. See also Education Week.

Serve Improving Learning through Research and Development
www.serve.org
Funded by the U.S. Office of Education, SERVE has a variety of documents on NCLB and programs and products to support NCLB. Also see the conservative Thomas B. Fordham Foundation (www.edexcellence .net) for analysis of NCLB.

Chapter 2

Planning for the Social Studies

Planning is necessary to meet the wide range of abilities and cultural diversity among students. Curriculum planning of units and lesson plans includes objectives, activities to achieve the objectives, and measurements to evaluate whether the objectives of student learning have been achieved. These topics are organized from the most general broad planning to specific daily lesson plans.

- Planning
- Long-Range Planning
- Instructional Objectives and Specific Standards
- Organizing Content and Skills into Units
- Alternative Forms of Units
- Lesson Plans
- Block Scheduling

■ PLANNING

"Teaching Positions Available: Only Good Planners Should Apply"

This is an extreme statement, but within lies a kernel of truth. Teachers who remain in the profession tend to be good planners. Planning is especially important to meet the needs of all students in the **inclusive classroom.** Chaotic classrooms in which the teacher does not know what to do next can overwhelm even the most dedicated teacher and student. Without planning, a classroom experience can be very frustrating for both students and the teacher. If you do not plan, you usually end up making decisions on the spur of the moment, and at times the consequences are not desirable in terms of student learning. In addition, not planning ahead can waste precious minutes of class time that are lost forever. Lack of planning can also create class management problems.

You may also be asked to plan as a member of a **teacher team.** In the middle school, teams are usually established by grade level. In the high school, teams may be formed with the English department or within the social studies department. It is essential to have an adequate planning period for team effectiveness. Otherwise, the team is only a team in name, not in reality.

In this chapter we are making artificial distinctions for the sake of clarity between planning and teaching methods/strategies and assessment. How to teach—instruction or strategies—is the emphasis in Chapters 3 and 4, and Chapter 5 is devoted to assessment. In planning, you usually have to consider what standard or content or skills are going to be your instructional objectives. For example, you want to use standards to improve student learning. Here is Standard 2C (p. 175) from *National Standards for United States History* (National Center for History in the Schools, no date): "Demonstrate understanding of the impact at home and abroad of United States involvement in World War I."

You now have to consider how this content you have decided is important is going to be taught. What learning experiences will be used to teach the reasons for President Wilson's intervention or the roles of women, labor, and African Americans during the war? Will your students have a debate on whether the United States should have maintained its neutrality during World War I? Will you teach skills and techniques such as comparing the roles of different groups in the United States before and during World War I? What assessment will you use to determine whether students achieve the standard? All units and lesson plans need to address the issue of how the content or skills are to be organized so that students will be able to learn and to measure their achievement. *Curriculum must also adjust to the level of the students and aim to meet the wide range of students' abilities.*

Planning for the Inclusive Classroom

Teachers usually face a diverse group of students who have a variety of learning styles. The reality is that not every single student benefits from your teaching, even if you are a teacher with great skill. Yet all students can learn. The first step is to *plan your lesson for the whole class*. Activities such as prereading and prewriting can help all students. Then you can adapt your lesson plan to specific learners, such as pairing up students, allowing other alternatives, giving more time, rewriting questions, using graphic organizers, and reducing complexity. Assistance from specially trained resource teachers may also be available.

It also takes time for English language learners (ELLs) or English as a Second Language (ESL) students to understand social studies concepts and skills taught in English. Support is needed throughout the semester, not just for one lesson plan. For ELLs and others, you may need to get materials at their reading level, use buddy or peer pairs in assisted reading, at times use homogeneous English competency groups (students who all know Spanish), use sheltered English, or use translation software that can translate material into the student's native language.

Sometimes, teaching students with a wide range of abilities is called **differentiated instruction** or the **differentiated classroom.** In this type of classroom, students take different and multiple approaches to content and skills. Teachers use a blend of whole class, small group, and individual instruction so that all students can make sense of ideas and express what they have learned. Teachers in differentiated classrooms realize that all students bring many commonalities to the classroom, but they also bring differences that make them unique. One important group that often needs more attention is the growing number of English language learners.

Almost every teacher supports the goals of differentiated instruction. The problem comes in trying to implement this important strategy. One of the most common techniques in differentiated instruction is to place students into small groups according to their abilities or readiness (more on small groups in Chapter 4). However, sometimes the groups are formed on the basis of student interest. Often this arrangement involves assigning different materials to the different students or think-pairs. For example, in studying the difficulties facing the Estates General at the beginning of the French Revolution, reading individual biographies on the Marquis de Lafayette or Marquis de Condorcet is often easier for challenged students. Other groups could be formed to investigate one of the Three Estates: the First Estate, the higher clergy; the Second Estate, the nobility; and the Third Estate: the remaining population. Within the Third Estate, one subgroup could examine the peasantry while another subgroup studies the bourgeoisie. As you can tell from this example, the teacher must gather up a wide variety of resources or at least check to see if the content is easily accessible from web sites. Always identify the web sites for students so that students can avoid long searches on the Internet. Another difficulty is that it may take the groups different amounts of time to complete their assignment to describe one of the estates using a chart or bar graph that illustrates the population, land ratio of each estate, the ideology of each class or individual, and the like. Differentiated instruction does take up the teacher's time. For this reason, one recommendation is that teachers start slowly with one unit at a time in implementing differentiated instruction. Differentiated instruction may also be more easily implemented in the middle school or high schools that operate with large blocks of time rather than the standard shorter high school period.

Adaptations

Planning does *not* mean you have to follow a rigid schedule without deviating an iota from your lesson plans. Being attentive to your students' reactions and performances is essential for making changes. In fact, when most middle and high school teachers repeatedly teach the same course, they find they change their lesson plan slightly each time they teach it. One year, they may see that more time needs to be spent on a particular concept. Another year, it may be clear that some students do not have the necessary skills to do the map exercise. There are clear advantages to teaching the same course more than once a day. It not only reduces planning time but also gives you a chance to quickly modify the lesson plans as needed. Probably the only complaint about teaching the same course more than once in a given day is that teachers soon memorize every line of the video they have shown, and they cannot always remember if they told or did certain activities for a given class.

Busy Teachers

Unfortunately, beginning teachers may not devote as much time as necessary to planning because they are so busy correcting papers. In addition, student teachers often have real time constraints, including outside employment so that they can support

Planning and grading students' work are important responsibilities of all teachers.

themselves. Planning does take extensive time for beginners, but eventually, as files of lesson plans and materials are collected, planning does become easier. However, teachers should not use the same *unchanged* lesson plans year after year. Beginners sometimes see experienced teachers walk into a class without written lesson plans. Although some experienced teachers carry their lesson plans inside their heads, even they can forget, and their teaching would be more successful if they had jotted down some notes or had written lesson plans.

Value of Written Lesson Plans

An asset for beginners is that planning gives you confidence. Writing out a lesson plan helps you better remember what is supposed to happen, because in the process of writing the plan you have used multiple senses. You feel more ready to face the class if you have done adequate preparation. As the old saying goes, "A plan a day keeps disaster away." Otherwise, it is unsettling to enter the classroom feeling that you are not adequately prepared.

In addition, planning can help get the creative juices flowing. How can you engage bored students when the topic is the weaknesses of the Articles of Confederation, or China's early empires? What can you do to set up conditions for learning? In planning you can look over some alternatives to gain students' interest and motivation. Would the Articles of Confederation lesson be helped if you were to include more information on the types of government? Maybe the students could present brief skits showing a dictatorship, anarchy, oligarchy, weak executive government, and the like. Could this concept be explored by discussing different ways that families make decisions? It would be closer to the background that students have experienced, but is this possibly too sensitive an area for some students? On the topic of China, should small groups decide whether Emperor Shi Huangdi's Great Wall project indicated that he was a cruel tyrant, or a great builder? Or would it be a good idea to compare Chinese children's obligations to their parents with what your students feel is "due" their own parents? Again, might that activity be an invasion of students' privacy? Maybe a comparison of Chinese children's obligations would be better if compared to another ancient civilization. Thinking over alternatives can help you to make better teaching decisions.

But even with good planning, successful student learning does not always occur. Despite the most careful planning, some lessons fail. No teacher is pleased every single day about how well every class went. And then at other lucky times, a teacher can walk into a class and "wing it" successfully without much preparation.

The critical thing is to critique and *reflect* on your lesson plans, especially the less successful ones, at the end of the day when your emotions relating to the lesson are calmer. Did the students lack the necessary background or skills needed for success? Did you fail to provide important directions? Were students little motivated or interested in the day's topic? What worked and what did not work? Going over these factors and other possibilities can help you improve your teaching to support student learning. Your reactions to the lesson's success are good clues to what happened for the students. Critiques by other teachers and college supervisors can also be valuable.

Make sure to jot down or type your comments so you will have them as a reminder for coming lessons or for repeating the lesson next semester or year. Scribbling notes on the back of an envelope is not as helpful as having written lesson plans using a word processor so you can easily incorporate corrections and suggestions. Written lesson plans should also be kept in labeled folders so you can easily find them next year. It is easy to forget what you taught a long time ago. This is the big advantage that experienced and organized teachers have with all their lesson plans and auxiliary materials. In a second, they can pull out appropriate plans and ideas.

In some cases, written lesson plans are also required additions to your portfolio, or must be available for substitute teachers to use. Before e-mail and fax capabilities, teachers were known to leave their sick beds to deliver lesson plans to their schools for their substitutes, because the written lesson plans required by the principal were not available at the school site. (Now they get out of their sick beds only to *make* lesson plans!) Some teachers have generic lesson plans for emergencies, often on skills. Written lesson plans are also valuable if any parent challenges what you are teaching. They are also used when an administrator comes in for observations and evaluation.

Getting Started: Locating Resources

One of the first things to do when planning lessons is to assemble all your resources. These include the following:

- Your state standards for the social studies; useful also are the standards for language arts or other subjects if there is to be an integrated curriculum
- Social studies state-mandated tests, if any
- Your district's curriculum guides, especially if updated to reflect standards
- Your textbook, teacher's guide, and the publisher's supplemental materials such as tests
- Sources available in the school bookroom
- Media catalogs for your county and district
- Suggestions from your school's media specialist, often the librarian, and your department chair for references, trade books, media, web sites, and maps
- Computer resources, including WebQuests, lesson plans from the Internet, virtual field trips and simulations
- Ideas and lesson plans from teachers in your department or the Internet
- Parent and community resources such as guest speakers and local newspapers
- As much data on the background and abilities of your diverse students as possible
- A school calendar (essential for knowing holidays, changes in schedules)

ON YOUR OWN	**PLANNING AND EMOTIONS**
2.1	*Although there are differences among teachers, a common experience while teaching is feeling frustration and anger. Students typically are the trigger for these negative emotions. These emotions often make teachers tense and intrude on their thinking. What can be done to help reduce teacher frustration and anger?*

■ LONG-RANGE PLANNING

The Curriculum Planning Process

What are the first steps in planning after you gather and have skimmed over your resources? Most teachers look at a calendar for a full year or full semester and then roughly block out how much time they will spend on each **unit,** the main divisions of the curriculum. Given the number of weeks of the school year, how much time will you spend on each unit? At this stage, you may want to use the units in the textbook as a guide. You are also probably using your own philosophy of education and your social studies rationale or approach to the social studies to determine what is important to teach and for students to learn. See Figure 2.1; the different terms within a given box describe the same idea.

By making these tentative choices, you are now doing **long-range planning.** Typically, in the social studies there is far more content to be covered than time. Trying to cover everything is counterproductive and impossible. Can any of the units be given less time or downgraded compared to the others? Give consideration to reduction of time for a given unit when students have already encountered the material from a previous grade level. Think also about examining some topics in depth, a

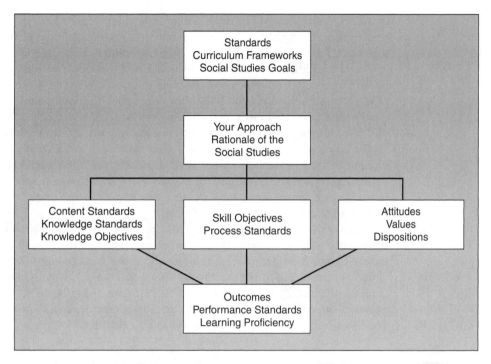

FIGURE 2.1 The Curriculum Planning Process

recommended practice to counter the "mile-wide, inch-deep" approach of textbooks that touch on everything but not with any in-depth exploration.

Remember that your long-range plans are not set in concrete. Usually adjustments have to be put into place, especially as you learn more about your students. However, as you are thinking about your plans in a given semester or year, do not be afraid to ask the teachers in your department or school for help. Experienced teachers have some feel for the ability levels and talents of the student body. In addition, to start from scratch in planning is a difficult task that can almost overwhelm a new teacher. For that reason, more schools are using mentor teachers to help new teachers with their curriculum. But do not rigidly follow someone else's lesson plans, because your class and your philosophy undoubtedly are at least somewhat different from the other teacher's. Be a creative borrower and always be on the lookout for new ideas and materials. This is why teachers attend conferences and workshops and also use the Internet to search for lesson plans. They want to get new ideas and materials for their teaching.

Looking at your tentative units, now check what your state and, if available, district standards require students to learn. In addition, look at the curriculum frameworks of your state and district (if any) to help give more meaning to the standards and goals. Some states have tons of materials and loads of detailed documents to help you, whereas other states have a bare outline of the goals and standards. Remember, the standards are there to help students learn and should not be regarded as a straitjacket. In practice, beginning teachers who do not yet have a considerable investment in prepared units have been more willing to examine their state standards and to try to use them. Using state standards usually has the high approval of administrators who are trying to get the whole school to use standards.

Analyzing the standards may show that there is not a match, for example, between the history textbook you have available and your state's standards in geography, economics, and civics. This may mean that the best solution is for you to incorporate these standards into your history course instead of teaching the geography or economics standards as separate units. Separate units on economics or geography will probably take too much time out of your history curriculum, and integration may be the best policy. Your state may also have some legal requirements on the significance of certain holidays, people, or topics. Again, your own views and rationale will determine what you think is important to teach and whether you should integrate the curriculum.

What you are doing at this stage of the game is thinking about what you want students to gain in content, skills, and values. There should be challenging subject matter that aims at higher-level thinking. This forces us to consider what are sound education practices for the age group we are teaching. Normally we want high student involvement with a connection to real life. To show us that students have achieved these goals, we also have to plan assessments as an ongoing process, integrated with instruction as well as at the end of the unit.

■ INSTRUCTIONAL OBJECTIVES AND SPECIFIC STANDARDS

Objectives, Learning Experiences, and Evaluation

The first two stages in curriculum planning (Figure 2.1) were the broadly stated standards, curriculum frameworks, and social studies goals together with your approach to or rationale for the social studies. At this stage, you still have very sweeping statements of what you want students to gain—responsible behavior toward citizenship and the community, problem-solving skills, and knowledge of history and the other social sciences. It is not a good idea to walk into a classroom only with the idea that you would like to teach democratic values. Your planning now must become more focused and has to zoom into a more concrete plan.

According to Tyler (1949) and many other curriculum writers, all subject areas, from physics to physical education, can be divided into three main questions:

1. What are your objectives or standards?
2. What learning experiences can be set up to meet those objectives?
3. What evaluation will you use to determine whether the objectives have been achieved?

In teaching, it is important that these three steps are **aligned** with one another. Nonalignment occurs when you set up inquiry or thinking activities but evaluate students with a true/false test that does not measure thinking. The most common failing occurs when teachers do not plan the assessments they will use. Too frequently a teacher constructs a chapter or unit test at the last minute without reflecting on the objectives or activities. Publisher's test items are then used even though they may not align with what really happened in the classroom.

For example, let us use the Era 4, Standard 2 in *National Standards for World History* (National Center for History in the Schools, 1994, p. 108), "Students should understand: Causes and consequences of the development of Islamic civilization between the seventh and tenth centuries." For activities, you concentrate on the geography of the Arabian Peninsula and read translated selections of the Qur'an. And then you test the students on the differences between Middle Eastern bazaars and malls in the United States. You can see the mismatch between objectives (the standard), activities, and evaluation. Some of the learning experiences are probably worthwhile and the test item may have high interest to students, but there is not a logical flow from objectives, to learning experiences, to evaluation. There is no continuity in student learning, which makes it more difficult for students to learn the major concepts.

Alignment might be improved if the effects of geography (the desert and oases) on the lifestyle of nomads and trading town-dwellers were investigated, and selections of the Qur'an were examined to see what made Islam attractive to new converts and why Arab Muslims were successful in founding a vast empire. Day-to-day assessment could include written reflections by students as well as informal feedback. Then the formal evaluation of the standard, perhaps an essay question, should flow from the content and skills that were set up.

Social Studies Standards and Instructional Objectives

Today we increasingly see teachers using standards instead of instructional objectives in their planning. Notice how for the standards approach (Table 2.1), the teacher designs the assessment first and then the activities. This is in contrast to the traditional approach. However, if either format for planning is followed carefully, both will likely encourage student learning.

You may have noticed that for standards the most frequent verb is **understand.** Typically you see "The student will understand how the values of those who founded our nation shape it today," or "Students will understand how sources influence the picture we get of historical figures and times." Not as popular anymore, perhaps because of the teacher work involved and also the controversy about the use of objectives (Eisner et al., 1967), are the use of **instructional** or **behavior** or **performance objectives,** which pinpoint more sharply what the student should be able to *do* as a result of instruction. The philosophy behind the use of performance objectives has always been that the verbs must be as clear-cut as possible so that the teacher can observe whether the student really has mastered the objective. In addition, the use of performance objectives enables teachers to determine whether they are concentrating on lower-level, "recall" objectives rather than including some higher-level *thinking* objectives. Pioneers in this field include Bloom (Bloom, Englehart, Hill, Furst, & Krathwohl, 1956) and Krathwohl (Krathwohl, Bloom, & Masia, 1964). Later in 2001, a revision and update of Benjamin Bloom's classic taxonomy was published (Anderson & Krathwohl, 2001).

From the instructional objectives perspective, "understand" is too vague. This means that, in general, *standards* have a broader or less exact verb than the more

TABLE 2.1 Comparison of Traditional versus Standards-Based Planning

Traditional Practice	Standards-Based Practice
Formulate objectives.	Select standard(s) that students need to know.
Design instructional activities.	Design an assessment that will allow each student to demonstrate what he or she knows or can do.
What resources will I need for the activities?	Design appropriate learning activities with resources to achieve the standard for all students.
Design and give an assessment, usually summative assessment.	Give an assessment(s).
Check to see if objectives have been reached; if necessary, reteach; modify next lesson plan or unit; give grades to students.	Use data from assessment to give feedback, reteach, or move to a higher level of the standard or a new standard.

carefully, narrowly defined *objectives*. A teacher may have to take the broadly stated standard and rewrite more concrete objectives.

What is a well-written objective? The ideal objective has three parts: the observable performance (the verb), the elaboration of the condition(s) under which the learner's behavior is to occur, and the criterion measure, the minimum level of acceptable learner performance (Mager, 1962). For example, *The student will **identify** today's nations in the Arabian Peninsula* tells what is clearly expected of the student. The conditions tell what will be provided to the students for the behavior to occur. These could be time constraints, equipment or materials allowed, or aid rendered. Conditions in this objective could be added, such as *When given an outline map, the student will identify today's nations in the Arabian Peninsula*. The next elaboration would be the criterion or evaluation of the student's identification. Would the student have to identify six of the nations to have mastered this objective? Or would four correct be acceptable? Criteria could be both quantitative, how many correct, or qualitative, such as the standard to which the performance is to be compared. Because the criterion is typically difficult to state, most often it is missing from an objective. This is also true of the conditions, which also are not stated. For practical purposes, most teachers believe that an objective that identifies the behavior or an observable performance is satisfactory for their purposes without listing either the conditions or criteria.

The most serious problem in writing objectives is the use of vague and unobservable verbs such as *understand, appreciate, comprehend, know,* and *demonstrate*. Although these general verbs are appropriate to use as objectives for a unit or a goal, they are not specific enough for daily lesson plans. The second most common error is that the objective is written in terms of learning *activities*, such as "The student will read Chapter 3"; "The student will listen to the lecture carefully." For these written objectives, you can see that the behavior is not really observable and may not be related to the objective. A book may be in front of the student or the student may appear to be listening, but there is no satisfactory way to establish that the student has really mastered such a vague objective.

Communicating Expectations to Students

Some teachers who do not use objectives draw on questions as the focus of the lesson. "How do people change the land?" "Why did some nations colonize when others did not?" "How do we find out what happened two hundred years ago?" Regardless of what organization is used for planning, students need to know what standards or objectives are being used. Many experts believe that if students do not know what they are supposed to learn, their chances to be successful are reduced. "If you do not know where you are going, there is less chance of getting there." This old refrain also applies to teachers. If teachers do not know what standards or objectives they have in mind for a lesson, they are not as likely to be focused on what to achieve and the lesson will not be as successful in terms of student learning.

Also pertinent is the issue of what is acceptable performance. How well does the students' work meet the standards? Students may think their essays or their portfolios are outstanding. But they may not know what is considered a good answer or product unless **rubrics,** descriptions of what student work must consist of to get a certain score, are used.

SMALL GROUP WORK	**DO TEACHERS USE OBJECTIVES?**
2.1	*Why do you think some teachers use objectives and others do not? Do you think you will use objectives? Why do clear verbs—outline, draw, create—help students know what to do?*

■ ORGANIZING CONTENT AND SKILLS INTO UNITS

Units

From discussing long-range planning, you know that teachers divide the year or semester into units. A **unit** is a series of sequenced learning activities related to a theme, topic, issue, or problem, which typically lasts several weeks. A unit also includes assessment activities, which are opportunities for students to show what they have learned. Reflecting the dominance of the textbook in social studies classes, teachers often use the framework of their textbook as the way to organize their units. A typical textbook is divided into several large units; within a unit, there are several chapters.

Textbooks have several advantages. Most social studies teachers rely heavily on textbooks for both classwork and homework. However, textbooks usually do not meet the needs of all students in a heterogeneously grouped class. The reading level may be a challenge for many students. Furthermore, most students find reading and answering questions from the text to be boring, especially if these two main activities are repeated day after day.

Therefore, many social studies experts recommend that teachers minimize their use of the routine exercises commonly provided in textbooks, workbooks, or worksheets. Instead, incorporate opportunities for students to develop higher-level thinking skills by using primary source documents. All the basic skills such as reading, oral presentations, listening, and writing as well as using media and technology also are strongly recommended. Moving beyond the textbook and its associated workbook means planning units with a wide variety of learning activities for your students.

Often units are divided into three parts:

1. Beginning the unit, often a motivating activity showing the significance of the topic/unit and how it relates to the students; frequently a video
2. A variety of activities to develop the topic
3. Culminating the topic/unit

Commercial and Free Units

Units are produced by organizations so that teachers will be more likely to insert the unit into their curriculum. These prepared units save the teacher time, because ideas and resources have already been formulated. Organizations ranging from dairy associations promoting dairy products to Proctor & Gamble and financial services have available units for teachers. Some of these units are very attractive, with posters and other colorful materials for students. However, teachers need to be concerned about bias in the materials. The publishers of the unit are producing the unit at their own expense in the hopes that their particular ideas will be incorporated into the classroom.

In recent years, more units and lesson plans have been made available on the Internet by government agencies, especially state departments of education. For example, the California Department of Education has course models for teachers grades 1–12 keyed to the California state standards (www.history.ctaponline.org). For each grade level, several units are available. A condensed version of this **standards-based unit** is used as an illustration in the Sample Unit Plan on Manifest Destiny.

Consider one teaching unit produced by the United States Institute of Peace, an independent federal institution. The goals of this unit are to examine the nature of conflict (particularly violent conflict) among and within nations, and to explore means of conflict management in the international community. Their web site (www.usip.org) is updated weekly with special news and materials. The Sample Unit Plan summarizes the activities, content, and skills for each of seven lessons designed for high school students in any course that includes the study of international relations (U.S. or world history, civics or government, electives, and the like). This 76-page unit includes a diary of a child's life in Sarajevo, cartoons from around the world, and a simulation of an international whaling conference. These are materials that the average teacher would have to spend a great deal of time to find. The focus is not just on content but also on developing complex thinking skills.

SAMPLE UNIT PLAN

MANIFEST DESTINY, TEXAS, AND THE MEXICAN AMERICAN WAR

Standard 8. Students analyze the divergent paths of the American people in the West from 1800 to the mid-1800s and the challenges they faced.

Elements of Standard 8

Six listed. Let us examine just one, **8.85** Describe the Texas War for Independence and the Mexican-American War, including territorial settlements, the aftermath of the wars, and the effects the wars had on the lives of Americans, including Mexican Americans today.

Beginning the Topic

Introduce the concept of Manifest Destiny with a series of art reproductions and maps (resource section indicates where sources are found).

Developing the Topic: Activities (only a few listed for brevity)

1. Class is divided into four document groups and each is assigned a different primary source. After each group studies their own primary source, they turn to another group, where representatives of the four primary source groups explain their own respective document using a jigsaw puzzle approach (see Chapter 4). A variety of questions are available for teachers or for teachers to give to the groups. Examples: What conditions did the Mexican government establish for settlement? How did Mexican officials view settlers who emigrated from the United States? What concerned Mexican authorities most about these settlers?

2. Divide the class into five groups representing the aspirations of Democrats, Whigs, Texans, Mexicans, and Europeans (principally British and French interests). The groups representing U.S. political parties should be larger than the other three groups. These two groups should subdivide to represent different regional factions in each of the parties. Within each group, examine the issues raised in the election of 1844. Extend the activity to allow for Democratic and Whig candidates' campaign speeches and press bulletins representing the attitudes of Texans, Mexicans, and Europeans on the political campaign.

3. Select several students to role-play a meeting between U.S. and Mexican officials to mediate the dispute in 1845. Was war inevitable? What were the alternatives, and were they reasonable considering the attitudes held by leaders of both republics?

Culminating the Topic

1. Have students in groups propose a boundary settlement following the Mexican-American War. Each group presents its boundary to the class in light of topographic

(continued)

maps and the interests of the two nations. Do the student groups' boundaries differ? How do they differ from the boundary established by the Treaty of Guadalupe Hidalgo?

2. Essay question. Support or refute the argument that the annexation of Texas and the Mexican-American War represented Manifest Destiny.

Source: Butte County Office of Education Center for Distributed Learning in collaboration with the California Department of Education.

ON YOUR OWN	A WORKABLE UNIT?
2.2	*Are the standard(s), activities, and assessment aligned for this unit? What is your reaction to this unit? It was designed for the eighth grade. Do you think it would be appropriate for that grade level? For the eleventh grade? Do you think that most of the students would acquire enough background to be able to do the many thought-provoking activities?*

SAMPLE UNIT PLAN

MANAGING WORLD CONFLICT

Goal

Students will understand the nature of conflict among and within nations.

Lesson 1. International Whaling Commission Conference

Activity	Content	Essay Preparation
Simulation of conference on moratorium on whaling.	Conflict among nations and international organizations	Developing clear point of view about a conflict situation
Write reports about conference effects on whaling conflict.	Conflicting points of view on whaling moratorium	Expressing points of view
Debrief reports on whaling conference.	Analysis of media and government reports	Identifying contrasting points of view
Assessment of likely outcomes of whaling conference.	Stages of development of international conflicts	Evaluating contrasting points of view

Lesson 2. Worldwide Conflict

Activity	Content	Essay Preparation
Mapping exercise to locate selected world conflicts.	Conflict (violent) as a worldwide phenomenon	Organizing and analyzing geographic information

| Classifying types of conflict as intranational and international. | Conflicts between nations and between people within nations | Clarifying differences between intranational and international conflicts |

Lesson 3. Case Studies of International Conflict: Causes and Development

Activity	**Content**	**Essay Preparation**
Student groups analyze six case studies of intranational and international conflict.	Types of reasons for conflict (ideological, territorial, racial, identity, etc.)	Contrasting points of view underlying current intranational and international conflicts
Apply diagram of conflict stage development to six cases.	Stages in life cycle of conflict development	Developing strategies to analyze international conflict

Lesson 4. Case Studies of International Conflict: Conflict Management

Activity	**Content**	**Essay Preparation**
Student groups continue analyses of six case studies.	Types of international conflict management activities	Analyzing the pros and cons of alternative approaches to conflict resolution
Apply diagram of stages of conflict resolution to six cases.	Stages in life cycle of conflict resolution or management	Organizing and analyzing political and social data

Lesson 5. Views on Peacemaking

Activity	**Content**	**Essay Preparation**
Paired writing exercise on personal views of conflict and conflict management.	Readings on international conflict and management in six case studies	Reflecting on information and expressing formative ideas in paragraphs
Discuss outcomes of paired writing exercise.	Cultural values underlying and affecting conflict management	Assessing changes in one's own thinking

Lesson 6. Editorial Cartoons on Conflict

Activity	**Content**	**Essay Preparation**
Student groups analyze a set of four editorial cartoons.	Pictorial comments on intra- and international conflicts	Identifying points of view about conflict situations
Discuss messages of editorial cartoons.	Reports of student analyses of editorial cartoon content	Identifying, analyzing, and expressing points of view
Student groups create cartoons that convey pictorial messages about conflict and peace.	Information translated into cartoon representations	Using alternative means of expression to convey cultural points of view on conflict

(continued)

Lesson 7. Reading and Writing about Conflict

Activity	Content	Essay Preparation
Student groups analyze four different forms of writing.	Poetry, excerpt from a fictional short story, diary entries, and a prize-winnning essay	Developing clear point of view about a conflict situation
Write reports about analysis of writing examples.	Points of view on impact of conflict	Expressing points of view
Students begin formal writing activities.	Information about processes of prewriting, prompting, and precomposing	Developing prewriting and precomposing skills

Source: *Managing World Conflict: A Resource Unit for High Schools* (pp. 8–9) by the United States Institute of Peace, no date. Washington, DC: United States Institute of Peace.

Before using this unit, or any commercial unit, the teacher needs to consider how it fits in with the standards and goals of the course. Is it even appropriate? Always look at the main purpose of the prepared unit and determine how it should be changed to meet the needs of *your* students. For example, in this sample unit, each of the lessons (most of which would last a day or two) ends with essay preparation. This is because this federal agency was sponsoring a National Peace Essay Contest with college scholarships. Many teachers using the unit but not having students entering the contest would modify this by using activities such as oral presentations or other ways of organizing students' conclusions.

Note that this unit does not use state standards, because the government agency wanted it to be useful for students regardless of the state they lived in. However, the assessment is built into the unit as students prepare to write an essay, or if the teacher decides to use oral reports.

SMALL GROUP WORK	ANALYZE THE UNITS: MANIFEST DESTINY AND WORLD CONFLICT
2.2	*Is there a wide variety of activities in these units? Provision for the teaching of skills and values? Do you like these units with their concepts and complex thinking skills? Do you think these units would be successful for most high school students? What modifications would have to be made for lower-ability students?*

Planning Your Own Unit: Teacher-Made Units

Teacher-made units have many advantages. A teacher-made unit can individualize the unit to match students' abilities and experiences. In addition, a teacher-made unit can use the teacher's own talents and experiences.

Usually a unit has the following three main parts:

- An introduction or initiating activity, often a motivating experience to help students understand why what they are learning is important
- Lesson plans with a variety of activities to develop the topic
- A final, cumulative experience in which students show what they have learned. In many social studies classes, this is a test at the end of the unit, but it need not be limited to tests.

Format for Units

This is a typical format for a unit. Other formats may be recommended by your district or your instructor.

1. **Title Page.** Include title of the unit, grade level, and your name.
2. **Standards or Framework.** How the unit meshes with the standards or curriculum framework of your state/district. In some districts, the identification number of the standard is given. Rationale for the importance of the unit.
3. **Three Unit Objectives or Focus Questions**
4. **Lesson Plans.** Activities that allow students to achieve the objectives; development activities to explore content or practice skills.
5. **Assessment.** A variety of measurements is best to see that students have achieved the objectives.
6. **Appendix.** Copies of student materials necessary to implement the unit and a list of other related resources.

The preceding format is a mere skeleton. The Sample Unit Plan shows a traditional teacher-made unit on the American Revolution. In contrast, the student teacher in the Sample Classroom Episode planned a literature-based unit.

ON YOUR OWN	**ALTERNATIVES FOR THE UNIT**
2.3	*Do you think using historical fiction is a good idea? What about the alternative of using biographies of historical individuals, such as the founding fathers? What other choices of themes and materials could be made for teaching the American Revolution?*

Integrated Curriculum

Before looking at teacher-made units, give some attention to **integrated curriculum,** or an **interdisciplinary approach.** Advocates of this way of shaping the curriculum believe subjects such as social studies and language arts should be interwoven instead of being taught separately at different times of the day. This recommended practice is more often implemented in the middle school, but you do find English and social studies teachers working together at the high school level, too. Although integration of social studies may occur in other subject areas such as science and art, it is most

SAMPLE CLASSROOM EPISODE

Bonnie Bailes, a student teacher in a middle school, thought about how the last two months had been going. She remembered the excitement and thrill in September of having a new career and how much she wanted to succeed. But along with the exhilaration there were also all those feelings of anxiety and uncertainty. Going into a new and unfamiliar school had also brought out self-doubts. What if she could not make it? Then the first few weeks or so there had been the lack of direction. The cooperating teacher, Elizabeth McGrath, did not seem to know what she wanted Bonnie to do. Bonnie had also felt isolated when her cooperating teacher did not seem to introduce her to the rest of the faculty or facilitate her as being a member of the team.

And there were the surprises! The amount of work was almost unbelievable. At times she felt exhausted because of the stress and time demands. She had not expected the nonteaching responsibilities such as meetings and communicating with parents. True, there were some positives. She was getting to like her eighth-grade social studies class and they seemed to like her too. And really, the discipline was less difficult than she had expected. Of course, there still were individual problems. Alexis was always trying to get her attention and was a real nuisance. Andrew was constantly ready to argue with her. Then there were the passive students who did not cause problems but just sat and did nothing.

Things were better because she was becoming more organized. The classroom had structures and routines. Negatives had been the school politics. The faculty seemed to be divided into cliques who differed enormously on what should be done to improve their school. They did not even seem very professional. The way some of them talked about their students was upsetting, and what a few of them thought about the administrators was almost unprintable.

What were now her major concerns? The first was selecting and organizing the curriculum. Pacing had been troublesome. At times she ran out of activities and other times she did not have enough time. The second problem was how to teach. What could she do to make the content interesting and meaningful? And trying to reach the right level of the students was a challenge. She had been told more than once that she was not teaching a college-level class.

Assessment was another bottleneck. Were they really learning anything? Grading was hard to do. Sometimes she knew certain kids were trying, but they really did not produce good work. Maybe she was too sympathetic and soft with her students.

But she now had to face a big problem. How should she teach the American Revolution? Would using historical fiction as recommended in her methods class work out? Should she stick to the textbook as the main source of information? From looking at the state standards, she knew it was important to help her students understand what it was like to live at that time. Bonnie also checked with the English/language arts teachers to see how they integrated novels into their classes. After discussion with the English department, Bonnie decided to use historical fiction as much as possible in this unit.

Bonnie borrowed from other teachers some "Novel Units," which are teacher's guides with vocabulary words, comprehension questions, and activities for one novel. She had noticed English teachers using published teacher's guides, although she knew she would have to modify some of the activities. She realized that for some classics there was a free unit available on the Internet, but she thought the commercial units would be easier for her to adopt. She also checked the quantities of relevant books in the bookroom.

frequently found with language arts. In some schools, an interdisciplinary team designs a unit.

In particular, historical fiction is highly recommended to bring historical events alive for readers and to explore how people lived at a particular time period. It is felt that literature is more interesting than a textbook and that adolescents will identify more with adolescents portrayed in the literature books. There are now more books available that offer exciting, in-depth portrayals of events, people, places, and issues that immerse readers in the past. New titles are appearing all the time. Each April/May issue of *Social Education* publishes the outstanding titles for social studies K–8. Some teachers also use literature to promote an understanding of justice and injustice at various historical times. For example, *To Kill a Mockingbird* by Harper Lee has been a classic that highlights the injustice of an African American man on trial.

Listening to other teachers' ideas can help you in planning.

The following skills can be emphasized when using historical fiction:

1. **Historical Content.** Learn about historical events from the novel.
2. **Historical Insight.** Make observations and inferences to see beyond obvious facts.
3. **Historical Accuracy.** Decide whether information they are reading is accurate.
4. **Relevancy.** Connect a historical matter in the novel with people and events today.
5. **Literature Skills.** Characterization, theme, plot.

By reading historical fiction, students not only learn content but also can improve their literacy and reasoning skills. Students can make comparisons between the historical novel and what their history textbook and other sources disclose about the same events. In effect, reading historical fiction offers the opportunity for students to improve their content and skills in both social studies and language arts. Observe how the literature focus is integrated into the American Revolution unit in the Sample Unit Plan on pages 50–51.

History through Literature

To illustrate how curriculum integration would be done, the following four books with adolescent protagonists are appropriate for a unit on the American Revolution. These books illustrate why there was conflict between families, friends, and communities.

1. Howard Fast, *April Morning* (New York: Bantam/Random House, 1983), paperback, 202 pages. A story of one day in the life of a young American boy in colonial Lexington, the day on which he joined the militia and saw his father shot down by the British.
2. James L. Collier, *My Brother Sam Is Dead* (New York: Scholastic, 1989), 216 pages. Young Tim Meeker watches his 16-year-old brother go off to fight with the patriots while his father remains a reluctant British loyalist in the Tory town of Redding Ridge, Connecticut.
3. Ann Rinaldi, *The Fifth of March: A Story of the Boston Massacre* (San Diego: Gulliver/Harcourt Brace, 1994), 335 pages. Fourteen-year-old Rachel March, an indentured servant in the household of John Adams, is torn between loyalties when she falls in love with a British soldier who participates in the Boston Massacre.
4. Esther Forbes, *Johnny Tremain* (New York: Yearling/Random House, 1987), 256 pages. Published in 1943 and awarded Newbery Award in 1944, still available in paperback. A young apprentice silversmith injures his hand, struggles with his limitations, and becomes a messenger for the Sons of Liberty.

Reading historical fiction alerts us to the problem of reading texts. The old adage that every teacher is a reading teacher is true. In the social studies as well as other subject areas, teaching vocabulary is essential. Terms such as *revolution, loyalist, indentured servant,* and the like exemplify that new terms must be defined using language and examples that are already familiar to students. In addition, the more ideas from background knowledge that the student can associate with the new term, the more likely the term will be remembered. Indeed, the importance of students' prior knowledge cannot be emphasized enough. Prior knowledge also influences how students relate history to current issues.

Using literature in a social studies class is not without its problems. The first practical problem is having enough copies of the book(s) for a whole class, although some teachers with only one copy of a book read chapters to their class daily. Usually you cannot have a literature-based curriculum unless you have books for your students. Fortunately, paperback editions can reduce the cost significantly, and language arts and library budgets may be used for the purchase. The second problem is the spectrum of reading abilities of the class, which may range from students with mild disabilities and ELL (or EL) students to students with college-level reading skills. For this reason, it is wise to include more than one book in the classroom and to see if an audiocassette edition of a popular and well-used book is available. If media are not available, "buddy" or "peer pairs," in which a stronger reader is matched with a weaker reader, are frequently used.

Most significant, critics are concerned about the trade-offs embedded in the literature approach to teaching social studies. In particular, the time spent on literacy is at the expense of social studies content because using literature in the social studies classroom will take time from the normal social studies topics. In addition, so much attention and time may be required to read the particular novel that the students lose the larger picture of social studies content, in this case, the American Revolution. Check with English or language arts teachers to see if they plan to (or could) use these books in their curriculum. Maybe they will save you the effort.

A novel about particular historical events must be placed in the broader framework of history. Otherwise, students may not realize that the Americans won the Revolutionary War. History content has to be addressed with activities such as timelines; additional investigation, using various sources, into famous people and events; and integrating map and visual information to fill in the background of the novel. Students should always be considering multiple perspectives about the events in the novel and coached to not always accept everything in the novel as being "true."

Given the trade-offs involved in a literature-based approach to the social studies, other planning decisions must be addressed in using literature. One is honoring the concept of student choice. Even if we think a book is a classic and deserves to be read by everyone, some students are going to find a given book boring, tedious, slow going, too detailed, not related to their interests, or perhaps depressing (with characters that die or suffer extreme hardships). One recommendation (Stix, 2000) is for the teacher to give a clear introduction to each book and then allow students to look over the books and to select one. When you have limited copies, have the students rank their choices. Otherwise, for example, more girls may choose *The Fifth of March* (because a young girl is the heroine) than you have books available. Then give a trial period of a day or so to see if the chosen book is interesting to students. Allowing students to switch at the beginning is better than trying to force them to finish a book that is not interesting to them.

SAMPLE UNIT PLAN

THE AMERICAN REVOLUTION, EIGHTH GRADE

Standards/Rationale

The American Revolution is important because it resulted in severing the colonial relationships with England and creating a new nation with a new system of government under which we now live. The American Revolution also had a worldwide impact at that time as well as today. (Note that with this standard, a variety of emphases are possible; focus on a theme such as the nature of conflict or the issue of what is "good government.")

Standard 1: The students will be able to describe the causes of the American Revolution, the ideas and interests involved in forging the revolutionary movement, and the reasons for the American victory.

Integration: Social studies, language arts

Unit Objectives

1. Students will reconstruct the chronology of critical events leading to the armed conflict between the American colonies and England.

2. By reading historical fiction, students will determine how the American Revolution affected the lives of people.

3. Students will demonstrate understanding of the factors affecting the course of the war and contributing to the American victory.

Day 1

Objectives

1. Students will identify three of their heroes and heroines. (An alternative is to use "role models" instead of heroes/heroines.)
2. Students will indicate their choice of a book to read.
3. Students will identify by a pretest what knowledge they already have about the American Revolution.

Procedure

1. Ask students anonymously to list on a worksheet (indicate gender, other categories) the names of three people who they think are heroes or heroines. "In a few words, also write the accomplishments of your heroes or heroines." Students then share their responses in a small group, with a secretary charting each name of a hero or heroine. Either manually or with a computer, tabulate the data for the whole class. Small groups then discuss what makes a hero or heroine. Then ask the secretary from each group to share their small group's working definition of a hero or heroine. Lead a whole group discussion on the characteristics of a hero or heroine. Ask if the characteristics that made heroes in the past are the same

characteristics that today's heroes and heroines possess. Do some further analysis if girls respond differently than boys or if the sports-minded students have different types of heroes or heroines. Many students will report a member of their family as a hero or heroine.

2. After you have introduced each of the four books on the American Revolution, students look over the four books and rank their choices.

3. As a pretest, give students a list of people and events in the American Revolution and ask them to briefly write about the significance of each. This will indicate how much of the fifth-grade American history course students can recall. Remember that assessment is included as an ongoing process during the whole unit.

Day 2
Objectives

1. After defining the concept of revolution, students will identify three of the major events of the American Revolution (see lesson on pages 57–58).

2. Students will make or use a timeline (computer timeliners are available) matching their protagonist's actions with the major events occurring during the American Revolution. (Grading rubric provided.)

Day 3
Objective

Students will compare different interpretations of the Boston Massacre (see lesson on pages 58–59).

For brevity, let us outline what is planned for the next seven days, beginning with activities involving the novels the students have chosen.

Literature Book Activities for the Rest of the Unit

Reading. Each day students read for about twenty minutes, or you may want them to read three days a week. Because the books vary in length, students will be given a list of how many pages are to be read each day for their particular book. This means that some will have to finish their reading assignments at home. To guide their reading, Stix (2000) recommends an open-ended question, such as "Some characters in the book take risks that are likely to cause themselves harm. How do people justify their actions to themselves?"

Small Group Discussions. Every few days there will be Same-Book Literature Circles, a small group discussion on an open-ended question. If five or more students are reading the same book, subdivide the group. After the various groups have discussed their open-ended question, count off students for Different-Book Literature Circles to discuss the same open-ended question in their new groups. This means that students hear from other students about what is happening to characters in the three other books.

In small groups, occasionally use the **hot seat** activity, in which one student is chosen to portray one character in the book, such as Johnny Tremain, and the other students ask that character questions about his beliefs, ideas, and actions, such as "Johnny, why did you. . . ." or "What might you have done differently if given the chance?"

Timeline–Protagonist Activity. Students continue to record what is happening to the protagonist on a timeline coordinated with significant events of the period.

Social Studies Activities for the Literature-Based Unit

This content is from a variety of sources such as textbooks, additional books, and web sites to be used for days 4 to 9.

The key issues of content/standards are the following:

- The background and causes of the American Revolution
- The Declaration of Independence
- Key individuals during this period
- The course and outcome of the war

1. Role-play how a loyalist and a patriot would view such events as the Stamp Act, taxes on tea, and the skirmish at Lexington Green. Repeat with several actors. Record differences and similarities on a Venn diagram. An alternative is to have students write as a loyalist or a patriot on a given event. Students read their response and can illustrate with a poster.

2. Analyze and discuss the importance of the Declaration of Independence. Why is this document the basis of our democracy today? To demonstrate their understanding of the meaning of the Declaration of Independence, students draw up their own document declaring their independence from something, someone, or a group. This can be an actual situation or one you make up. Include four parts: introduction, beliefs, wrongs, final decision.

3. To study key individuals of the American Revolution, view selected parts of the film *1776*. Do character profiles on selected people—George Washington, John Adams, Benjamin Franklin, Thomas Jefferson, and the like. According to the film, what kind of person was this? Students write at least three characteristics and indicate in what circumstances the characteristics were shown. Students can also write short poems about key individuals or events. To learn more about George Washington, visit Mount Vernon at www.mountvernon.org.

4. Examine the course and outcome of the war. Compare how the Revolutionary War was fought with how wars are fought today. What are the similarities and differences? In particular, discuss guerilla warfare, medical care of the combatants, treatment of prisoners, the roles of women, and alliances. These topics can be developed by small groups.

5. Role-play two young African American slaves in Virginia who are uncertain whether to enlist for either the loyalist or the patriot cause or remain on the plantation.

6. On a map, locate the major battle sites and the territorial changes agreed upon in the Treaty of Paris.

7. Using a famous painting of the American Revolution such as *Washington Crossing the Delaware* (often found in textbooks), ask students to interpret what is taking place. What message is the artist trying to convey?
8. Why was music important during the American Revolution? After hearing selected songs and reading a reproduction of the lyrics on an overhead, discuss the meaning of the songs and the historical events.

Assessment

Book (One-half of the grade)

1. Ongoing assessment of participation in small groups during the unit.
2. "Using a five-star rating chart, tell if you liked the book you read (two paragraphs)."
3. "Complete the timeline, coordinating real events with those of the main character in your book."

Social Studies (One-half of the grade)

1. Participation in ongoing activities and written work during the unit.
2. Test items placing events in proper chronological order (see Chapter 5).
3. Multiple-choice items (see Chapter 5).

Read Novel outside of Class?

To avoid taking class time away from teaching social studies, some teachers assign the novel to be read outside of class. Here a major problem is getting students to actually read the novel. This is what one teacher (Heath, 2005) did to ensure that students read outside of class, usually 20 pages a day, or about fifteen minutes at home. Motivate students to do the reading by using prereading questions and teaching the essential vocabulary. Each day the student completes a log on the number of pages read.

Objective 1. You (the student) will complete each day's reading on time with a record of the time spent and pages read each day.

Objective 2. Each day write a minimum of five how, why, and/or what questions that you want answered, including the page number and paragraph where the question arose.

Objective 3. Each day, complete a diary entry of at least half a page reacting to that day's reading in the novel.

Objective 4. Be prepared each day to share questions prepared the previous night for discussion in class the next day.

To be successful using this approach, the teacher carefully reads each day's assignment, noting important paragraphs, quotes, and how each page and paragraph contribute to an idea.

■ ALTERNATIVE FORMS OF UNITS

Using Technology to Teach a Unit on the American Revolution

Teachers are urged to make use of technology to enhance the learning of all of their students. How can this be done with the topic of the American Revolution? Using a

Google search, you or your students will get thousands of hits for the topic of the American Revolution. It is better to use specific educational sites that are more limited and have ready-made lesson plans with the needed resources. **Gateway to Educational Materials (GEM)** (www.thegateway.org) is the Department of Education's mandate for federal agencies to improve and expand access to teaching and learning resources on the Internet. From GEM, after typing in "American Revolution," you could choose the Sample Unit Plan "Was the American Revolution a Revolution?" You could also use other question/problems cited in this particular web site.

SAMPLE UNIT PLAN

QUESTION/PROBLEM: WAS THE AMERICAN REVOLUTION A REVOLUTION?

Objectives
1. Describe the British and American strengths during the Revolutionary War.
2. Explain the importance of key battles in the Revolutionary War.
3. Define the concept of "revolution."
4. Compare and contrast the goals of national leaders, loyalists, women, American traders, and slaves during the Revolution.
5. Evaluate the success of different groups of Americans at achieving their goals during the Revolution.
6. Critique one historian's view of the Revolution.
7. Interpret primary resources.
8. Write an organized essay supporting a point of view on the significance of the American Revolution.

Activities (Not all of the eight lessons/activities have been listed from the web site, and some are abbreviated.)
1. The teacher asks students to brainstorm a definition of *revolution*. Students' responses should be shared and discussed by the class as a whole. The answers should emphasize the concept of change. Revolution implies dramatic change, a radical departure from what existed previously.
2. Students learn about the perspectives of various groups by using readings A–E available from the web site. The teacher should decide whether students will be able to read these passages and interpret them on their own or whether there should be an oral reading.
3. Distribute "American Revolution: Concluding Activity." Some students could answer "yes," "no," or "yes and no" to answer the question of whether the various groups achieved their goals. Or students could answer by writing an essay using "Assessment Criteria: Concluding Activity."
4. Distribute "American Revolution: Two Historians' Views" and answer questions on the worksheet.

From these objectives, you can see that students could be challenged to higher levels of thinking as well as use skills such as reading and writing as they investigate the results of the war from the perspectives of different groups of people. The objectives also lend themselves to students working individually or in small teams as they explore the status of various groups before and after the American Revolution (more on the project method in Chapters 3 and 4). But probably most useful is the availability of handouts suitable for students, although these handouts will need to be supplemented with other information from textbooks and other resources. This use of GEM and other teacher-friendly resources is almost always better than simply sending students to search by themselves on the Internet on such topics as the American Revolution. As critics have noted, web sites that students find often merely reproduce available textbook information and other forms of media that are readily available in the classroom or school library.

Using Concepts on the American Revolution as a Framework for a Unit

Concepts are abstract ideas or categories, such as "family," "cooperation," "justice," and "revolution," that embrace the characteristics of many particular examples. They are the building blocks of organizing our experiences as well as the key ideas in any of the social sciences and history. Unfortunately, too often in history the concepts tend to get buried and "facts" are emphasized.

Concepts can be used to organize a unit on the American Revolution, and these can be tied to your state's standards. Here are some concepts that could be used to organize the content on the American Revolution.

Concepts on American Revolution

Conflict	Equality
Continuity	Government
Independence	Power
Justice	Protest
Nation	Representation
Rights	Revolution
Values	Taxation

You have already seen that one objective on the American Revolution was organized around the concept of "revolution." One recommendation is to choose one concept or more to use as a theme for your unit. Then let the standards of your state dictate the introduction and treatment of the concepts you wish to teach. Concepts cannot be taught as a list. They must have many examples that relate to your students' experiences. However, facts without concepts to organize them result in confusion for students and little retention of the content.

Combination of Traditional and Project Unit

Many teachers want to plan exciting and relevant lessons but are worried that their students will not do well on tests. Here is one high school teacher's solution to the problem (Duvall, 2005).

SAMPLE UNIT PLAN

COMBINATION OF TRADITIONAL AND PROJECT UNIT

Unit Introduction (1–2 Days)

- Motivation, anticipatory set activity (often a video).
- Introduce primary standard.
- Review unit topic.

Teacher's Summary Guide (5–7 Days)

- Review all standards.
- Students read and highlight the 5- or 6-page outline the teacher has prepared.
- Students answer written questions prepared by the teacher.
- Journal entries.
- Timelines for cause and effort.
- Unit test (retakes possible on questions missed; give one-half credit per question to improve grades).

Unit Project/Extension Activity (5–7 Days)

- Performance-based assessment (individual or group).
- Examples: posters, debates, skits, simulations.
- Explore one topic in depth.
- Using primary sources (maps, photos, songs, selections from novels, etc.), students in small groups move to centers and answer questions in packets; two days to finish all the centers (often around eight).

You can see that in this type of unit, the teacher provides learning experiences for about the first half of the unit, stressing the standards. Unique is the unit test taken around the middle of the unit. After the unit test, students focus more on projects and extension activities. Do you like this type of balance?

In summary, the various formats/units presented on the American Revolution all use skills such as thinking and reading as well as achievement of the content objectives/standards. All try to make the activities interesting and meaningful for students. These formats/units also show the variety and creativity that can be developed with the same topic. However, the results in student learning about the American Revolution may vary among the formats/units in terms of both specific content and skills that are emphasized.

■ LESSON PLANS

Detail Is Important

Lesson plans indicate what is expected to happen in a given day. However, most teachers concentrate on the content that is to be presented. They will cover the Declaration of Independence or the Peace of Paris. Often teachers briefly review the content before they teach it. Effective teachers usually introduce new content daily. Nevertheless, consideration must be given to the entry level or the ability level of the wide range of students and what methods will be used to help students learn. Thus, the lesson plan should be written at an appropriate but challenging level.

To meet this consideration, a variety of materials and aids are useful. In addition, student participation is valued. And as mentioned before, the lesson should be aligned with the objectives and evaluation. Also try to get some daily evaluation in, to see how well the students are achieving the objectives. On some days, this evaluation may consist merely of a glance at the students' written work or observation of their participation in a small group.

Teachers use different formats for their lessons plans. Often these include the following items:

- Objectives or standards
- Initiating activity/motivation
- Instructional activities and strategies to achieve objectives/standard
  Alternative strategies for all learners?
- Materials and resources
  What textbooks, documents, etc., support the student during the activity?
- Time element
- Closure/assessment
  What should the student be able to do at the end of this lesson?
- Rubric

What criteria will be used to evaluate or score the student work/performance? In standards-based lesson plans, the assessment comes right after the standard instead of at the end.

What is probably the most serious error in designing lesson plans? Not enough detail! Lesson plans that state only the content such as "The 1920s" or the "Mongol Empire" to be covered, without the activities clearly defined for students to achieve the objective, are a waste of time. In addition, the emphasis on content issues may cause you to neglect skills development. Lessons made day by day may also lose sight of larger goals, such as citizenship education and civic participation—the ultimate purpose of the social studies.

Now, examine a few more lesson plans related to the American Revolution.

SAMPLE LESSON PLAN

DAY 2: INTRODUCTION/OVERVIEW
TO THE AMERICAN REVOLUTION

Objective
Students will identify several of the major events of the American Revolution.

Introduction
Have prepared on a handout, on the board, or a projector foil (transparencies) the following quotations: "Give me liberty or give me death." "No taxation without

(continued)

representation." "There ought to be no more New England men, New Yorkers . . . but all of us Americans." " . . . that all men are created equal, that they are endowed by their Creator with certain unalienable Rights, that among these are Life, Liberty, and the Pursuit of Happiness."

Initiating Activity

1. Ask the students if they recognize any of these quotes. Do they know who said the statements or what group of people would have probably said them? What do they mean?
2. Why, from the quotes, were the American colonists so angry, and what were some of the causes of the American Revolution?

Activities

1. Using the timeline at the beginning of their text's chapter and using what students have remembered from yesterday's identification of people and events, review the important events in the American Revolution.
2. Students make or are given a timeline from 1760–1783 to fill out on the American Revolution. They will also record, below the main timeline, what is happening to the protagonist in their novel.

Closure

Be careful about having students check one another's work for accuracy if used for grading purposes, as it may be considered an invasion of privacy. Self-checks may work satisfactorily.

Further Development

Many documents suitable for primary-source analysis are available for analysis from National Archives and Records Administration. One possibility would be Benedict Arnold's Oath of Allegiance, considered in relation to his behavior and his career. Also check web sites listed at the end of the chapter and those on your state Department of Education's web site.

SAMPLE LESSON PLAN

DAY 3: THE BOSTON MASSACRE

Objectives

1. Students will compare interpretations of the Boston Massacre.
2. Students will interpret historical evidence.

Procedure

Pass out a copy of the engraving of "the Bloody Massacre" by Paul Revere. This is frequently found in textbooks. Explain that this is an engraving printed in the newspapers in the colonies in May 1770. Ask the students to tell you what they think is happening in the picture. Questions to ask:

1. What was the Boston Massacre? Who is involved?
2. What are they doing?
3. What is the surrounding environment like?
4. What can be generalized about the event that the picture shows?
5. As a colonist, how would you feel about the picture?

Hypothesis Making

Have each student make a hypothesis about the event from the information in the picture. Read or print out another interpretation (this can be from one of the novels).

1. Does this description differ from the picture?
2. Why do you think the engraving is different from this description?
3. Does your hypothesis need to change because of the new information?

Closure

It appears that this historical engraving was printed with exaggerations. What reaction did Paul Revere want the colonists to have? Do you think the engraving was effective?

Bringing It Up to the Present

Using current pictures and cartoons from newspapers and magazines, discuss with the students how exaggerations in cartoons appear today. Where? Why?

Further Development

Available from the National Archives and Records Administration are artwork on Ethan Allen, Valley Forge, General George Washington, Benjamin Franklin at the Court of France, Surrender of Burgoyne at Saratoga, and the like. Use a similar format for analysis. Also check web sites listed at the end of the chapter and those on your state Department of Education's web site.

SMALL GROUP WORK	ANALYZE THE UNIT
2.3	*What are the strengths and weaknesses in the various units on the American Revolution? More specifically, critique the following questions: (1) Is it challenging? (2) Are there opportunities for students to act as historians? (3) Are skill development and values integrated with the content? (4) Are there opportunities for assessment of instruction throughout the unit? (5) Would students find the unit interesting and engaging?*

■ BLOCK SCHEDULING

A New Block of Time

What goes on in a classroom begins with the scheduling of classes. Then, in detailed planning for lessons, one of the first things to consider is how much time you have in your period. Some teachers mark in their lesson plans the approximate time each activity will take. There is an old rule of thumb that middle school students need at least three different activities per period because of their more limited attention span. You may rarely get to do three activities, but there will be times when you are glad you had three planned. This advice also applies to the high school level.

Because "time" is so important in teaching, many middle and high schools have moved into some type of **block scheduling.** Instead of having seven (or so) separate, disconnected class periods lasting forty-five to fifty minutes, block schedules typically double the length of a period. Wide variations exist in block scheduling, such as alternative day (A/B or eight-block), trimester plans, and the like. In most block schedules, the equivalent of formerly two periods are blocked together for ninety minutes, and the class meets every day. In this way, a former whole year's time period is condensed into one semester. The student takes half the normal courses in one semester, usually four, and therefore usually interacts with a fewer number of teachers but for a longer daily time period. Still other variations may include giving everyone a twenty-minute sustained silent reading time at the start of the day or a split forty-five-minute class. In some schools, team teaching is combined with a block schedule. Other schools schedule students to meet at times in large groups and then in smaller seminar groups.

Among the advantages cited for block scheduling are the following:

- There is more time to teach and students have more uninterrupted time on task because some unnecessary and unstructured passing time between classes is eliminated.
- Longer periods can support interdisciplinary experiences and reduce lesson fragmentation by allowing activities that take longer than a typical period, such as hands-on class activities, research, speakers, experiments, and projects.
- There is better rapport between students and teachers when there is increased individualization. By staying a longer period of time with the same students, teachers get to know their students better, probably the greatest advantage of all attempts to redesign schools.

Block scheduling can have both positive and negative outcomes. More student-centered learning practices allow students to be more actively engaged in learning; cooperative learning, Socratic seminars, and inquiry learning can be done when there is a longer period of time. However, some teachers struggle to make effective use of the longer time block and may fall back on lecturing. The success of block scheduling requires implementing several instructional strategies to avoid student boredom and wasting time (Chapters 3 and 4). A more recent trend is to return reading to subject area classrooms. All teachers are encouraged to use part of the period to improve reading skills, and this may be facilitated by block scheduling.

SMALL GROUP WORK	**TREND OF THE TIME: BLOCK SCHEDULING**
2.4	*It appears that more schools are adopting some form of block scheduling. This means that you are more likely to teach in a block schedule school. Why would you have to do more planning in a block schedule school? Would there be more*

or less time on administration—attendance, grades, and the like? More or less time on classroom management problems? More or less help for individual students?

| **LARGE CLASS DISCUSSION** | **CONTROVERSIAL ISSUE** |

Differentiated instruction and inclusion are recommended for all classrooms. Do you think these policies are realistic in light of the responsibilities that teachers face? Do they meet the needs of the students at the extreme ends—gifted students and students with disabilities?

■ SUMMARY

Planning is essential to meet the wide range of abilities in a classroom and to motivate students. Teachers usually block out what units they want to teach during a year or semester. A unit approach, with its objectives, learning experiences, and assessments, can best meet the needs of students by focusing on learning. For the same standard/objective, a unit can have different formats. Lesson plans should be detailed enough that what students are to learn is clearly delineated.

■ REFERENCES ■

Anderson, L. A., & Krathwohl, D. (Eds.). (2001). *A taxonomy for learning, teaching, and assessing: A revision of Bloom's taxonomy of educational objectives.* New York: Addison Wesley Longman.

Bloom, B., Englehart, M., Hill, W., Furst, E., & Krathwohl, D. (1956). *Taxonomy of educational objectives: The classification of education goals. Handbook I: Cognitive domain.* New York: Longman Green.

Duvall, R. W. (2005). Getting students to think historically. Presented at the California Council for the Social Studies Conference, Burlingame.

Eisner, E., et al. (1967, Autumn). Educational objectives: Help or hindrance? *The School Review,* 250–282.

Heath, B. E. (2005). Novels to teach the American West. (De Anza Middle School, Ontario, CA). Presented at the California Council for the Social Studies Conference, Burlingame.

Krathwohl, D., Bloom, B., & Masia, B. (1964). *Taxonomy of educational objectives. The classification of educational goals. Handbook II: Affective domain.* New York: David McKay.

Mager, R. F. (1962). *Preparing instructional objectives.* Palo Alto, CA: Fearon Publishers.

National Center for History in the Schools. (No date). *National standards for United States history: Exploring the American experience.* Los Angeles: University of California.

National Center for History in the Schools. (1994). *National standards for world history: Exploring paths to the present.* Los Angeles: University of California.

Stix, A. (2000). Mixing it up: A multilevel book room and flexible literature circles. *Social Education, 64,* 217–220.

Tyler, R. (1949). *Basic principles of curriculum and instruction.* Chicago: University of Chicago Press.

■ WEB SITES ■

Awesome Library K–12 Lesson Plans
www.awesomelibrary.org/social.html
Lesson plans and downloadable readings.

Council for Exceptional Children
www.cec.sped.org
Helps learners with disabilities and their parents.

ESL Lounge
www.esl-lounge.com
Lesson plans, worksheets, and teaching tips.

ESL Party Line
www.eslpartyland.com
Students can access interactive activities.

Gateway to Educational Materials (GEM)
http://thegateway.org/
Lesson plans, curriculum units, etc. by grade level and topic. GEM is the Department of Edcuation's mandate for federal agencies to improve and expand access to teaching and learning resources on the Internet.

The Internet TESL (Teachers of English as a Second Language) Journal
http://iteslj.org
Games, conversation questions, and more for ESL learners.

National Association for Gifted Children
www.nagc.org
Nonprofit group that wants to improve the quality of education for the gifted.

SCORE History/Social Science
http://score.rims.k12.ca.us
California's web site for lesson plans by grade level and topic.

Social Studies Lesson Plans
www.csun.edu/~hcedu013
Select from the lesson plans and teaching strategies to plan classes or complete projects.

Chapter 3

Basic Instructional Methods

Variety in methods is necessary. Using mainly one instructional method does not meet the needs and interests of all students, nor is it appropriate for the teaching of all types of content and skills. Addressing cultural diversity means using a wide repertoire of teaching methods. After reviewing what happens in real classrooms, this chapter concentrates on four primary instructional methods associated with a more direct teacher role that social studies teachers use: teacher lecture, direct teaching, whole class discussions, and questioning. Attention is also given to independent projects. These topics follow:

- The Need for Variety
- What Happens in Real Classrooms?
- Teacher Lectures
- Direct Teaching or Direct Instruction
- Whole Class Discussions
- Questioning
- Independent Projects

■ THE NEED FOR VARIETY

Methods

How to teach troubles beginners and even experienced teachers. What method or combination of methods is best to use in the classroom? Should I put into practice the constructivist approach from my educational psychology class? Or would I be better off following more traditional methods? Typically the terms *methods, instructional techniques, teaching strategies, strategies, and instructional strategies* are used loosely and interchangeably. Once you have gained competency in a teaching method to enhance learning, it is referred to as teaching skill.

As indicated in Chapter 2, almost at the same time you decide **what to teach**—the standard, content, key questions, concepts and skills such as reading and writing—you are also thinking about *how* to teach. Part of the difficulty in making a decision is that the good teaching of social studies, like any other subject, cannot simply be a matter of using the "right" method or strategy. Any method may be more or less effective depending on its fit with the school, the classroom, the teacher, and the needs of individual students. No school, classroom, or student is exactly like any other. Therefore, it is advantageous for every teacher to have a large repertoire of teaching methods or strategies to use. In addition, the teacher must be highly adaptable when classroom management problems occur or the environment changes, as with schedule adjustments.

In practice, some teachers plan for at least three different activities in a class period, often with about half of the classroom time devoted to instruction of content material. Usually a teacher implements a mix of activities within a class period. Balance is achieved when a more teacher-centered method is succeeded by a more student-centered activity. For example, a mini-lecture is followed by cooperative learning experience in which students can more actively participate after listening actively but quietly to the teacher talk. Or, after viewing a video, pairs of students get a chance to talk by sharing their reactions to the video and answering questions about the video. It is usually not productive to have students do the same activity again and again in the same period, such as first reading primary documents, then reading the textbook, followed by reading historical fiction.

It is particularly important to have variety in methods for the following reasons:

- The diversity of learners and their needs
- Multiple intelligences
- Cultural differences
- Language skills of students
- To motivate interest in the subject

Increasingly, more teachers consider cultural and gender sensitivity and give attention to special needs as many classrooms become more culturally diverse and inclusive. This does not mean that traditional methods are wrong. However, traditional methods do not work for all students. Offering a variety allows students to learn in ways that are in line with their communication and cognitive styles.

Remember that methods do not take place in a vacuum. Teachers always want to promote a positive classroom environment that facilitates learning. Always try to encourage students to communicate in positive terms and not to criticize other students. Students also need to feel that they are in a safe environment in which they can express their own point of view on controversial issues.

■ WHAT HAPPENS IN REAL CLASSROOMS?

Two Instructional Perspectives

There are two main instructional perspectives on how to teach. One is called **direct** or the **structured** or **effective teaching** model. According to this perspective, the effective teacher reviews the previous day's work, presents new content or skills, and provides for student practice, feedback, and reteaching—thereby allowing students to work independently on the new material. The other approach is called **constructivist teaching,** as outlined by Brooks and Brooks (1993). This approach asserts that students learn new concepts by expressing their own ideas, being challenged by the ideas and questions of others, and then reformulating their understandings. Students make sense of their school experiences. Constructivist practices, building on the ideas of Dewey (1933) and of Vygotsky (1978), emphasize the importance of students' prior learning by asking what students already know and organizing learning and instruction around important ideas. The constructivist approach de-emphasizes whole class teaching such as lecturing, strives for less student passivity and memorization of facts, and stresses activities that involve higher-order learning, with students being more responsible for their own learning. They "construct their own knowledge."

The contention of this book is that teachers need to use methods from *both* perspectives. This chapter emphasizes the traditional, basic approaches, and Chapter 4 focuses on student-centered approaches.

What methods do social studies teachers actually use? A national survey of teachers' instructional practices by the U.S. Department of Education (Henke, Chen, & Goldman, 1999) used recommended practices of national professional groups (Figure 3.1) as criteria for teachers' instructional practices. (These "recommended practices" were influenced by a constructivist perspective.) Neither the quality nor the effectiveness of the teaching methods was assessed by the survey—teachers simply reported what methods they use.

Grades 7–12 social studies teachers were less likely than teachers in the other core academic subjects—English, mathematics, and science—to use alternatives to whole group instruction. Social studies teachers were also less likely than mathematics and science teachers to work with small groups, and less likely than English and mathematics teachers to work with individual students. Most social studies teachers talked with students (85 percent), led a question-and-answer session (88 percent), or had students answer recall (91 percent) or open-ended questions (87 percent) on a weekly basis. Fewer had students lead discussions (38 percent) or talk with one another (61 percent) on a weekly basis.

With regard to materials, nearly all social studies teachers had students read textbooks at least once a week, both in class (94 percent) and at home (95 percent). The use of supplementary printed materials at least once a week was the lowest (66 percent) of the core academic areas. On use of technologies, with the exception of using the board or an overhead projector at least once a week (95 percent), social studies teachers were well below the average on using media, manipulatives, hands-on materials, and school computers for writing. On the use of portfolios, another recommended practice for assessment, only 9 percent of middle school social studies teachers used this approach during the past semester and 6 percent of high school social studies teachers used portfolios during the past semester, again the lowest compared to the other core academic areas.

What conclusions can be drawn from this national survey? Discouragement may be the first reaction. Perhaps one inference is that, compared to teachers in the other three core areas, social studies teachers unfortunately are not using recommended practices in their own field of history/social studies as much as are teachers in other

FIGURE 3.1 Social Studies Instructional Practices Recommended by National Curriculum Standards

Recommended Grouping Practices and Use of Group Work
Students engage in discussion primarily with other students.
Students work on group projects for individual or group grades.
Students confer with others about work.
Whole class discusses work done in small groups.

Increased Use of Technology and Materials
Students use supplementary printed materials other than textbooks.
Teacher demonstrates concepts using manipulatives, models, etc.
Teacher demonstrates concept using electronic media.
Students put events or things in order and explain organization.

Recommended Types of Tasks
Students explain how class relates to real world.
Students evaluate and improve their own work.
Students solve problems with several appropriate answers.
Students work on projects that require at least one week to complete.
Students work individually on projects or presentations.

Source: Henke, R., Chen, X., & Goldman, G. (1999) *What Happens in Classrooms? Instructional Practices in Elementary and Secondary Schools, 1994–95* (p. 37). Washington, DC: U.S. Department of Education, the National Center for Education Statistics. From standards published by the National Council for the Social Studies, the National Center for History in the Schools, and National Geographic Research and Exploration.

core academic areas. There could be many reasons for this. What it means is that when you observe many, though not *all,* social studies classrooms, you are more likely to see traditional methods such as the teacher providing whole group instruction and students reading the textbook in class and answering questions versus them getting information from a variety of sources, using technology frequently, and participating in group work. This raises an important question: Are the majority of students really being prepared to think and to use citizenship skills for the twenty-first century? Teachers using a variety of methods could help improve this situation.

SMALL GROUP WORK	**ARE THE RECOMMENDED PRACTICES A GOOD IDEA?**
3.1	*Examine one by one the recommended practices in Figure 3.1. Which ones do you think you would like to implement? Why? Which ones do not appeal to you? Why? How would usage depend on the type of class you had?*

Teaching Vocabulary/Reading

Social studies teachers spend a lot of time teaching "concrete" vocabulary, such as the names of famous people and historical events. This instruction is often done by direct teaching, helped by visual aids, which are especially helpful for linguistically or culturally diverse students. Many times the vocabulary must be explicitly taught for the students to make sense of the reading or oral presentation. **Vocabulary** is the primary obstacle facing comprehension in social studies. It is most efficiently learned through direct instruction but is more than a matter of memorizing definitions. Vocabulary instruction is most effective if it relates to prior knowledge and experiences of the students, and is best learned through context rather than a separate vocabulary list.

More difficult to teach is the *conceptual* vocabulary or concepts such as patriotism, progressivism, or implied powers. These concepts are important for understanding social studies because they are the main building blocks of the academic disciplines. To teach concepts successfully, teachers can make connections with students' personal experiences and current events. Then students need to apply the vocabulary and concepts to reading, writing, or discussions in multiple lessons.

Just learning vocabulary is not enough. It is estimated that about 25 to 40 percent of U.S. students do not read well enough, quickly enough, or easily enough to comprehend the content in their courses in the middle and secondary schools. Students must comprehend 75 percent of the ideas and 90 percent of the vocabulary in reading a social studies textbook. To help these students, teachers can add prereading activities, graphic organizers, vocabulary development activities, and media to typical lessons.

Students must learn comprehension strategies to make sense of their reading. Successful reading requires more than just the ability to recognize words. It also requires adequate background knowledge of the historical period or subject area. Otherwise, students read but do not comprehend. In addition, teachers can select concepts related to the reading. These important concepts such as power and culture are not always explicitly labeled in the text. See the Sample Classroom Episode for one teacher's approach to teaching vocabulary.

SAMPLE CLASSROOM EPISODE

TEACHING VOCABULARY

Emma Egan, a seventh-grade middle school teacher, is responsible for the content of a unit on medieval and early modern times. Three other different subject area teachers are part of Emma's team. Every teacher in the school has been charged with improving students' reading skills. Furthermore, Emma and the other team teachers are to follow the same instructional sequence for teaching each new vocabulary word (Figure 3.2) regardless of subject matter. Therefore, an important consideration in buying the new social studies textbook was its explicit attention to how to improve reading skills and especially to build vocabulary. Emma's whole class has the same textbook.

(continued)

FIGURE 3.2 Teaching New Vocabulary

1. The teacher pronounces the word.
2. Ask students to repeat the word, at first slowly and then quickly.
3. Clarify the part of speech.
4. Provide an accessible synonym and/or a brief explanation.
5. Provide a visual representation of the word and/or illustrate with a sentence.
6. Rephrase the simple definition/explanation, asking students to complete the statement by substituting aloud the new word.
7. Assess comprehension with a brief, focused question or task.

Source: From Kinsella, K. (2005). *Narrowing the 4–12 achievement gap: The pivotal role of robust school-wide academic vocabulary development.* Presented at the California Council for the Social Studies, Burlingame, CA.

The social studies textbook is organized with a high-incident and high-utility 500-word list appropriate for academic subjects. If Emma and all members of the team teach students these words, they can help students to read more fluently and to understand the text. In addition, for each lesson, the textbook provides a list of more specific key terms and people. For example, for the unit on the Mayas, high-use words include *hemisphere* and *core.* The more specific key terms and people vocabulary include *Mesoamerica, slash-and-burn agriculture, drought, elite, hieroglyph, codex, stela, alliance, extended family,* and the names of Mayan leaders. Emma feels that at least half of her class, especially the English language learners, normally benefits from her explicit teaching of vocabulary. The strategy calls for students to hear and say the word correctly. The students usually need at least two examples before they can use the word accurately in a sentence. The philosophy behind this approach is as follows:

- Vocabulary is best learned in context.
- Words are learned through repeated exposure.
- Active learning of words is most effective, as opposed to silently working at a desk.
- Students learn more words in context when the context is challenging.

Emma follows this instructional sequence of teaching a new word because it is the school's policy and because of her loyalty to her team. Emma has only one problem in teaching vocabulary. What should she do about the one-third of the class that does not appear to need the explicit teaching of vocabulary? Sometimes on the previous day, she has previewed the vocabulary list and asked students to write down whether they recognize and understand the given vocabulary. Typically the same group of students has already mastered the vocabulary, with the exception of names of people. Yet the explicit teaching of vocabulary, especially if there are more than five words, is taking both planning time (creating a visual) and class time.

Do you believe that a social studies teacher should explicitly teach vocabulary, as is the policy of Emma's school? To all students?

SMALL GROUP WORK	**HOW TO TEACH VOCABULARY**
3.2	*How helpful is directing students to look up a word in a conventional dictionary? A glossary in a social studies textbook? Vocabulary "skilled sheets" done silently at students' desks? Teaching vocabulary when needed and "on the fly"?*

Let us now examine the more traditional methods of teaching social studies, starting with teacher lectures.

■ TEACHER LECTURES

Teacher talk is essential in a classroom and is used more than any other single method. Teachers introduce units, provide information not easily obtainable by students, teach a skill, and direct a review session, just to name a few examples. Some critics say that many teachers are talking far too much. In this context, it may be important to differentiate informal teacher talk from formal lecturing.

Critics of the Lecture Method

Some constructivists will not even address lecturing methods for fear that will encourage teachers to lecture. Constructivists are especially concerned about lectures that are too long and believe that lecturing is used far too often. As with any other method, there are advantages and disadvantages to lecturing. The key advantage is that much content can be covered within a short period of time—although how much is really retained by students is another question. In teaching social studies there is always an oversupply of content. For this reason, delivering lectures is one of the oldest forms of teaching and is common at all levels except the primary/elementary level.

At both the middle school and the high school levels, a lecture may last only ten minutes or so and may be more properly called a **mini-lecture**. However, as students grow older, their attention span for listening to a lecture may increase. Even so, it is often only in AP and honors history/social science classes for juniors and seniors that the lecture may last for a longer time period, more than fifteen to twenty minutes. Many teachers report that their students' attention span for listening is equal only to the time from the beginning of a television program to the first commercial break. After that point, effective listening on the part of some students may decline. In addition, ELL students or others with limited listening skills probably can concentrate on listening for only a short time. So high school social studies teachers should plan for lectures that last no longer than twenty minutes.

Formal Lecture

A **lecture** conveys information and ideas to students from the teacher and, for our purposes, includes the mini-lecture. It is associated with a more formal teacher presentation. Many experts believe lecturing is a poor technique because lectures are a passive student experience without much real learning taking place. Students, it is reported, also may retain little of what was said. They are not active listeners. Instead of listening, students can be engaged in doing homework for other classes, passing notes, or dozing. Yet lectures can be intellectually stimulating and can be an invaluable learning experience. Students can be guided to become more active listeners. However, delivered ineffectively, lectures can make for a boring and barren learning experience.

Lecturing puts the personality and intellect of the teacher or the guest speaker on the spot. Your voice and delivery (too fast, too slow, monotone) are on show. This means that what works for another teacher may not work for you because of individual differences and styles of lecturing. Some teachers and guest speakers can convey enthusiasm about what they are talking about, whereas others do not. If you decide to lecture, you have to discover what kind of lecturing works best for you. Practicing with a tape recorder may help. Even more beneficial is viewing a videotape of yourself.

Lecturing is a form of communication, and the vocabulary used by the teacher must be clear and not beyond that of students. You may have had the experience of listening to a lecture on physics or some other subject unfamiliar to you. The words went on and on, but they did not make much sense to you. Students often feel this way when the teacher lectures on an unfamiliar topic. You as a teacher are well versed in the subject matter, but the students are not.

To be effective, a lecture should be structured, as shown in Figure 3.3.

A framework or **advance organizer** is needed so that the students can put the material into a meaningful learning experience and can see the relationship to their background and interests (Ausubel, 1968). During a lecture, good lecturers typically help students to focus by making statements such as "Look at that timeline" or "This is *really* important." Teachers may also use nonverbal clues such as gesturing to call attention to important points. Then there is a good summary for reinforcement of the learning. Ideally, this should be followed by some form of evaluation of whether the objective was achieved.

FIGURE 3.3 Lesson Plan for a Lecture

Lecture

1. Objectives

2. Entry: Framework, relationship to students

3. Presentation

4. Closure: Review of learning

5. Evaluation

Preparing the Lecture

Lecturing's poor reputation may come from the fact that many teachers do not really prepare their lectures. It is essential that you organize the basic ideas you will present, especially if you expect the students to take notes. Without clear organization, students spend more time puzzling over what they should be putting down instead of listening and thinking. What, if anything, will you do to help students in taking notes?

At worst, a lecture may consist of only anecdotes, jokes, or trivial material. A further problem is that often the teacher merely repeats what is in the textbook or other student materials. The lecture then becomes a rehash of what the students should have read, without new material being presented. This encourages the students not to read the material, because they know it will be covered in the lecture.

A lecture should focus on concepts and ideas, but you always have to remember your audience. Students may need concrete examples and illustrations to make the ideas relevant and alive to them. Good lecturers are always on the lookout for material that will enrich and enliven their lectures. This can include cartoons, newspaper or magazines articles, humorous or dramatic stories, and a very limited amount of relevant personal anecdote. Too many jokes will prevent your students from taking you seriously as a teacher and view you instead as an entertainer. Also avoid giving too much of your personal history or personal incidents.

Interactive Slide Lectures

Visual aids can also do a great deal to add substance and detail to your lecture. **Interactive slide lectures** are recommended (Teachers Curriculum Institute, 1999). The teacher selects powerful images from a variety of sources. Each slide is projected onto a large screen in the center of the room, and there is an overhead projector with a smaller screen in a front corner of the room. For each slide, the teacher prepares a series of questions that move from the basic to the complex. The teacher records the students' responses to the questions on the overhead projector, supplemented with pertinent historical information that was not obvious from the slide. The students then copy these notes into their notebooks. Keep the same slide in front of students for a short period of time or they will lose interest. Yet allow time for the students to do their note-taking.

The teacher also dramatizes the history with **act-it-outs** (Teachers Curriculum Institute, 1999). Slides showing human interaction such as slaves working in the fields in the pre–Civil War period or children working in factories could be demonstrated by standing in front of the slide and acting the roles of the people in the slide. Some teachers give a few minutes for a group to prepare the act-it-out. The rest of the class then can prepare questions for the actors. In this case, the teacher or a student acts as an "on-the scene reporter" to interview the characters about what is happening and how they feel. These methods have moved the typically passive teacher-centered lecturing into an activity with much more student involvement.

PowerPoint and Overhead Projector Presentations

Computer slide shows such as PowerPoint presentations generally take too much preparation time for most teachers unless the lecture will be given several times so that the time investment pays off. However, publishers have prepared PowerPoint slide sets. When slide shows are used, the teacher should not put too much information on a single screen. In place of PowerPoint presentations, simple equipment such as an overhead projector can help students gain insight. With either slides or overheads, make sure that all the students can easily see the material on the screen. Some teachers move the class into two main sections with a center aisle so that heads are not in the way of the screen.

Notes?

You have to decide if you are going to use notes or speak from memory. Beginners are advised to use an outline and notes. You may want to mark in color the most important ideas. Be careful when using notes that you keep an eye on your audience and do not become too stilted. Kinetic variation—the lecturer moving around freely—helps students to keep alert.

Have good eye contact with your students. This helps to maintain rapport with your students and gives clues to their understanding. Looking down all of the time is often a disaster in terms of both delivery and classroom management. However, avoid gazing only at one part of the room or looking at the ceiling or the floor.

Speaking more extemporaneously, if done well, can be very effective. This is partly because the speaker can look directly at the class and note their reactions. But beginners are often worried about running out of material and feel more secure with notes. Speaking without notes requires a good memory, which usually requires going over the lecture before the presentation.

You cannot decide what room you will teach in and may find yourself hampered with a poor physical layout or noise from outside. Nevertheless, try to speak loudly and forcefully so that all can hear you and you do not appear unsure of yourself. If you are to use even simple equipment such as a chalkboard, make sure you have chalk and an eraser. If several teachers share the same room during the day, it is a good idea to carry your own supply of chalk, especially (if you use it) colored chalk.

Student Note-Taking

Can students become more active listeners? Student note-taking can help and is an important student skill. More students are now attending college/universities, but often their first grades are a disappointment to them because they have not mastered **learning strategies,** the new term for old-fashioned **study skills.** Effective note-taking is one of these strategies or skills and is essential for success in many college classes. However, many students relied on their high school social studies teachers to signal what is important, or had outlines available of the material to be covered. In high school, some teachers model learning strategies by handing out a one-page **graphic organizer** to highlight what is important. Other teachers have each student use an **interactive student notebook,** in which the entire class takes notes on a common set of information and then processes this information by making diagrams and flow charts, expressing their reactions to the material, and similar exercises. Needless to say, this is not the typical situation once students get to college.

Teachers should initially help students to understand the organization of their lectures. This is especially important for ELL or ESL learners. Then gradually the students should be weaned from these teacher props, especially in AP classes, so the students can recognize what is worthwhile to take down and what is a digression. Students should be encouraged to read over their notes nightly. Each day in class, the teacher should ask if there are any questions or clarifications needed from yesterday's lecture. Too often, students look over their notes only just before a test, and they cannot figure out why or what they have written. Other students do not even use their notes at this time or any other time. For this reason, it is worthwhile to sometimes allow students to use notes for tests. This can reinforce the value of keeping and understanding their notes. The purpose of note-taking is to help the student, and if notes are not used, they are worthless. In the future, more note-taking will be done using computer technology, but the computer is only a tool.

Some, but not all, students are helped by being in a group review session. There they can compare notes and tutor one another, as often the best way to master material is to be able to explain it to someone else. Some schools have arrangements for tutoring, but for many students, an informal group review session among friends is ideal. In general, too many students spend too little time studying social studies outside of class compared to their other academic subjects (Chapter 8).

Should You Encourage Student Participation?

Besides note-taking, another decision you make is whether to combine lecturing with discussion. In other words, will you move in and out of your own presentation by asking students questions or eliciting their reactions? This is probably the most common procedure found in classrooms and is more informal than a straight lecture. It is sometimes called an **interactive lecture.**

Often your physical movement signals when you want to interrupt yourself. Moving away from your usual lecture spot and stepping into the aisles or in front of the desk may signal students that you are inviting questions. Most teachers want their students to interrupt if they have questions. However, often teachers must make choices if the questions appear to be irrelevant or of little value. Other times teachers say that questions will be answered at the end of the lecture, especially if they plan on covering the topic later in the lecture.

In summary, a lecture is what your speech or English teacher always told you to do when giving a speech. Tell your audience what you are going to tell them, then tell them, and finally, summarize what you told them. For teachers, this means tell students your objectives, tell them how the lecture is to be organized, give a well-planned presentation, and then summarize your points. Better yet, after a clear summary, assign an activity that ties together and reinforces the learning. This activity also provides the variation from the more passive lecture experience to a more student-centered activity.

In some flexible high school time schedules, we are seeing more large group lecturing, later balanced by small group classes in which the lecture material is discussed. Here a PowerPoint presentation for a large audience may be used with advantage. However, it is uncertain how long this large-scale lecturing trend will continue.

SMALL GROUP WORK	**DOES LECTURING DESERVE ITS POOR REPUTATION?**
3.3	*In your opinion, what are the pluses and minuses of using lecturing in middle schools or high schools? Should all students take notes on the lecture? Should the notes be graded later?*

■ DIRECT TEACHING OR DIRECT INSTRUCTION

Correcting the Faults of Lecturing

To combat the offhand and meaningless efforts that pervaded too many classrooms, Hunter (1984) and others advocated a more focused plan of teaching called **direct teaching.** Sometimes this method is called *active teaching* or *structured teaching* or *effective teaching.* With the emphasis on testing, direct teaching and its related formats are getting more attention. Realize, however, that effective teaching can occur with methods other than direct teaching or direct instruction.

Direct teaching tries to correct the faults of the lecture method. As the term implies, the teacher directly teaches the whole class. The Hunter method has been modified by many districts and is shown in Figure 3.4. The lesson model there is especially suitable for teaching **concepts.**

Teaching a Concept: Privacy

See how this five-step direct teaching model would work for teaching the concept of **privacy.** The Center for Civic Education's (1994) National Standards for Civics and Government for both grades 5–8 and grades 9–12 includes a content standards that the student "define and distinguish between private life and civic life." Here the teaching of the privacy concept, one of the most important and controversial issues in the field of individual rights, is appropriate. This lesson could be taught in several grade levels with modifications, though the classroom in the Sample Classroom Episode is at the high school level.

SAMPLE CLASSROOM EPISODE

Teaching the Concept: Privacy

To get the students' attention (**anticipatory set**) is not too difficult, because the privacy right involves use of the Internet and of abortion, both areas of high interest to high school students. Also, privacy issues directly involve students through their high

FIGURE 3.4 Five-Step Direct Teaching, Generic Lesson Plan

1. Anticipatory set (get students' attention)
   a. Focus students.
   b. State objectives of the lesson.
   c. Establish purpose.

2. Instruction
   a. Stimulate recall of previous learning.
   b. Provide new information.
      Explain concept.
      State definitions.
      Identify critical attributes.
      Provide examples.
      Model.
   c. Check for understanding.
      Pose key questions.
      Ask students to explain concept, definition, attributes in their own words.
      Have students discriminate between examples and nonexamples.
      Encourage students to generate their own examples.

3. Guided practice
   a. Initiate practice activities that are under direct teacher supervision.
   b. Monitor closely and constantly to check for understanding.
   c. Provide specific feedback to students.

4. Closure
   a. Make final assessment to determine whether students have met objectives.
   b. Have each student perform behavior on his or her own.

5. Independent practice
   a. Have students continue to practice on their own.
   b. Provide feedback of results.

Note: Thanks to Bill Crandall, one of my former students, for the development of this material.

school transcripts and medical records. The teacher, Sarah Ravitz, states that the objective of today's lesson is to learn about the concept of privacy. Students will distinguish whether in a variety of cases the individual is protected by the right of privacy, is not protected, or it is a gray or controversial area and why the particular decision.

In **instruction,** Sarah Ravitz recalls previous learning on individual rights, and defines the *privacy right:* (1) the right of individuals to be left alone to decide for themselves what their private actions should be; and (2) what information about themselves and their private conduct should be communicated to others or made public. She then gives the conditions that restrict private actions. Then she starts with a relatively simple example using smoking; Sarah Ravitz asks if Haley Lee, a

(continued)

young adult, can smoke in the following places: (1) in her own room in her own house; (2) on a commercial airplane; (3) in her own private plane; (4) on a hiking trail in a National Park; and (5) inside a local restaurant. (Note: Sarah Ravitz prepared by first researching local restaurants' antismoking regulations.) Next she checks for understanding with many more examples, such as asking, "Does Josie have the right to visit a web site with sexual content on her home computer? Can she visit the site when working for an employer? Or can your student transcript of grades be sent out without your permission? What about your medical records?"

For guided practice, Sarah Ravitz hands out a worksheet with several examples: "Can Amazon.com keep track of where you visit on their web site? Can an individual make bombs in his mountain cabin to mail to people he hates? Can Haley play a guitar quietly in her own home? Can Julio practice his drums in an apartment complex? Can DeMarco join the local American Red Cross chapter? Can the government use wiretapping?" As students fill out the worksheet, Sarah Ravitz monitors whether they are making good choices by glancing at their decisions. She sees that most students are having difficulty with the privacy of credit ratings and reteaches by giving more explanations. For the closure portion, students summarize what they have learned. For homework, students are given another sheet of situations in which individuals may or may not have the right to privacy. For example, "Can your server keep track of what web sites you visit and sell them to businesses? Can a Mormon family practice polygamy in an isolated community in Utah? (The Church of Jesus Christ of Latter-Day Saints abandoned polygamy in 1890.)"

Sarah Ravitz is pleased with the results of her direct teaching. She feels that students better understand the complexity of the right to privacy and will not be as likely to use gut reactions when tomorrow she uses examples in which the right to privacy may be more controversial. Students in further lessons will be in small groups discussing privacy controversies. Then she will ask each group to report on the results of their discussion after examining several controversial privacy issues. Sarah Ravitz feels that by explaining the concept first and having the students go through numerous examples of high interest, they are now highly motivated and will be better able tomorrow to think clearly about the more controversial issues of the right to privacy.

Notice that this direct teaching had one main concept. Part of the difficulty for many students while listening is that too much content is piled on them during a given lecture. They are then unable to sort it out into a meaningful experience. It is helpful for the teacher or the students to sketch the main concept(s), supporting elements, and bridges that represent the complexity of the concept.

Evaluating Direct Teaching

Looking closely at the lesson plan for direct teaching in Figure 3.4, you can see the strengths. In all classes, the teacher spends a certain amount of time talking to the students. For some learning, direct instruction is the most effective and efficient method. Think how you learned to use e-mail. Probably someone taught you—you did not learn by reading the computer manual or using trial and error (discovery learning).

How did you learn to find resources in a library using a computer? Hopefully, someone taught you rather than you having to use trial and error by yourself.

If a teacher-centered talking approach is used, too frequently students are given a brief explanation or lecture, told to read the textbook, and then to answer the questions. Being unaware of the value or purpose of what they are to learn, they do not listen attentively to the explanation. Then they do not have a clue about how to do the homework. The direct teaching method aims to remedy these problems by establishing a purpose, using direct instruction to convey the information, and allowing students to practice the activity under teacher guidance; then the students are able to successfully work independently. The direct teaching method has been successful in many classrooms, including schools in low socioeconomic neighborhoods.

Are there any drawbacks to the direct teaching method? Constructivist's claim that the direct teaching method encourages student passivity and neglects students' personal meaning making. These are valid concerns. Yet direct teaching or structured teaching methods are essential skills for any teacher. A teacher must often talk or explain material to students.

Still, as with any method, you always need to consider whether another method or strategy would work better for your class. Would a handout with the main ideas about the right to privacy be more effective? Some ELL students might appreciate having the definition of privacy printed out. Of course, a handout for the lecture could be given to students. It takes time to prepare student materials to go with a teacher presentation, but it may be worthwhile. As is true for all methods, direct teaching requires thoughtful planning to be successful and additional time to individualize or adopt a lesson plan to meet the needs of all students.

In some districts, direct teaching has been controversial because zealous administrators have expected every teacher to follow this approach all the time. Teachers then are concerned that they lack flexibility in teaching. Also, some teachers think the format is more suitable for teaching math or in situations in which small increments of new information are given daily. A neverending argument is that some administrators believe that some teachers object to direct teaching because they would have to do more planning, while teachers respond that they have little time for planning.

In summary, successful direct teaching or the lecture mode can be divided into three main parts. The first part is the beginning, during which the teacher tries to capitalize on student interest or experience. Here the teacher focuses students' attention and uses a structure or framework to help students prepare to learn the material or skill. The objectives for the lesson are clearly stated. The second or middle part of the lesson is the instruction. Ideally, the teacher uses a concept, states definitions, and provides examples. The teacher poses key questions and asks students to explain material in their own words. The final part of the lesson is the end or closure. Here the teacher and students review or summarize the points made in the presentation. Last, some form of assessment occurs so students can demonstrate that they have met the objectives.

SMALL GROUP WORK	**WHAT IS YOUR REACTION TO DIRECT TEACHING?**
3.4	*How much direct teaching do you think you want to do?*

■ WHOLE CLASS DISCUSSIONS

Informal Discussions

Teacher-led **whole class discussions** are a more informal type of teacher talk than lecturing. A discussion starts with the **identification of a problem, issue,** or **topic.** In the course of the discussion, there is **clarification** and **explanation** of the topic. At the end of the discussion, there should be **closure** or a **summary.** A discussion is a reflective process. Discussion is advocated for its usefulness in the development of critical thinking and building a class community, and its value in discussing public issues in preparation for adult civic participation (Engel & Ochoa, 1988; Parker, 1996).

A whole class discussion is distinguished from a **question-and-answer** session. In a question-and-answer session, the teacher assigns material to be studied and then checks to see whether the students have learned the material. Formerly this was called **recitation,** but because of its old-fashioned connotations, teachers frequently call this teacher–student interaction pattern "a discussion." The recitation method is good for making a diagnosis about student knowledge of basic facts. In contrast, however, in a whole classroom discussion, students are to receive information, consider arguments, and orally respond in an open format, all of which are high-level cognitive skills.

Thus, "real" discussions are more than simply a question-and-answer session or recitation. But in actual practice, what are labeled "discussions" are frequently just recitations or question-and-answer sessions with a purpose of facilitating students' recall of knowledge. Sometimes these recitations are called "quiz show" sessions, and students try to give the right answers quickly to the teacher who is asking low-level, convergent questions. Recitation or question-and-answer sessions require little planning and can fit into practically any part of a lesson. For that reason, many teachers overuse this method.

For a whole class discussion to be successful requires the interaction of two factors: the teacher and students. The teacher needs to create a climate conducive to discussion in which it is safe for students to express their views. The teacher must choose topics in which the teacher and students have the necessary background and potential student interest, often a more controversial issue or an open-ended question. A class discussion also needs student engagement, and this factor cannot be automatically assured.

It is true that a successful whole class discussion can be an effective learning experience. It can provide students with opportunities to further skills such as listening, oral expression, critical thinking, and skills in *clarifying* their thinking. Students use what is being said as a thinking device. They listen to one another and build on one another's comments. The teachers and other students can ask a respondent to support her or his opinions.

As a result of a good discussion, a teacher often has a feeling of success at the end of the period and students walk out saying, "Today we had a good class." But whole class discussion can dramatically fail, as countless teachers have found out. Teachers then say: "There was no sparkle," "They just do not respond," "The class was dead." Sometimes a failure may be partially or wholly outside your control, influenced by factors such as the weather, flu, the mood of your students, and the class atmosphere.

Essential for effective classroom discussion is the willingness and ability of at least some students to participate. Some consideration must also be given to classroom etiquette. In a discussion, only one person can speak at a time and respect must be given to all comments, without groans and comments like "Here he goes again." By monitoring and enforcing these rules, you will promote a better climate for discussion. Sometimes students want to participate but they lack the necessary background, either because they have not done the reading or they do not understand the material. In addition, students may not have the verbal skills to process information given at a rapid pace and to participate. Furthermore, too many students lack the confidence or willingness to respond orally in front of the whole class. Peer pressure can be enormous, and students do not want to be perceived as "losers."

Equity issues are also important in a classroom discussion. Teachers have to encourage all students to participate. It would be ideal for every student to make at least one comment during the discussion. This may mean limiting the contribution of the few outspoken students, and especially curbing offensive remarks directed against other students. In many cases, a few students, sometimes males, dominate the discussion. The teacher also has to decide whether to give students credit or points toward a grade for their class participation. Many teachers do this to encourage participation.

Remember that discussions are not just opportunities to have students talk, talk, talk. What they say should be important and relevant to the topic. This means that the teacher asks others for their interpretation, asks whether they agree with what has been said, or, by questioning, moves the discussion along. The classroom discussion should support the objectives of thinking and responding. It should push students to new levels of understanding. Students do not benefit from a classroom discussion if they do not learn anything new during it.

Socratic Method and the Socratic Seminar

In leading a whole classroom discussion, a teacher can use the Socratic method. Most of us are more or less familiar with the Socratic teaching method: The teacher asks thought-provoking questions, students respond to the answers, and both teacher and students ask more questions. Often this requires asking for clear definitions and calling into question what most students assume about a given problem or issue. Students have to give reasons for their answers and consider other points of view. Ideas are challenged and clarified. Students hear about ideas they have not thought about. Sometimes this means the teacher acts as a skeptic and asks students to question their assumptions and to use knowledge to find and to solve problems.

Perhaps this method has a poor reputation among some teachers because they fear that their students will not appreciate being held to such high thinking standards or that their students will think they are being "mean." Some teachers also believe that the Socratic method is confrontational, pitting the teacher against a student or one student against another student. (For this reason, some teachers prefer to call this method a **seminar.**) However, the Socratic method need not be confrontational. The purpose of this method is not for students to acquire information, but rather to learn how to think about assumptions and the meaning of the text or issue. This means that the teacher needs to have skills in managing the discussion and have self-confidence that the method will work.

How much the teacher directs the discussion also varies. It is best to let students explore their ideas by questioning one another, with the teacher redirecting the discussion only when necessary. Sometimes this is called a **reflective discussion.** This is the most difficult form of discussion for teachers to conduct and therefore the one that is least used. Unless students are experienced in the Socratic seminar, most teachers assume a more active role when using the Socratic method. **Deliberation,** when a decision has to be made by a group, is less frequently found in the classroom but could be used by the student council as they look at alternatives.

Regardless of what particular emphasis is used, the following steps are needed to produce good whole classroom discussions.

Preparing for Discussion

To increase the probability of a fruitful discussion, both the teacher and the students have to be prepared. The teacher must be familiar with the material and place it in its proper context. It is advisable for a teacher to prepare a list of questions, issues, and problems to pose. In turn, students need to be prepared before the discussion. This usually includes reading assigned materials or completing certain assignments. To ensure that students are prepared for a discussion, the teacher can try in advance to make the reading or background material as exciting or relevant as possible. Students cannot productively discuss anything unless they first have some understanding of the topic. Good teachers know that the best motivation for participation in discussion is not fear of being called on, but a real interest in the topic.

Starting a Discussion

There are several ways to start a discussion. You can ask the first question and remain silent until there is a response. Or you can read a brief passage and ask for comments. In some experienced discussion classes, students will start the discussion. The best questions to ask are those that lead to multiple answers, as good discussions thrive on multiple points of view.

Sustaining a Discussion

To sustain a discussion, make sure you give positive reinforcement by smiling, nodding, and complimenting students' responses even as you avoid *evaluating* the responses. Do not let misinformation go unanswered, but at the same time do not discourage or embarrass students. Writing students' comments on the chalkboard or the overhead projector shows students that their answers are valued. Always give enough time for students to think, and be careful not to quickly call on the first raised hand.

Sometimes a classroom discussion gets bogged down, becomes repetitive, and moves away from the issues. It can fizzle into silence with no student participation.

What can be done to revive a lagging discussion? You might become a devil's advocate for an unpopular or unacceptable approach—but warn students when you are taking this approach. Sometimes you can read a brief text passage. You can ask "What if" questions about what the effect would have been if a person, group, or nation had acted differently. Or you can bring the discussion to an end and ask students to summarize what they have learned. If the momentum has run out, it is best to end the discussion and move on to another activity, ideally one that reinforces or applies what has been covered in the lecture. This means a teacher needs at least one backup activity for times when discussion no longer is productive. Sometimes teachers allow a discussion to drag on because they have planned nothing else. Even in this worst of cases, a brief summary the following day can reinforce the important points of the discussion and salvage some value.

There are many possibilities for following up on discussion learning. Students can create advertisements urging action on a policy or design political cartoons or illustrated timelines. They can write a personal response in the form of a historical journal or diary, make a postcard, or write poetry about a certain person or event. They can explain what grade (from A to F) they would give to a historical figure such as Stalin or a particular president. Students can also make flowcharts, Venn diagrams, and the like on the content that has been covered in the lecture. Another possibility is to have students write a reaction page to the discussion.

To summarize, in some cases, small group discussions might be more productive and elicit more student participation than a whole class discussion. In other cases, whole class discussions can be fruitful if the teacher has carefully planned and the students participate with gusto. More information on the **issues-centered approach,** a form of classroom discussion, is found in Chapters 6 and 8.

■ QUESTIONING

Importance of Questioning

As indicated in the previous section on whole classroom discussions, adroit **questioning** is an essential teacher skill. Questions are used in a variety of teaching methods that range from whole classroom discussions to the teacher's role as a coach in any inquiry exercise or when working with an individual student. The most important purpose of questioning is to stimulate students' thinking, especially advanced levels of thinking, and to help them reflect on ideas. Good questions can trigger new understandings from previous experiences. The **type** of question asked, the **sequencing** of questions, and the **wait time** a teacher allows for students to formulate answers—all these affect the success of the teacher's questions. Good questions encourage student participation in the class as well as their thinking.

Types of Questions

In some classrooms, about 80 percent of classroom talk is devoted to asking, answering, or reacting to questions, usually questions about the subject. Some teachers ask hundreds of questions a day. Typically, teacher questions dominate, and students

Why are questioning skills so important for teachers?

ask very few questions. Of course, some teacher questions are related to routines in a classroom, such as "How many have finished the reading or the worksheet?" However, here we concentrate on questions that guide student thinking and learning. Critics have complained for years that during a class period teachers ask many questions, sometimes many more than one a minute, but most of these questions are factual, such as "What is the capital of Brazil?" or "Where did the Industrial Revolution start?" Most questions do not require substantial thinking and depend only on rote memory for a correct response.

This is not to suggest that students do not need a basic understanding of a topic. Knowledge questions are essential, and students cannot do higher levels of thinking without the necessary background. But a concentration on factual questions that have only one answer (*convergent* rather than *divergent* questions) does not encourage students' higher-level thinking processes. Too often teachers overuse factual, nondebatable questions. Other times students have little or no conceptual framework for the additional information; consequently they rapidly forget the answers to the questions.

Question Levels

What can be done to improve teacher questioning? An obvious recommendation is to use carefully sequenced questions that start with basic concepts and lead to higher-order thinking questions. (This sequence presumes that students did not already have the basic knowledge.) A more sophisticated suggestion is to formulate questions using Bloom's (1956) taxonomy, which outlines six levels of cognitive processes. Each level of the taxonomy includes the verbs that indicate the level of thought involved in answering a question at that level.

1. **Knowledge** (students recall or recognize information)
   - "Who, what, where, when"
   - Verbs: *recall, identify, define, describe, locate*

2. **Comprehension** (students use previously learned material to rephrase, describe, make comparisons)
   - Verbs: *describe, compare, rephrase, contrast, summarize*
   - Verbs: *tell in your own words, explain, tell the main idea*

3. **Application** (students use previously learned information to solve a problem)
   - Verbs: *apply, classify, use, choose, demonstrate*
   - Verbs: *solve* (only one answer is correct)

4. **Analysis** (students identify reasons or causes; analyze material; reach a conclusion)
   - Verbs: *tell why, analyze, identify the cause of, infer, compare, categorize*
   - Verbs: *detect, determine the evidence, determine a conclusion*

5. **Synthesis** (students produce original work, make predictions)
   - Verbs: *construct, plan, design, develop*
   - Verbs: *write, predict, draw, synthesize, compose*

6. **Evaluation** (students judge the merit of an idea or solution to a problem)
   - Verbs: *evaluate, judge, appraise, decide, support, criticize*
   - "What is your opinion?" "Which is better?"

Bloom's taxonomy has a hierarchy and requires more cognitive skills as a student moves from one level to another. This format for planning, thinking, questioning, making test items, and even designing state and national curricula has been used for around fifty years in schools throughout the nation. The use of Bloom's taxonomy is a well-established procedure that you will encounter in lesson plans of teachers who have created meaningful lesson plans. Bloom's taxonomy may also be used by some of your instructors.

However, in 2001 one of the major authors of Bloom's taxonomy, along with his team members, revised this well-known taxonomy. Their new recommendations were influenced by the more recent research on how learners learn and how they think. The first level is now called "Remember" and the second Level "Understand." The fifth level is "Evaluate" and the highest level, level 6, is "Create," a reverse pattern. This new cognitive organization is illustrated in Figure 3.5. In addition, the Knowledge

FIGURE 3.5 Illustration of Levels of Questions for Cinco de Mayo

1. Remember

What is a holiday in May that is celebrated in Mexico and other parts of the Spanish-speaking world? *Cinco de mayo*

What does *Cinco de mayo* mean? *May 5th*

2. Understand

Explain why Cinco de mayo is celebrated in Mexico. *To celebrate the victory over the French in 1862.*

3. Application

What is a similar holiday that we have in the United States? *Fourth of July*

4. Analysis

Why is Cinco de mayo celebrated in the United States? *Remembering heritage*

Who celebrates Cinco de mayo? *Mainly families with roots in Mexico, Americans*

Why would some Hispanic immigrants not celebrate the holiday? *They want to leave their pasts behind*

Does your family celebrate Cinco de mayo? Why or why not?

5. Evaluate

Should Cinco de mayo be celebrated in the United States?

6. Create

Design a Cinco de mayo celebration for the school.

Write a speech you would give to a group celebrating Cinco de mayo.

---

dimensions are now organized hierarchically into the following four categories, from the lowest to the highest:

   a. Factual knowledge
   b. Conceptual knowledge
   c. Procedural knowledge
   d. Metacognitive knowledge

You may see either of these taxonomies being used in education.

There are other approaches to improving questioning besides using Bloom's taxonomy, but those methods are not widely used or familiar to most teachers. These alternative methods include asking *inference* questions, as when students are shown a photograph and asked to provide missing information, or *interpretation* questions, such as "Explain the meaning of" a cartoon or editorial.

Sequence the Questions

Normally you cannot simply ask questions as they occur to you. Questions often have to be **sequenced**, in a planned order. It usually is not wise to immediately jump to a high-level synthesis or evaluation question before the knowledge basis is established. This might, however, be done to get an opinion at the beginning of the discussion. For example, "Should we have capital punishment?" or "Should we have genetically modified food?" Then more factual questions could be asked. However, teachers typically spend most of the class time making sure that the basic who, what, where, and when questions are answered. The result is that students do not move on to a higher level of thinking. You will have to decide on the proportion of time given to lower and higher levels of thinking questions. Give some careful thought to this decision.

Look at the questions in Figure 3.5. Are they clear? Are they focused? Frequently, teacher questions are ambiguous and poorly phrased. Avoid using too many words and clauses. Be as explicit as possible. When questions are not clear, you will end up repeating or rewording the questions, wasting time as well as frustrating your students, who must try to figure out what you meant. Also, avoid yes/no questions that lead nowhere. This means, ideally, you should write questions into your lesson plans so the questions can be thoughtfully worded. Also, try not to reveal your own conclusions in the wording of your questions; first, let students do their own analysis.

Wait Time and Probing

Even with clear questions, the questioning process can be less than ideal if the wait time (Atwood & Wilen, 1991), the students' "think" time, is too short. In many classes, teachers use a shotgun approach, allowing only one second for students to respond—with the natural result that students have little time to think. When you increase the wait time to five seconds or more, students can formulate longer answers, you get more volunteers, and many of their answers will reflect higher-level thinking. This seems awkward at first, partly because your own teachers probably did not wait, either. Most teachers do not like silence and fear that the class might grow uneasy; they quickly move into rephrasing or answering their own questions.

If a student response is not correct, try to **probe** using a follow-up question to encourage the same student to complete, clarify, or support the earlier response. By asking more specific questions, you hint that the answer is at least partly wrong. In this situation, you want the student to continue to participate, but you also need to clarify what is accurate. Probing is also a way of adapting questions to the ability of the student. You can provide clues or rephrase the question at a lower level. You can use questions of clarification: What do you mean by _____? Or can you explain further? At times, redirecting the question to other students is helpful.

Foster Participation and Equity

To increase participation, avoid attaching a name, as in "Maria, compare the values of the Athenians with the Spartans." As soon as you say "Maria," the rest of the class believes they have escaped answering the question and may tune out. Also, do not habitually repeat student responses, as this may encourage students not to listen to their peers because they know you will always repeat the answer. However, sometimes, for emphasis, it is wise to repeat.

Equity in interaction, in terms of gender and ethnic/racial groups, means encouraging and calling on all students—females and males, the bright and the more intellectually challenged students, those in the back of the room as well as in the front, the most vocal and assertive as well as the shy and quiet students. It is easy to get into the habit of calling on a few students. It takes an effort to break the established pattern. Try to encourage all students to participate, and especially call on those who are reluctant to volunteer if you think they do know an answer. One clue is if they make eye contact with you.

Encourage Student Questions

Encourage students to ask more questions (beyond those such as "Where do I put this reference book?"). Even if you say a million times there is no such thing as a "dumb question," most students are reluctant to admit in front of their peer group that they do not understand something. Students have to be encouraged to ask questions in the discussion. In many cases, the way to find the answer can be thrown back to the student to encourage independent learning, or other students can help answer their fellow student's question. In addition, admit that you do not know everything; if a student asks a question you cannot answer, model aloud how you would go about finding the answer.

In summary, good questions by the teacher cannot be underrated, because they are vital to the success of many teaching methods. We cannot quickly make changes in our personality and other areas, but teachers who are willing to plan (and write out) the questions they will use, and to critically evaluate their own patterns of wait time, sequencing, and student involvement, can make their questioning skills truly shine.

■ INDEPENDENT PROJECTS

Value of Projects

Independent student projects have been advocated for years in education. Do you recall doing any independent social studies projects while you were in school? A **project** requires a student task and a resulting product. It usually takes at least a week to complete and uses several skills such as reading and oral or writing skills. The project should present a challenge to the student but still be doable.

You will recall the recommendations in Figure 3.1 that students work **individually** on projects or presentations and that these projects require at least one week to complete. Or the project could be done by a group (Chapter 4). For many classes, the independent project, made once a quarter or semester, can be valuable experience for the student because it requires students to exercise higher-level thinking skills. Students can make use of what they have learned by producing a meaningful project or performance. Furthermore, projects can encourage students to work independently

Why are independent projects important for students?

and be in charge of their own learning. Often, years later, students will remember the project they developed.

The teacher has to decide whether part or most of the work will be done during class time or if the project will be done mostly outside of class. Because many teachers are reluctant to devote a week or more of valuable teaching time to independent projects, often these assignments are to be completed outside of the classroom. This, of course, presumes that most of the students have both the skills, such as finding resources and evaluating different interpretations, and the motivation to start and to complete the project. If these skills are lacking, for students to complete the project the teacher will need to provide direct teaching for the whole class or coaching for small groups and individuals. Sometimes teachers forget how many skills are necessary to do a project; often students must read for main ideas, track down specific details, take and organize notes, write a report or speech, and make an oral presentation. Often, spending class time in the library can be worthwhile. Librarians are usually happy to introduce students to appropriate sources.

The independent assignment requires careful planning on the part of the teacher. One decision a teacher makes is whether students should choose their own topic or whether the topic comes from a list the teacher has drawn up. Some teachers allow both choices. A student can choose any topic with the approval of the teacher, or a student can choose from the list of acceptable projects. In practice, most students will choose from a list, but occasionally a student will want to work on a topic of his or her own choosing. The latter choice normally requires more independence on the part of the student.

Types of Projects

Probably the most common project is an oral presentation, frequently about a less-known figure in history, such as Catherine Beecher, or Frederick W. Taylor (the father of scientific management), or a group such as the Patrons of Husbandry ("the Grange"). This type of project is especially found in history classes. Taking a more in-depth look at an individual or a group of the time period can supplement and personalize the broad picture of a historical era or a controversial issue. In government and civics classes, projects might be service learning (Chapter 8) or involve school or local issues. Oral presentations can also take other formats, and the use of media is encouraged. A good project for a group is to dramatize a trial or protest march. An oral presentation can include both written and oral work as a student explains her or his own designed poster about a person or an event.

The second most common project is a written research paper on a manageable topic such as women's clothing and dress styles in a certain time period or the growth of a specific department store. But there are other variations. In a project involving a *primary source paper,* a student takes a short primary document and first examines the origins or the impact of the text. Then the student can explore the audience, the social climate, and the message of the document. Another type of project is a *review* paper on a book. This is commonly found in AP classes, where it is typical to assign a nontextbook to be read at least once a semester. Students can also be asked to review television programs, documentaries, and local cultural events such as tribal dancing and neighborhood civic activities.

Other written choices are *policy memos* on controversial issues. Here, the student gives arguments and relevant evidence to support his or her point of view. Some students have produced storybooks or an annotated mural. Some schools have a community service requirement (see Chapter 8), and students are required to write up their experiences on an individual project. Or schools may require a project for a portfolio. On written projects, attention must be given to *plagiarism,* a growing problem with students using the Internet. Some students are not citing the sources of their data and are now "lifting" pages of text from the Internet.

As you can see, no single project assignment works best for every student. Each choice has its own advantages and disadvantages. However, regardless of the assignment, to avoid overwhelming students the teacher needs to specify the standards and deadlines for the project. It is highly recommended that you provide a rubric (see Chapter 5) for how the work will be evaluated and then give specific feedback for improvement. If possible, show outstanding projects that former students have done in the past—but be sure to obtain permission from the former students before you do this.

When assigning an independent project, you cannot simply announce it and expect all students to work independently and complete the project on time. You need to explain the rationale and the benefits of doing the project and show how the content and the skills are related to their lives, especially for being able to work independently. Explain also how the project relates to their course grade. Coaching and encouragement are required to support struggling students, who need to know that they really have the ability to do the project but must work through the difficulties. Check to see that they really understand what they are to do. Frequent monitoring of how students are pro-

FIGURE 3.6 Checklist for Projects

1. What have you completed this week (or last three days or today)?
2. What went well? How can you duplicate this success in the future?
3. What didn't go well? How can you fix this problem and how can you avoid this problem in the future?
4. What remains to be done in your plan?

Points can be given to students for answering these reflection questions.

gressing and what snags they are encountering is essential (see Figure 3.6). These steps encourage success. Then, if at all possible, all written and oral student work should be shared with the whole class and—if possible—other classes or on the Internet. Sharing their projects can make students more aware of the quality of their own work. Students may also put in a little more effort in their work if they know there is an audience beyond the teacher.

In summary, there is a strong rationale for trying to use independent projects for middle and high school social studies students. If done well, successful projects can produce a growth in knowledge and skills. However, teachers normally have to plan carefully, monitor student progress, and take the time to fully evaluate the projects so students can gain specific feedback on their performance.

ON YOUR OWN	**WHAT WAS YOUR EXPERIENCE WITH INDEPENDENT PROJECTS?**
3.1	*Did you ever feel proud of a project you completed for a social studies class? Did you feel it was creative and that you gained a lot from it? Do you believe there is value in using projects at least once a semester for your students?*

LARGE CLASS DISCUSSION	**CONTROVERSIAL ISSUE**
	Mark C. Schug (2003) says that research consistently shows that, although student-centered instruction (cooperative learning, hands-on experiences, projects, etc.) may work in some cases, teacher-centered instruction (direct instruction and lecture) works better with most students and with most teachers. Do you agree with this statement?

■ SUMMARY

Recommendations have been given for social studies teachers to use more group work, more technology, more supplementary materials, and more tasks such as projects. But not many social studies teachers have followed the recommendations when compared to teachers in other core academic areas. Teachers need skills in direct teaching because direct teaching is appropriate at times. Teacher questioning skills are essential in conducting whole class discussions as well as being used in many other methods. Use of individual projects is also highlighted and recommended.

■ REFERENCES ■

Anderson, L. W., & Krathwohl, D. (Eds.). (2001). *A taxonomy for learning, teaching, and assessing: A revision of Bloom's taxonomy of educational objectives.* New York: Addison Wesley Longman.

Atwood, V., & Wilen, W. (1991). Wait time and effective social studies instruction. What can research in science education tell us? *Social Education, 55*(3), 179–181.

Ausubel, D. P. (1968). *Educational psychology: A cognitive view.* New York: Holt, Rinehart & Winston.

Bloom, B. S. (Ed.). (1956). *Taxonomy of educational objectives, the classification of educational goals. Handbook I: The cognitive domain.* New York: David McKay.

Brooks, J., & Brooks, M. (1993). *The case for constructivist classrooms.* Alexandria, VA: Association for Supervision and Curriculum Development.

Center for Civic Education. (1994). *National standards for civics and government* (pp. 45, 89). Calabasas, CA: Author.

Dewey, J. (1933). *How we think.* Boston: Heath.

Engle, S., & Ochoa, A. (1988). *Education for democratic citizenship: Decision making in the social studies.* New York: Teachers College Press.

Henke, R., Chen, X., & Goldman, G. (1999). *What happens in classrooms? Instructional practices in elementary and secondary schools, 1994–95.* Washington, DC: U.S. Department of Education, National Center for Education Statistics.

Hunter, M. (1984). Knowing, teaching, and supervising. In P. Hosford (Ed.), *Using what we know about teaching.* Alexandria, VA: Association for Supervision and Curriculum Development.

Parker, W. C. (1996). Curriculum for democracy. In R. Soder (Ed.), *Democracy, education and schooling* (pp. 182–210). San Francisco: Jossey-Bass.

Schug, M. C. (2003). Teacher-centered instruction: The Rodney Dangerfield of social studies. In J. Leming, L. Ellington, & K. Porter (Eds.), *Where did social studies go wrong?* (p. 101). Washington, DC: Thomas Fordham Foundation.

Teachers' Curriculum Institute. (1999). *History alive! Six powerful teaching strategies.* Palo Alto, CA: Author.

Vygotsky, L. S. (1978). *Mind in society: The development of higher psychological processes.* Cambridge, MA: Harvard University Press.

■ WEB SITES ■

Kathy Schrock's Web Guide
http://school.discovery.com/schrockguide
An abundance of lessons organized around content areas.

The WebQuest Page
http://Webquest.sdsu.edu/webquest.html
A WebQuest is an inquiry-oriented activity in which most or all of the information is drawn from the Web.

Chapter 4

Active, Student-Centered Strategies

Continuing a focus on what we want all of our diverse students to gain from citizenship goals, this chapter concentrates on teacher methods that refigure the traditional roles of teachers and students. These methods are based on the concept that the students should have a more *active* role in their learning and that students should ask more questions, discuss concepts and ideas, and then revise their ideas and misconceptions. Active approaches include more student talk, reading, and writing, areas that are getting more attention. The teaching methods that deepen understanding and improve skills include cooperative learning, "Jigsaw," group projects, Co-op Co-Op, other small group strategies, inquiry, role playing, and simulations. These more indirect methods are intended to balance and complement the direct methods described in Chapter 3. All students need a combination of basic knowledge along with **skills**—the ability to think critically, read a timeline, map, write a response paper, and the like. The main divisions of this chapter are listed below.

- Active Learning

- Cooperative Learning

- Group Projects

- Co-op Co-op

- Other Formats for Small Groups

- Inquiry and Problem-Based Learning

- Role Playing and Simulations

ACTIVE LEARNING

Let us now look at the following more active methods of teaching both content, skills, and values (Table 4.1). Skills, problem solving, creativity, and teamwork are now especially needed by all students in today's changing world.

TABLE 4.1 Active Methods of Teaching

Model	Goal/Objectives
Cooperative learning	Students increase interpersonal (group) skills and content knowledge.
Problem-based learning, inquiry, and inductive teaching	Students increase thinking and analytical skills.
Role playing	Students inquire into personal and social values.
Simulation	Students experience various social realities and examine their reactions to them.

■ COOPERATIVE LEARNING

The Critical Importance of Small Group Discussion Skills

First, consider how essential small group skills are for students and for individuals in all walks of life: In the real world, we all need social skills to communicate with our families, our friends, in work situations, and with others. The interpersonal skills that students can develop, such as listening to others, encouraging others, offering ideas, being a team player, and learning from others, are invaluable to them, both now and in the future. Small group skills are also necessary for participating in a democratic society, because students need to learn to work with all types of people and to hear different ideas from their classmates. Therefore, small group experiences have enormous applications to real-life experiences. For these reasons, in recent years, small group practices have been strongly advocated. Yet students in small group discussions are not just learning skills. Small groups offer a learning context in which students can reflect more critically on the material and their work. In addition, small group activities can help students build a better team climate in the classroom, instead of focusing solely on individual, competitive achievement. Furthermore, students take a more active role in their learning in small groups.

One of the greatest advantages of being in a small group is that it allows more student participation. If you are a member of a class of twenty-five, you have one-twenty-fifth chance of speaking at a given moment. If you a member of a group of three, you have one-third chance of speaking. This opens up the possibility of far more interaction in a small group than a whole group discussion, including more opportunities for personal feedback about the other members' ideas and responses.

In ensuring success for small group work, the teacher has two important tasks: (1) **planning the small group activities**; and (2) **teaching the skills** crucial for participation in small groups, such as listening, respecting members of the group, and giving constructive criticism. These invaluable skills need to be taught, monitored, and rewarded.

Look at the teacher's role in the small group environment (Figure 4.1). It includes determining the group size and composition, dealing with conflicts, resolving status

FIGURE 4.1 Teacher's Facilitator Role in Small Group Learning

- Plans the activity, usually the academic content
- Explains the goals and objectives of the activity
- Monitors the small groups
- May have to teach specific cooperative skills
- Encourages groups to evaluate and process their experience
- Evaluates by giving feedback (oral and written) on what was accomplished; rewards group success

problems, identifying the task, seating the groups, and arranging the materials. Interspersed are the tasks of teaching students small group skills.

Definitions of Small Group Learning

Collaborative learning is a less structured process in which the group members explore a problem, develop procedures, and produce knowledge. Collaborative learning could even include students from different schools working together on a shared assignment by using new technologies. Collaborative learning need not be a face-to-face experience. It has been used by the college/university level, especially in the sciences. And because of the Internet, it is becoming more common in the middle and high schools. In usage the terms *cooperative learning, collaborative learning, complex instruction, group investigation, student team learning*, and *learning together* are often used interchangeably.

The most popular format of small team grouping is **cooperative learning** (Johnson & Johnson, 1994; Slavin, 1990), in which three or more students are bound together by a common purpose to complete a task. In this face-to-face activity, every group member is included and the group works as a team. Students use small group skills and processes or think over their effectiveness as a small group. Students are held accountable individually, and now more often students hand in written work. The group work is also assessed. Note that cooperative learning is not the same as *peer teaching*, which involves two students.

Teachers practice different variations of cooperative learning. Let us first examine the most commonly accepted model for cooperative learning and the planning and teaching the teacher must do to help ensure success. Although the student is the center of attention in cooperative learning, teachers actually may have to do more careful planning, using indirect forms of teaching, than if they were using direct teaching methods such as lecturing or devising questions for the whole group. Teachers still choose the overview of the content in small group work. Teachers also have to make clear to students the objective of the group work and how this is related to learning goals. Teachers monitor what is going on in the groups. Teachers also devise **rubrics** or outlines of their expectations. Giving these to students at the beginning of the assignment can help to guide students in their small group work.

Forming Teams

Group Size and Physical Setting

A cooperative group has at least three members and not more than five. Everyone in the group should be able to contribute. In terms of the physical setting, each group member should be able to see the nonverbal actions of all members of the group—the eyebrows going up, the moving a seat back from the group indicating disapproval and not wanting to be part of the group, the drumming of fingers on the desk indicating impatience or boredom, or members eager to speak. In addition, every member must be able to hear the comments of each group member.

Most teachers seem to prefer pairs and groups of three or four. The size of the group reflects the old advice about hosting a successful dinner party: Everyone should be able to hear and to see everyone else. Did you ever regret that you were seated at the end of the table or in an even more isolated position so that you could not talk to the rest of the group? You must also have experienced a situation in which there are too many people in a group, and individual members started talking to the person next to them instead of addressing their remarks to the whole group. Yet, in the right size group, you probably have felt comfortable and more willing to be friendly.

Ability Levels

A big advantage of having the teacher form teams is that it is a better method than using convenience groups by saying, "Form a small group with your neighbors." If you use this convenience method, often the unpopular students are squeezed out and not invited to be part of any group. Student selection of teammates also runs the risk of having groups of the same gender, ethnic group, and friendship together. In addition, the more disruptive students will attract one another, causing classroom management problems. Another effective method is random assignment by counting out 1, 2, 3, and the like to form groups by their number.

Formerly, almost all experts recommended using mixed abilities or heterogeneous groups when forming the small groups. In fact, this was one of the reported advantages of using small groups; it mixed students of different abilities and could promote positive intergroup relations and self-esteem (Slavin, 1990). According to this point of view, the teacher, based on the abilities of the students, assigns a top, bottom, and two or three middle achievers to each group. In addition, the teacher avoids putting best friends into the same group, because best friends tend to talk and to interact only with each other. The teacher also avoids making groups of all the same gender, or teams that do not proportionately reflect the racial and ethnic makeup of the class.

However, recently there have been debates about what to do about high-achieving students. In some situations, the most expert member explains more to the below-average member of the group, thus helping the below-average member to achieve more, but the middle achievers do not gain as much (Webb, Nemer, Chizhik, & Sugrue, 1998). In contrast, a group of high-achieving students may learn more if put in a group with other high-achieving students, especially when they then work on more complex material (Fuchs, Fuchs, Hamlett, & Karns, 1998). To put it plainly, gifted students can be held back when grouped with weaker students.

This is a real dilemma for teachers. Your decision about grouping probably depends partly on how you view high-achieving students and whether you think the norm should be heterogeneous grouping. Should high-achievers be put in groups to help other students or should they be grouped together and challenged with a more complex assignment? This is not an either/or proposition. Teachers must consider when and how to use heterogeneous and homogeneous groupings. You can alternate groupings depending on the task. In some circumstances, you may want to form groups according to the abilities of the students, and at other times you may form mixed-ability groups. Students can be regrouped for different purposes on a temporary basis.

How Long Should a Group Remain Together?

It usually takes a certain amount of time for a group to develop a team spirit. To be effective, every group needs to develop a good atmosphere. For this purpose, the teacher can set up exercises for team building, which includes having each group establish their own identity with a name. Another team-building exercise is the **round-robin format,** in which students take turns sharing some information with the other team members. In the round-robin exercise, the purpose is to participate equally and to get acquainted with teammates. The task could be naming your favorite sport or interest, or—with a more social studies orientation—the historical figure who you think has influenced the world the most, or which U.S. president or political person you admire the most.

Some teachers keep groups together for a whole semester. Successful small groups of the same students meeting together almost every day of the semester have been reported. Other teachers change every six weeks or even more often, working under the assumption that more frequent changes allow an individual student in the class to get to know all the members in the class and to learn about the wide range of individual responses. Each time a new group is formed, a certain amount of time is usually needed for team building. Of course, how long a small group stays together also depends on how frequently a teacher uses cooperative learning. If small groups meet only once a week, it is perhaps better to keep them together for a much longer period. If groups meet infrequently, it is also a good idea to post the names of members of each group so that after a week or so students do not say, "What group am I in? I forgot." Students have been known to "forget" what group they belong to, hoping that they will be able to join a different group, one with friends.

Conflicts

In many cases, conflict in a group triggers student learning by encouraging the disputants to give explanations or seek alternative explanations. Other conflicts may be on a more personal level. Students need to learn how to resolve personal conflicts. A student may come up to you saying: "I don't like my group; they don't listen to me." Or a few students may complain about a member of the group who is "too bossy" or uncooperative. More than once, teachers have observed someone in tears during cooperative learning. Groups, although usually considered a more pleasant and "fun" activity than listening to a teacher's lecture, can be at times an unpleasant experience for some students. Were you ever in a group of three in which two members of the group intimidated you into agreeing with them? Small groups can generate group pressure and disagreements, and these are not always comfortable experiences. The teacher needs to teach basic conflict management skills such as identify the problem, brainstorm a satisfactory outcome, and agree on a solution.

Status, Gender, and Racial Problems

Status problems affect participation in a small group as well as in the whole class. Classroom status is often based on high ability in reading and writing and a facility for public speaking. Students initially come together in small groups already having a sense of who is smart, average, or slow, coupled with the peer status of who is most popular. In general, the more popular or smart students are, the higher their status.

Because of status, even if a member with lower status gives a good response, often the group will reject it because of their perception of the respondent as someone who does not know very much. Thus, because of status differentials, frequently there is not true acceptance of all members of the group, and a trust relationship never develops. This results in an overparticipation by the "smart" students and an underparticipation by the "slow" ones. Those who are left out feel frustrated and are ready to engage in off-task behaviors. Or, some high school students do not cause any obvious difficulties in the group but simply do not do their share of the work; they lie back, "hitchhiking" and letting the others do the work. This places a burden on the stronger students, who do most of the work and naturally have negative feelings about small group work. The single most serious problem in cooperative learning, after "lacking or not applying skills to participate in small groups," is the lack of individual accountability.

Another problem is gender and racial inequalities in discussion. Males may discredit the ideas of females, and non-minorities may discount the contributions of minority students. Yet all-female or all-minority groups may also have their disadvantages. As with the question of grouping by ability, you may decide not to use the same format for setting up groups all the time.

Teachers can help reduce status differentials by asking for evaluations by the group near the end of the cooperative learning process. Have the group review their group skills by asking, "Did every group member participate? Did the group use its time wisely? Did every member do his or her job? Did group members encourage one another?" Sometimes the teacher assigns one student the job of logging participation during a cooperative learning experience. In addition, the teacher constantly observes what is happening in the groups. Teachers may provide slower students training in the skills and knowledge that are vital to the group so that the group will value them more.

In some student groups, as in adult groups, there are power struggles over who will be the leader and whose ideas are best. There can also be personality clashes, bickering, and insults. After hearing these complaints, the teacher, if not previously aware of the situation, should observe the group in action to see if the undesirable behavior persists for more than one day. Given enough time, with some feedback and encouragement to review their participation, are the group members likely to be able to work out their problems? The teacher can talk to the group to demonstrate how to use conflict management techniques to prevent future problems. Does the teacher need to have a private discussion with one or more students about working together in a group? Many teachers hope for the best because they know that if they make one change, they will be pestered by other students who also want to leave their groups. Sometimes students can "hang in there" if they are told that all of the groups will be changed in two weeks (or some other given time period).

To avoid these problems, a recommended practice is the use of **roles** to encourage more equal participation and to help groups accomplish their tasks. This technique is particularly helpful in the middle school if the groups are relatively inexperienced in the use of cooperative learning. The **facilitator** or chairperson organizes the group's work and makes sure the group understands what its job is. A **checker** makes sure that everyone can explain and agrees with the group's response. The **encourager** keeps up the reinforcement of the group efforts. A **harmonizer** tries to settle conflicts and disagreements. All members of the group should eventually be both encourager and harmonizer at all times.

Some teachers combine the roles of **recorder** and **presenter,** creating one person who writes down the notes on the discussion and later reports the group's responses to the whole class. If these two roles are separated, sometimes the presenter cannot read the recorder's notes very well and has to interrupt to ask the recorder what this scribble means. There also may be a **timekeeper** or a **materials manager.** The timekeeper makes sure the group stays on task to get work done in time. These roles should be rotated among group members so that all get a chance to play the different roles.

The problem with the assignment of roles is that often students do not follow these roles but allow more dominant and higher-status members of the group to take over the coveted roles, especially that of chairperson. Constant monitoring and feedback to the group on its efforts are needed if roles are to be truly rotated.

The Academic Task

The work of Elizabeth Cohen (1994) has been especially helpful in stressing the importance of the task in designing group work. Her criteria for setting up the task are as follows:

- The task should have more than one answer or allow more than one way to solve the problem.
- The task should be interesting, rewarding, and challenging.
- Different students should make different contributions.
- A variety of skills should be used by the group, such as reading, writing, and illustrating.

In other words, the task should not allow for a single right answer or work that can be done quickly by one person. The task should not consist of low-level memory questions, such as "Who was Alexander the Great?" or "What were the weaknesses of the Articles of Confederacy?" A task could involve making a poster urging citizens to enlist in the Civil War or any other war. Tasks should promote dialogue, even controversy, such as rating U.S. presidents according to given criteria.

Perhaps this recommendation that a task require more than one answer is the reason for the less than enthusiastic response of social studies teachers to the implementation of cooperative learning in social studies classes. As they teach history, they may not feel that the subject matter lends itself to multiple-answer questions given their students' variable ability to read for understanding and their own time commitments for locating source documents with multiple perspectives.

But a careful examination of the content can give rise to good questions. For example, "Were the Indian reservations a good idea?" offers more possibilities as a question for designing group work than "What happened to General George Custer at the Battle of Big Horn?" "What were the multiple causes of World War I?" is a better question for small groups than "How did World War I start in Sarajevo?" Of course, these questions presume that students do know something about Indian reservations or the pre–World War I period before the small group discussion begins. A discussion without the necessary background is generally unproductive in terms of either learning or skill development and often ends up as a pleasant but unproductive social chat.

The task needs to be understood by the group members if they are to work productively in a small group. It is often best for the teacher both to explain the task orally and to have it written on a chalkboard or on an overhead transparency so that the groups can look up to remind themselves of what they are supposed to accomplish. The best tasks are clear but have more than one answer. Poor explanations lead to confusion and reexplaining the task.

To ensure that the group stays on task, each group is usually held accountable by having to report back to the rest of the class; this is made clear to the groups before they start the task. This also raises the question of how much **time** should be allocated to the task. Teachers have found that some students will spend the entire period looking for a pencil if they allow this to happen. A **kitchen timer** is useful in cooperative learning and other activities. One recommendation is to set the timer for seventeen minutes of cooperative learning. Of course, the amount of minutes depends on the task; the time could be only a few minutes or an entire class period. After the buzzer goes off, you can decide whether the class needs more time. The timer provides a sense of urgency and helps students get to their work more quickly. This tends to maximize time on task.

It is often wise to announce that the group has only ten minutes or whatever time you decide on for group work. Otherwise, the groups will act more casually about accomplishing the task. It does mean, however, that some groups may not complete their discussion. Even so, many teachers prefer this option to having many groups who have finished their task sitting around with nothing to do. But this time allocation can cause students to engage primarily in lower-level thinking rather than critical higher-level thought. It is necessary to experiment with various time structures depending on the complexity of the topic.

After announcing that the time is up, the teacher asks for reports from the groups for a whole group discussion. The teacher needs to be a facilitator of ideas for the whole class. If groups start repeating the same ideas, the teacher may ask if there are any presenters whose ideas are dramatically different from what has already been given. A good technique is for presenters with different views to argue their points. In addition, the whole group discussion gives the teacher the opportunity to correct inaccuracies or give alternative explanations. If you do not call on every single group, remember next time to call on the groups that did not give their input on the previous cooperative learning experience. Be careful not to always start on the same side of the room.

Many teachers assign a group task but also require each student to record information individually, often on a worksheet or notebook. This gives students a record of what was discussed for review later.

Room and Materials

Ideally, each small group is seated in a circle where group members can both see and hear one another, so usually furniture in the classroom needs to be arranged for small group activities. Nevertheless, remember to have students put furniture back in its original place at the end of the period if another teacher uses the room. One of the disadvantages of small group discussions is that with increased student participation (an asset), in many crowded classrooms the noise level swells as groups work closely together. Some individuals are more sensitive to noise than others and do not work their best in a noisy environment.

Teacher observation of the groups provides clues as to how groups are coming along. Do all members of a group appear to be listening to one another? Or have some members withdrawn from their circle, perhaps actually listening to another group? More teachers in the future will use a handheld computer with appropriate software to record anecdotal notes about behavior in small groups—"on task," "encouraging others"—onto their electronic grade book. Teacher observation is also critical in determining how many groups have finished the task.

Regarding the mechanics of physical arrangements, the teacher also has to decide whether the group will share materials or whether each student in the group will have a copy of a reading. These teacher decisions can promote interaction among students. Some teachers feel there should be only one set of materials for each group, to promote the feeling that "we are all in this together." Other teachers believe that giving each student a copy of the materials is more efficient and does not waste time, as may happen when one student reads the material to the rest of the group. However, the amount of reading should be limited—ideally, not more than a few pages at most. Sometimes the students can be asked to read the material in advance, as in the case of a textbook reading. This means each student needs a copy of the material, whether it is in the textbook or a handout. If there is new vocabulary or concepts, the explanation should be given before the class breaks up into small groups.

SMALL GROUP WORK	CRITICS
4.1	*Some critics believe that cooperative learning has been oversold and that too many teachers just relax during this activity. Others claim that students are not held accountable for their work and are often unclear about the objectives of the work. How valid are these criticisms?*

Jigsaw II

A different small group format is **Jigsaw II.** With this format, the purpose is to have a group of students teach one another material that can be broken down into sections (VanSickle, 1994). This technique is more likely to be used with high school students. In contrast to cooperative learning, in which multiple answers to a question are desirable, here the emphasis can be on factual content. But the goal also could be the analysis of primary source documents, such as having each group examine how a different person reacted to a crisis such as the Great Depression. The Jigsaw II strategy works well if the goal is for students to understand and to review content material for an exam or to cover a less important chapter.

In the first step, each student on the home team becomes an "expert" on one topic by working with members from other teams assigned the same expert topic. These study groups meet and study together to become experts on their assigned topic. It is essential that each study group teaches and tests each member until all members thoroughly understand the assigned content. Otherwise, they will not be in a good position to teach their content to members of their home team. Next, students go back to their home team to teach their teammates the content they have learned in the study group. In the third step, all students are assessed on all of the material covered by all of the teams. It should be noted that there are many variations of Jigsaw (Steinbrink & Stahl, 1994; Priest, 1994). In the original Jigsaw I, students in a group were given only part of the "pieces of a puzzle." This forced cooperation of the small group to solve the puzzle.

The pluses of Jigsaw II are that students acquire new material and then present that material to others. If done well, this strategy is strong not only in terms of students reviewing material, but also for status equalization. The Jigsaw II strategy can be effective if the teacher wishes to divide factual content and have groups of students study, for instance, the geographical features of particular regions, or have each group take a different nation (England, France, Spain, Austrian Empire, Russia) to learn (and then teach) about the rise of monarchies. This may also be a practical solution if there are not enough materials on a given subject for the whole class to investigate. For example, for World War I studies the teacher could divide the content along the following lines: trench warfare, women's jobs during the war, role of African Americans during the war, role of propaganda, and submarine warfare. Recall that the Jigsaw II strategy is more effective if there are definite correct answers to content questions. Answers to questions with multiple and complex answers are too difficult for students to teach to one another. It is most suitable if there is a concrete list of people, places, and dates that all students are to master.

In the Jigsaw strategies, students' test scores are partially dependent on the team average. Typically, each student receives two grades: one individual test score and one for the team average. The use of the team average is to encourage students to stay on task and to help teach their team members, because one of their grades is dependent on how well the whole group does on the test. This lends itself to status equalization because it forces upper-status students to pay attention to how well all the members of the team are learning the content. However, the grading system has to be clearly understood by all, or some students will strongly complain that it is not fair. You can always point out to students that group grades are also used for group projects.

Another good strategy for review and mastery purposes is the **Numbered Heads Together** activity (Stone & Kagan, 1994). Here the teacher asks a question and then students in each small group consult to make sure everyone in their group knows the answer. Then one student is called on by the teacher to answer. Often the successful answerer gets a point for his or her team. This strategy can be good for tutoring students and checking for understanding.

■ GROUP PROJECTS

Value

Group projects or **problem-solving group work,** in which a group researches a question and develops a product such as a colonial newspaper or a dramatic presentation on some aspect of history, has had a longer history than cooperative learning. In group projects, students get together to further their understanding and then share it with the whole class. Unlike cooperative learning, with its stress of group interdependence, group projects may be less structured and have more status differential among students. Because of the wide variety of skills needed, group projects are more appropriate for longer-term projects and older students. They can be used for learning more than just content—as in a debate on perspectives of different groups toward genetic research or the perspectives of landowners, farm families, factory owners, professionals, city officials, and the poor toward the Industrial Revolution. These projects can culminate in a skit or a minidrama of a person facing a crisis in a wartime period, a strike, or revolution. Students can create scenes from the lives of peasants or any other social class, or create a mural. The group project can be used concurrently with the traditional class structure, as students work one or two days a week on their projects. Or a whole week or more can be set aside so that students can work daily on their group project.

Compared to cooperative learning or giving an independent oral report, the success of a group project depends more on a group leader and often a secretary who keeps track of what work has been done and what needs to be done, because the topic is subdivided. For example, for work on producing either a Northern or Southern Civil War newspaper using a date late in 1863, some students could choose to research and then to write a column and a sketch on the fall of Vicksburg, the need for nurses in hospitals, the Battle of Gettysburg, varied responses of Native Americans to the war, changing women's fashions, or editorials on the course of the war. Some of these topics are more difficult than others. It would be worthwhile if one group produced a Southern newspaper and another group a Northern newspaper so that comparisons could be made. *Written work can use higher-level thinking skills.* Easier than written work, for most students, are oral presentations re-creating historical events or the lives of people at a given time period. However, some teachers ask for written documentation for the oral work, plus a full description of sources.

Thus, work in a group project has to be delegated, and each member must clearly understand his or her responsibilities. Some roles may be assigned, such as the role of an actor or a stage manager. If the assignment is not carefully defined and accepted

What might these students have learned about Stonehenge?

at this point, students normally will feel frustrated and be unable or unwilling to move ahead.

Note the variety of skills needed by students to be successful: reading, locating appropriate research materials, analyzing the data, writing and public speaking—*plus* social skills for working with the group, which include careful listening and sharing skills. Ideally, group projects are best used with students who already have developed some group skills. If this is not the case, a smaller, shorter project that will take only a few minutes for the students to act out may be a good first step. For example, students could adopt different roles and present skits about how the French Revolution is changing their lives: a peasant, an aristocrat in exile, a priest, a Parisian working-class woman, a young man about to be drafted, Thomas Paine, and the like. Or the topic could be how the U.S. involvement in the Philippines was regarded by different individuals. The results of the group's efforts, ranging from excellent to poor, are clearly visible to all, especially in an oral group presentation.

Evaluations

You need to assess students' work, including self-evaluations. Some teachers, using a rubric, ask students to mark how they rate their project as they hand in their work or after their presentation. Usually you and your students will pretty much agree on the quality of their work. However, if you feel that students have inflated their assessment, explain to them how you rated their work and offer suggestions for how it could be improved.

At times, teachers have almost given up using group projects after seeing how little some groups accomplished or—even worse—having a group that is totally unprepared for their presentation. This points out the need to coach students and to monitor each phase of the project. However, one good or excellent group presentation can be a model for the rest of the class of what is expected. A good presentation such as one on whether to surrender or continue to fight—George Washington, Napoleon, Robert E. Lee, Churchill in 1940, Gandhi, rebels in various countries—may help other students see what their shortcomings were. Poor results also may indicate that many students do not have the wide variety of skills necessary to do a project and that some direct reteaching may be necessary. Otherwise, students will continue the cycle of unpreparedness unless they learn these skills. Of course, unsatisfactory results also may reflect some students' lack of motivation or lack of ability to be self-directing in planning their work. It is helpful for all students to do a self-analysis exercise on what they could do to improve before undertaking a subsequent project. What we want is for students to learn from mistakes and accept suggestions in a positive way.

Using Technology for Group Projects

More and more students are using technology for their group projects. In some cases, such as CultureQuests (www.culturequest.us), students in the whole class choose a nation such as Ghana or India and link up with another class in the chosen nation. Small groups then focus on areas of culture that are of particular interest to them. This could be literature, art, music, daily life, or traditions of the nation. In turn, the students in the other culture communicate with the class to the mutual benefit of both groups. The class may create and design a web site to publish student work or use videoconferencing. This is really an updated version of the pen pals, now called ePals (www.epals.com), technique of communicating with students of a similar age who live in another country.

In addition, more students are now getting information for their group projects from the Internet. As when using any other data, students must search and evaluate their Internet resources for bias and accuracy. Students must also become aware of their own frame of reference or preconceptions as they read information about other cultures or controversial issues. Students must learn to assess resource materials for fairness and honesty. The Internet may be especially valuable in searching for information on today's headlines such as stem cell research, cloning, genetically engineered food, the death penalty, and the like. Videotaping projects also can help motivate students to do good work.

What factors might have made this group project successful?

■ CO-OP CO-OP

Co-op Co-op shares many similarities with group projects (Kagan, 1992; Stahl, Meyer, & Stahl, 1994). In Co-op Co-op the student first cooperates in small groups in order to cooperate with the entire class. Compared to traditional group projects, with Co-op Co-op there is a greater attempt to have each team member contribute more equally. Students get to choose what they want to investigate, what contribution each will make, and how the project will be presented. However, teacher guidance may be necessary to ensure each team has a fair sampling of students. To tap multiple intelligences and ability levels, the research material may include more non-text materials: a variety of media such as photos, artwork, and audiotapes.

This form of group learning has four main steps: (1) identification of topics; (2) formation of teams; (3) investigation of a selected subtopic; and (4) preparation for presentation. Let us look at how this might work on a unit on the Christian European Middle Ages or the medieval period. After asking in small groups what images students have of the Middle Ages—knights in shining armor, lavish banquets, kings, queens, bishops, monks, wandering minstrels—the teacher and the students could choose what they would like to learn in order to develop a more realistic picture of this time period. From the teacher and the class come the following topics: religion, homes, clothing, health, arts and entertainment, town life, the roles of women, a European castle, knighthood, the Crusades or a particular Crusade, guilds, universities, the Jewish community, and a Gothic cathedral. Teams then are formed on given topics. Teachers should check ahead with librarians to make sure resources are available, including web sites. Check that the web sites are current to prevent students wasting hours tracking down resources. If there are not enough resources, a group's topic might need to be changed or modified.

Follow what happens to one team that selected a European castle as their topic. First the group has to examine the topic and then decide how to divide their work. Would they be better off sticking to one castle, such as the well-known Windsor Castle, or would it be better to include many castles? Will one person make a model of a castle or would it be less work (or more interesting) to show many transparencies of several castles, created using a scanner and research materials? Will another person examine the fortifications of the castle and demonstrate with sketches on a large piece of paper? Should one team member address the daily activities in and around the castle? Or investigate how families lived? Or will another group be covering "the family" when they study homes?

After each member chooses his or her own subtopic, students research their subtopics using all the information available, including the Internet. Then each student presents those findings to the team, and the group prepares for a presentation to the entire class. Formats such as skits, or **debates,** in which a small group divides into two subgroups, giving pros and cons on a given policy, create high interest. One promising presentation is to create an **imaginary newscast** of "current" events such as a castle being attacked, with group members taking the roles of news anchor, foreign correspondent, reporters, and interviewers—plus one person behind the scenes creating the visuals. Each group member can speak for at least one minute to ensure equal participation. A **panel discussion** occurs when a small group of students, usually seated in front of the class, hold a discussion on a topic, issue, or problem. This format is more appropriate for presenting different points of view on a topic.

In summary, in Co-op Co-op or any of the variations, students have to first plan and then do their required share of the labor. A first point to note is that groups often vary in the length of time they need in order to accomplish these objectives. Second, as students engage in their reading, library work, and further research, modifications may have to be made if they find too much or too little data, or discover that their topic overlaps another one. Frequently the group has to help a member who has difficulty getting started. Third, the group plans the presentation together. The typical format is oral, although a group could write out their results to give to the whole class in the form of an outline or notes.

In the presentation, as much verbal interchange among the group as possible should be encouraged or the presentation will degenerate into a series of individual oral reports. A skit consisting of a conversation between enemies who are thinking of attacking a castle, discussing its defenses and weaknesses, would be much more interesting than a mere description of a castle. An illustration of the seating arrangements for a meal or banquet—or better yet, a tableau of students at a table—might be more effective for teaching about the social class system and food served than just reading a report on food or on social classes.

All these necessary steps point out the problems as well as the promises in Co-op Co-op. Multiple evaluations should be used, because normally this activity involves a lot of work on the part of students, often a major undertaking for the semester. These evaluations would include the teacher using rubrics to assess both the use of work time and the quality of the presentation. The teacher may also ask the group to evaluate how they think each member performed. Although often students diplomatically rate everyone highly in their group, at times they will be honest and express their annoyance about anyone who has slacked off. Make sure this process is anonymous to achieve more accurate responses. Some teachers also ask for the whole class to evaluate each presentation, but you do have to be careful because the popularity or unpopularity of students may affect the results.

SMALL GROUP WORK	**SUCCESSFUL PROJECTS?**
4.2	*In your experience, how successful have group projects been? Advantages? Disadvantages?*

■ OTHER FORMATS FOR SMALL GROUPS

Brainstorming

The amount and type of discussion in the small group is also affected by the small group format or structure or purpose the teacher chooses. In a small group, **brainstorming** may be used. The rule in brainstorming is that no one discourages any idea, even silly ones. Typically, brainstorming focuses on a problem relevant to the students' interests and backgrounds. A brainstorming question might be: "Name ways to reduce traffic problems" or "List ways to reduce discrimination." The advantages of brainstorming are that it is fast and many ideas are brought forward.

Students usually build one another's ideas, coming up with many more original ideas than they would if they had to do the exercise by themselves. Students often really enjoy the process, coming up with many ideas. Ideally, one secretary/recorder notes all of the ideas. Sometimes this exercise will diffuse the heavy load of emotions associated with certain issues. The disadvantages of brainstorming are the lack of time to contemplate which ideas are best and the fact that the more verbal and vocal students may contribute more—if not downright dominate the discussion. Typically the lists from each group are read to the whole class. If they are not read, the lists should be collected by the teacher. This fosters group accountability.

However, if you ask a small group to move toward **consensus** on what are the three best ideas to reduce traffic problems or discrimination, you will find that this process takes more time. This is because all members' views must be considered. There is also a tendency for individuals to think their ideas are best and so to hold fast to their own point of view. In some groups, a numerical value (ranking) can be assigned to each idea to indicate what ideas are most popular. Sometimes consensus is not possible, because the students have different values. This is not surprising; often adults cannot reach consensus on what should be done. In a case like this, the group should report that they could not achieve consensus and describe the main different ideas.

Think-Pair-Share

In this strategy, first on their own, students think and write reactions to a question posed by the teacher. For example, "Why did some American Indians (mound builders) in the eastern and central United States build mounds and earthworks?" In an economics class, the question could be "What are the best policies to reduce poverty?" The individual student writes down her or his hypotheses and then discusses them with another student. Then the pair shares their thoughts with the whole class. Some teachers really like this particular strategy because it first forces an individual student to think and to write for herself or himself. Teachers may want to counter the possibility that students feel they can think of good ideas only when they are in a group—that there is no inspiration when they work alone. This technique also is helpful for generating and revising hypotheses and encourages concept development as well as participation and involvement.

Response Groups

After viewing a presentation such as a film or debate, students in a **response group** give their reaction to the presentation. This strategy is especially promising if students respond emotionally to the presentation, because it allows more airing of reactions than could be done with whole class discussion. The reactions of the group can be written or orally given to the rest of the class.

Corners

Each student moves to a corner of the room representing a teacher-determined alternative. One corner could be "End affirmative action," another corner, "Support present alternative action policies in the state," and the like. Students discuss the reasons for their point of view, listen to other points of view, and then paraphrase ideas from the other corners. This activity forces students to listen to alternative arguments.

Summary of Small Group Work

To repeat, a teacher cannot throw together small groups and expect all groups to be successful, because students may not have learned the skills necessary to function and to produce good work in a small group. It may be necessary to first teach and reinforce small group skills. The advantages of small group work are that students can learn both content and skills, and it promotes social skill development.

SMALL GROUP WORK	WOULD YOU USE SMALL GROUP STRATEGIES?
4.3	*One of the best ways to decide is to try for yourself the various small group strategies with others in your class. Remember that at the college or university level, almost all members of your peer group have developed small group discussion skills, and the activity may go much better than in a grade 6–12 classroom. Try out the following: (1) for brainstorming, ask, What could be done to improve the teaching of social studies?; and (2) for consensus, Choose the three best ideas to improve social studies teaching.*

■ INQUIRY AND PROBLEM-BASED LEARNING

Importance

Although discussion skills are needed by all people in their everyday life and work, problem-solving skills also are extremely valuable, with real-life applications ranging from daily life problems such as "How to earn money" to global problems of peace and security. Today's society requires adults to be able to solve problems effectively. For our purposes, the terms *inquiry, problem solving, problem-based learning, discovery learning, inductive thinking, WebQuests* and *thinking skills* are often casually used interchangeably. **Problem-based learning (PBL)** is now the most popular term, and it has many definitions. Usually PBL is focused on a concrete problem such as how should the student council raise money or how should social security be reformed. Other definitions may emphasize *argumentation* in which the central claims are well supported and counter-arguments are addressed. Yet, given the enormous importance of problem-based learning to thinking skills, too many adults after years of schooling are not confident of their problem-solving or thinking skills. This is partly because most schools have concentrated mainly on teaching content (facts) rather than on nurturing inquiry or thinking skills.

Thinking skills have been difficult to teach in all subjects, but math and science teachers have made the most serious attempts to foster the process of inquiry. But a **thinking curriculum** means recognizing that all real learning involves thinking and that thinking ability can be fostered and encouraged in everyone. Sometimes thinking is divided into the following three categories:

- **Practical thinking:** Apply, use, or implement what students have learned
- **Creative thinking:** Create, invent, discover, or predict
- **Analytical thinking:** Analyze, compare and contrast, assess, "critical thinking"

The New Social Studies

In the late 1960s and 1970s, spurred by federal funds, the **new social studies** movement, with at least fifty national projects, emphasized the importance of inquiry or problem solving. **Inquiry** can be defined as "seeking information by questioning, resulting in useful knowledge." The emphasis was on the development of logical thinking processes or the scientific method, and on helping students learn how to ask and answer their own questions. In other words, inquiry is teachers having students use critical thinking skills to analyze and to solve problems in a systematic manner. It is an emphasis on "how we come to know" rather than "what we know."

It was generally agreed, on the basis of personal observations, that—when done well—inquiry methods could improve students' thinking skills, foster higher interest and more involvement as students directed more of their own learning, intensify the retention of ideas, and improve students' self-concepts about their abilities to think. Negatives noted were that inquiry seems to appeal only to certain types of students; it was not efficient for the typical large classes; it required even greater teacher skills; and there was a de-emphasis on basic facts because students examined a smaller number of topics in depth. A few critics also thought it was not a creative process but followed too structured a format. On the whole, little research was done on inquiry's effectiveness in the social studies. This was because inquiry was not widely used in social studies, and it was hard to measure improvements in effective thinking—or to be certain they were the result of a given inquiry program.

In the 1990s, however, some similar ideas about the importance of the major concepts and methods of the four disciplines of history, geography, civics (political science), and economics received renewed attention as these disciplines published their standards that every student should master (Chapters 1, 5–8). In a new format, inquiry became more popular. Thinking skills, *powers of understanding*, and *habits of the mind* are now being emphasized more, partly as a result of the growing body of information that suggests students need skills that involve how to understand and make sense of data and the world. In addition, teaching and learning are now viewed from a constructivist perspective, which believes that students make sense of their classroom experiences and reach a greater understanding of ideas, issues, and values. In the future, more problem-based learning will take advantage of the electronic environment, often using collaboration with distant partners.

Formal Stages in Thinking or Inquiry

Students need to be taught the strategies for thinking in the social studies and in other subject areas so they gain a greater understanding as well as learning the skills and the values associated with thinking. This often means breaking down the task into segments such as John Dewey's four steps, more or less the classic scientific model used in all of the social sciences.

John Dewey's (1933) model was one of the first about thinking that still is frequently used as a starting point for inquiry or thinking. The four simplified steps outlined in Figure 4.2, however, are not used in every problem-solving situation, and many other inquiry models are used as well. A further difficulty is that in real life, individuals often do not have all the necessary data available when they make decisions or solve problems.

Inquiry in the Social Studies Classroom

Let us see how this inquiry model would work in a classroom in which the focus is on learning content as a means to develop information-processing and thinking skills. One of the first questions is "What problems will be tackled by the class?" Answering

FIGURE 4.2 Dewey's Steps for Problem Solving

1. Define the problem.
2. Suggest alternative solutions to the problem or make hypotheses.
3. Gather a wide variety of data to support or negate these hypotheses.
4. Select or reject hypotheses.

this often involves finding out what students already know and what they want to know. Is the problem initially chosen by the teacher, as, for instance, when the teacher asks what the students want to learn about the juvenile court system or the conflict on Lexington Green? Could it be a combination of teacher and student interest? Obviously, inquiry should not be asking questions and searching for answers about minutiae or trivial questions.

Because you cannot think without having something to think about, the selection of the problem or issue deserves careful consideration. You cannot think in a vacuum, and the topic or particular content associated with the problem is critical. Therefore, regardless of how the inquiry is initiated, thought must be given to how a problem or issue is related to the students' experiences and the questions that trouble them. If there is not high student interest in the problem, it may not be worth pursuing. Likewise, some familiarity with content and the conceptual framework of the disciplines usually is necessary to be able to follow the typical steps in problem solving. Looking at primary source documents on the conflict at Lexington Green requires some understanding of how historians work and knowledge of the American Revolution. This obviously points to the importance of a teacher's background in the topic. It is difficult to ask probing questions to help students think if you yourself are not familiar with the content and the methods of historians and social scientists.

Often a distinction is made between inquiry about problems on various levels: personal problems such as "Should I spend my time with my friends or do my homework?"; a school problem such as name calling or graffiti; local problems a community is facing such as traffic or garbage disposal; and last, national and global problems such as growing world population, poverty, the military and disarmament, wars, economic development, terrorism, human rights, and refugee problems. Global problems may be of long-standing duration, complex, and not easy to solve. One has to be careful about asking students to solve problems that have defied easy answers or solutions for generations. Inquiry may not result in the "right answer." Nevertheless, awareness of such problems and the alternative solutions to them is certainly essential as part of a good social studies program.

Some students may be ready to tackle tough issues such as sexism, racism, and inequality, especially if limited to a consideration of their school and community. Another distinction is sometimes made between value analysis (see Chapter 8) and problem solving. Questions such as "Should we control population?" and "What should be done about the worldwide refugee problem?" obviously involve value judgments, but value questions also permeate the whole process of problem solving. What you consider to be a problem involves your values, as well as the way you select data and favor certain policies.

Let us see how problem solving might work out for the topic of justice for teenagers in the juvenile courts. Notice how the process is divided into steps. Note also the need for a wide variety of resource materials.

1. **Introduction—problem, question, or dilemma posed**
   What are our images about juvenile crime? Juvenile courts?
   - Small groups brainstorm; report back to the class.
   - Teacher presents news items about high-profile violence committed by juveniles and public demand to treat juvenile offenders harshly as adults.
   - Teacher judges student interest in the problem.
   Problem defined: Are we in the midst of a violent juvenile crime epidemic?

2. **Development of hypotheses (tentative answers)**
   Teacher-led discussion of ideas from brainstorming; selection of hypotheses.
   - Does our state (or county) have more violent juvenile crime than ten years ago?
   - For violent juvenile crimes, the juvenile justice system mirrors the adult criminal justice system.

3. **Gathering data** (Internet and wide variety of resources)
   Students collect data—individual or group research:
   - How much crime are juveniles involved in, and what kinds of crimes do they commit?
   - How often are juveniles the victims of crime, and what is the nature of their victimization?
   - What are the trends in juvenile violence?
   - Recent state legislation on juvenile justice.
   - How frequent is the transfer of youth to the adult criminal justice system?
   - How common is school crime, and how many juveniles carry guns and other weapons to school?
   - Is school crime going down?
   - Review of history prior to establishment of juvenile courts.
   - Goals of juvenile courts; differences from adult courts.
   - Will there be an increase of violence among youths if there is an increase in the teen population?
   - 1967 Supreme Court *In re Gault* decision that informal procedures used by juvenile courts deprived children of certain rights.
   - Promising intervention methods to help juveniles involved in the legal system.
   Students classify and interpret data.

4. **Hypotheses accepted or rejected**
   Teacher/class evaluate data and methods of research.
   Teacher/class accepts or rejects the two hypotheses.
   Students suggest further questions for investigation.

SMALL GROUP WORK	**THE JUVENILE COURTS PROBLEM**
4.4	*Do you think that this problem-solving inquiry into juvenile courts would be of interest to students? What skills do students need? Is it helpful to divide the process into steps?*

As an alternative, inquiry could be done on a more traditional social studies topic, such as Turkey. What problems is Turkey presently facing? After student discussion and reading, the hypothesis could be that "Turkey, a secular nation, is a nation divided over Islam's revival." Data gathered could include history from Mustafa Kemal Ataturk's reforms, the success and failures of Ataturk's reforms, the role of the military, minorities, economic changes, and the Islamic movement. Acceptance or rejection of the hypothesis could also include further questions about what might happen to Turkey.

Teacher's Role in Inquiry

Notice how the work of the teacher is critical as the teacher facilitates inquiry. First, teachers have to know and value the process of inquiry and apply this knowledge to help students. For example, the hypotheses must be worded carefully, and the teacher should usually critique them. In the juvenile justice problem, there are two hypotheses, but there could be only one. Whereas problem definition and development of a hypothesis might take only one period, the bulk of the time will be devoted to gathering and analyzing the data. This may require teacher assistance and certainly requires a good school library along with access to the Internet. This job could be done by small groups or individuals, ideally students being given a choice.

In addition, the teacher's role is that of a coach: asking more reflective questions and encouraging students. These could include the following: *Understand:* What are you trying to do? How should the question be investigated? *Plan:* What strategies could you use? *Results:* How do you know? What is the evidence? *Evaluate:* What was the best example of the team working together? In the future, for problems similar to this, what would you do? By seeing the model of the teacher's questions, the hope is that students will do self-initiated questioning. In assessment, the focus should be on both the content and skill development. This means careful teacher observation and feedback to students as they move along the inquiry stages.

Students' Role in Inquiry

What does the classroom look like during inquiry learning? Students should willingly engage themselves to learn more. In the juvenile justice problem, students would need to recognize, in interpreting the data, that there are two main positions here. There are those who want the juvenile courts to retain power over juvenile offenders, stressing the rehabilitation function, and those who want a shift toward a stronger adult criminal justice system focused on more accountability and punishment of juveniles. To answer questions, students plan their investigations and use a variety of resources to find answers. Finally, they critique their work, reporting its strengths and weaknesses.

As with successful group work, students need a variety of skills to be able to do inquiry or problem solving: generating ideas, gathering data (which includes finding information from a library and the Internet), thinking during listening and questioning, and especially being aware of bias in both materials and one's own perspective. If students have not yet learned these skills, snags and difficulties can occur in problem solving. However, students have to start somewhere. But focusing on *how* to answer a question is better than merely focusing on the correct answer to a question. Through inquiry, students can learn strategies for completing any task independently and generate a deeper understanding of the topic. The payoff for using inquiry can be high but is not automatic—which is true of all methods.

Can critical thinking be done every day in a classroom? Try to make students summarize what others or you have stated. Try to relate topics to students' own knowledge and experience by giving many examples. Ask students to evaluate the consequences of judgments and reasoning: What would happen if. . ., or what would have happened [during an event in history] if. . .

■ ROLE PLAYING AND SIMULATIONS

Dramatic Play

Before describing role playing and simulations, let us first distinguish them from **dramatic play,** in which students depict characters other than themselves. In a social studies class, students in dramatic play typically reenact a historical event. In dramatic play, the events must be *accurately* portrayed. Joan of Arc dies—she is *not* freed after her trial and is *not* rescued at the last moment by the French. Ferdinand Magellan is killed in the Philippines and does *not* live to see one ship arrive home safely. Dramatic play can be spontaneous and unrehearsed, or it can be a structured activity in which students know exactly what each player will say and do.

Another example of dramatic play occurs when, for local centennials and other milestones, individuals in some schools and communities dress in costumes to reenact certain historical events. **Mock trials** can also be an example of dramatic play if they are accurately portrayed and students do not change the verdict. Often mock trials are based on real court cases and simulate a real trial with a judge, jury, lawyers, witnesses, cross-examinations, and closing arguments.

Dramatic play can be effective because students can better remember the event acted out for the class, especially if it focused on one historical person. Effective dramatic play can require someone or a very small team to write a script, usually a task for students with both understanding of the time period and good writing skills. Otherwise, the unrehearsed version may not be accurate. One other alternative is readers' theater, in which the script is already written for students. Scripts are available on well-known persons and events such as George III or the Constitutional Convention meeting in Philadelphia in 1787.

Another format of dramatic play is **experiential exercises.** In this the teacher, often using an overhead transparency, outlines exactly and clearly what the whole class is to do. These are typically exercises such as having students crouch down on the floor as if they were soldiers in the trenches; then the teacher closes the curtains and reads selections from *All Quiet on the Western Front.* Next the students could write letters to their families about what they are experiencing in the trenches. The feelings of workers on an assembly line could be demonstrated as the students repeat the same task again and again. The teacher has to decide how long such activities will last: part of a period or the full period. The benefit of experiential exercises is that students remember them, mainly because they were so uncomfortable and unpleasant.

But it is not enough to go through the experience. Students need to be debriefed on how they felt and how their simulation was both like and different from what really occurred. They then can make connections to the history. However, to avoid student and parental complaints, do not force all students to participate. If someone does not want to participate, an alternative assignment should be available. It may be wise to alert administrators and parents beforehand as to why you are using these learning experiences. In addition, if you have a crowded classroom, experiential exercises may not be practical.

Role Playing

In using role play, the teacher hopes for high student interest and active involvement. **Role playing** tries to bridge the world of the classroom and the real world outside of the classroom. Typically, role playing starts with an unfinished story reflecting real problems, situations, and questions that students at a given age typically face and must resolve. These could involve responsibilities and commitments to oneself and others, or political issues. In contrast with dramatic play, role play is always unrehearsed, although the role players get guidance before they play their role. Role playing can be especially effective in helping students see different perspectives.

The impetus for role play is often provided by reading or viewing a story, a law case, an open-ended film, or a photograph showing conflict or a problem. The problem story or incident is left in the form of a dilemma that opens up various alternatives for action. Two or more students finish the story by role playing how they think it would or should end. This is followed by a discussion. Often there is a further enactment and discussion as students and teacher explore different alternatives.

A more precise and structured method of role playing was outlined by the Shaftels (1982) as a problem-solving method that requires several different alternatives. Through this method, students confront situations and learn to solve problems in a supportive group. Role playing permits a "wrong" choice, which can be discarded as students explore consequences. Figure 4.3 shows the steps outlined by the Shaftels.

According to the Shaftels' model, each student who is role playing follows the suggestions of the group on how to play the role: hostile, willing to compromise, and other likely responses of the particular role player. According to the Shaftels, students

FIGURE 4.3 Shaftels' Steps in Role Playing

Steps

1. Warm up the group.

   Identify and introduce a problem, which could come from a variety of sources.

2. Select participants.

   Describe roles and choose role players; set line of action.

3. Prepare the observers.

   Stress importance of the nonplayers; the observers must listen and observe carefully.

4. Enactment.

   Can be brief or extended; often an emotional conflict of values and ideas shown. Teacher may stop the enactment when it becomes repetitious or unproductive.

5. Discuss and evaluate.

   Focus on how well the actors portrayed the roles and how well the problem was solved or not solved. Shift to alternative ways of acting next reenactment.

6. Reenactment.

   Play revised roles, using another alternative.

7. Discuss and evaluate.

   Judge the effectiveness of alternative way of responding; a second (or third or fourth) chance to solve a problem.

8. Share experiences and generalize.

   If possible, formulate a general principle of action or a concept.

should not leave with the impression that there is only one way to respond to a problem or situation. In addition, the teacher must always stress that students are playing roles they have been told to play. Therefore, it is also best not to place the more aggressive student or the shy student in a role that reinforces the general perception or image the class has of that individual. Instead, put students in some other person's shoes so they can see from another perspective.

In general, students enjoy the improvised solutions reached by other students, especially as they express the emotions and values of the role player. Students almost always smile or laugh when a role player lies and says something outrageous. But role playing does not work in all situations—as, for example, when students act out and reinforce stereotypes. Although initially it may be difficult to get volunteers to play roles, through eye contact with the teacher and other means, students "volunteer."

Role playing is an appropriate strategy for social studies content that has a conflict dilemma and is open-ended. For example, in economics courses students can play the roles of consumers and sellers, labor and management, stockholders and management; global problems or international conflicts can be promising topics. Role playing has also been used effectively in law-related education classes on issues such as who should be given parole, the right of public assembly for demonstrators, and the right to privacy and other Bill of Rights issues.

The teacher's role in role playing is to initiate, to end events, and to lead discussion. The students assume a more active role compared to the traditional learning experiences in a classroom. A plus is the immediate feedback that is also part of the process of role playing, as students evaluate different decisions and alternatives.

Simulations

Like role playing, simulations used in education are designed to increase student interest and active involvement. A **simulation** is a simplified model of a situation. It creates realistic experiences to be played out by participants, such as members of the city council, in order to provide students with lifelike problem-solving experiences with hypothetical consequences. Thus a simulation is an elaborate and structured form of group activity in which students take assigned roles, as in well-known computer programs such as *Oregon Trail* or the many versions of *SimCity*. Students act out their roles and, in many simulations, interact with others. They make decisions and see the consequences of their decisions. Thus the purpose of a simulation is to develop students' thinking and decision-making skills, worthwhile goals related to the world outside the classroom.

Similar to role playing, a simulation has the following stages: (1) introduction to the simulation and in some cases the explanation of the rules; (2) participation preparation if needed; (3) simulation/enactment; and (4) debriefing discussion. Some simulations last for several class periods, whereas others can take less than one class period. See "Game of Farming" in Sample Classroom Episode. The debriefing session is most essential because that is when students review their actions, relate how they felt, and connect the learning to social studies goals. Yet some teachers slight this important step.

SAMPLE CLASSROOM EPISODE

METHODS FOR AVERAGE AND AP CLASSES

Jonathan Meyers, a high school social studies teacher with twelve years of experience, looks over his lesson plans for the coming week. For variation in pace, he chooses the simulation "Game of Farming, 1880–1882" for U.S. History.

In this noncomputerized simulation, students are placed in groups of two: husband and wife, two sisters, or two brothers. Jonathan always makes the choices because there is a little embarrassment if he asks students to select a husband–wife partner. He has used this game before and has found that it does not cause any problems to put a below-average student together with an average student.

This simulation also requires a little math, as each team has to decide what crops and animals they want to "buy." The more competent student can usually take care of any calculation that is needed. However, the below-average student does participate in making decisions on the farm for the years 1880, 1881, and 1882. The fact that the game produces more losers than winners is good for illustrating the problems that farm families faced in the 1880s and even relates to farm dilemmas today. At the end, the students really feel concern for the farm families of that period and have had an interesting and motivating class experience. When given the unit test, they always remember the problems of farm families of that time period.

Jonathan looks at the content requirements for the AP history course.

National Politics, 1877–1898: The Gilded Age
A. A conservative presidency
B. Issues
   1. Tariff controversy
   2. Railroad regulation
   3. Trusts
C. Agrarian discontent
D. Crisis of 1890s
   1. Populism
   2. Silver question
   3. Election of 1896: McKinley versus Bryan

Here is what he is thinking: "No simulation for the AP class! Simulations take too much time. Agrarian discontent is just a small piece of the week's content. I had better do lecturing with questions and answers to make sure students understand all that content. However, I will try to make a more creative homework assignment, since the AP class also needs writing practice in order to take the exam. For homework, I will ask them to imagine that they are a farm family in the 1880s and, by referring to primary sources, to write about the problems they are facing and what political action farm families should take. That should do it.

"For the AP class, I have to concentrate on content and writing skills this week. That means I will have to put aside time to correct those papers more closely. Those students and their parents are likely to expect a careful reading. I know that some AP classes use **peer editing,** which allows a greater volume of essay writing with rapid student feedback and less time for me to spend on grading. But I have to be sensitive to complaints. It seems I can do practically anything in the other classes and no one cares. I usually spend more time preparing the lectures and grading papers for the AP class than for any of my other classes, but I get my rewards because the students are alert and knowledgeable. The simulation for the average class needs almost no prep time. I already have the necessary worksheet and I only need to form the pairs, then observe and debrief at the end. I realize the Game of Farming would be a motivating learning activity for the AP class, but I feel pressure to cover the content by lecturing."

Research supports Jonathan Meyers in his feeling that he devotes more time and planning to his advanced classes. Surprising too is the finding that teachers of advanced social studies classes generally do not use recommended teaching strategies such as small groups and simulations compared to teachers who teach lower-ability students. With homework assignments, however, teachers of higher-ability classes are often more likely than teachers of lower-ability classes to use recommended practices such as analyzing primary sources and writing.

SMALL GROUP WORK	**WHAT WOULD YOU DO? YOUR IDEAL CLASS?**
4.5	*Do you approve of the choices Jonathan Meyers has made of the methods to use in the two different U.S. history classes? His allocations of his own time?*

To ensure success, students must have sufficient understanding of what the characters or roles might think or say, such as a diplomat from a given country at the United Nations, or colonial merchants' views on smuggling and the slave trade. Student preparation before the simulation is valuable, such as some knowledge of pioneers' or legislators' behavior—otherwise students do not know how to play their roles. A few teachers require students to write a brief résumé of a character or type before the simulation to help them in their actions.

Often in a simulation there are winners and losers, and students are in a competitive situation to achieve power, status, and economic advantage. Because of the competitive focus of some, but not all, simulations, some teachers are concerned that students will become too emotionally involved in the simulation. Noise may also be a problem as students interact with one another in the contained room. Some teachers are rightly concerned when students resort to cheating (such as manufacturing more pretend money), planning to assassinate a public figure, starting wars, or ruling as dictators. Other teachers think that simulations on such topics as the Holocaust or slavery distort or simplify the issue and should never be used.

Although the teacher is an observer during the simulation, she or he does not interfere unless unsocial behavior becomes too offensive. The actions of students must be debriefed at the end of the simulation and the behavior of the participants analyzed.

Currently, some simulations are computer based and these are valuable, especially if the computer can do some of the calculations needed on the supply of money or other resources. But the equivalent of *Oregon Trail* and its many variations can also be played without a computer. Such games are available at a relatively low price compared to a computerized version. Interact (www.interact-simulations.com) is one of the best-known sources, with over 300 simulations ranging from prehistoric studies (Bones & Stones) to the future (Galaxy).

As an example, "Egypt: A Simulation of Ancient Egyptian Civilization" is divided into six phases called "cataracts." Each cataract focuses on different aspects of Egyptian history, culture, or geography. To navigate these divisions, students travel as citizens of one of five ancient cities. Among the tasks are to make a 3-D map of the Nile Valley; use Egyptian numbers and hieroglyphs; construct masks to wear in the afterworld; study ancient Egyptian myths, religion, art, and architecture; create costumes; and participate in a festival and living museum. Typically part of the time is spent in small groups. Teachers could spend weeks on this simulation for the middle and high school level.

In contrast, the simulation "Martin Luther King, Jr." takes only one or two periods as students portray the people who had great influence on the life and work of Dr. King. Among the participants are his wife and parents, Henry David Thoreau,

Mahatma Gandhi, Rosa Parks, Malcolm X, and Robert Kennedy. Interact provides role descriptions, a teacher's guide, essay and objective test questions, and ideas for a follow-up press conference. This simulation can be played with ten to thirty-five players and is designed for grades 7–12. These are but a few of the many noncomputerized simulations available to social studies teachers.

Sources of Simulations

Usually teachers do not design complex simulations. The easier alternative is to use the noncomputerized versions, which are relatively inexpensive and in some cases are free in journals. However, teachers do use formats such as **town hall meetings,** a simulation of a **city council,** or of any other government body such as the **Supreme Court.** In the last case, nine students become Supreme Court judges and the rest of the class is divided into the two opposing sides who prepare and present their arguments. In these simulations, it is extremely important that students have time to prepare for their roles (Passe & Evans, 1996) and that they understand the issue.

As with most activities, remember that not all students "enjoy" simulations, especially if they have a low-status role. Who wants to be a peon without power or resources? Having students walk in someone else's shoes is not always pleasant for them, although it does give them the opportunity to realize how it feels to be a slave or disenfranchised person. The most important step is to discuss what the students gained after participating in a simulation. As in role playing, debriefing is essential in order to discover what has been learned or if attitudes have changed.

LARGE CLASS DISCUSSION

CONTROVERSIAL ISSUE

James Leming (2003) states that there are difficulties in teaching higher-order thinking because of the stages of adolescent cognitive development. Should teachers even spend time on teaching critical thinking? Does it result in student frustration and negative feelings toward civic issues? If thinking skills are so highly valued, why are more teachers not spending time teaching them?

■ SUMMARY

Methods that permit students a more active role in their learning include the many variations of small group work, inquiry, role playing, and simulations. These methods, combined with more direct methods of teaching, can help meet the needs of the wide diversity of students that teachers face in their classrooms. Each of these methods has the potential to help motivate learning, but both teachers' skills and students' skills are essential to achieve good results. In all cases, opportunities to improve reading and writing skills should be incorporated when using these methods.

■ REFERENCES ■

Cohen, E. (1994). *Designing groupwork* (2nd ed.). New York: Teachers College Press.

Dewey, J. (1933). *How we think*. Boston: D. C. Heath.

Fuchs, L. S., Fuchs, D., Hamlett, C. L., & Karns, K. (1998). High-achieving students' interactions and performance on complex mathematical tasks as a function of homogeneous and heterogeneous pairings. *American Educational Research Journal, 35,* 227–267.

Johnson, R. T., & Johnson, D. W. (1994). *Learning together and alone* (4th ed.) Englewood Cliffs, NJ: Prentice Hall.

Kagan, S. (1992). *Cooperative learning*. San Juan Capistrano, CA: Resources for Teachers.

Leming, J. S. (2003). Social change, "higher order thinking," and the failure of social studies. In J. S. Leming, L. Ellington, & K. Porter (Eds.), *Where did social studies go wrong?* (pp. 132–133). Washington, DC: Thomas Fordham Foundation.

Passe, J., & Evans, R. W. (1996). Discussion methods in an issues-centered curriculum. In R. W. Evans & D. W. Saxe (Eds.), *Handbook on teaching social issues: NCSS bulletin 93* (pp. 81–88). Washington, DC: National Council for the Social Studies.

Priest, Q. G. (1994). Student teams-achievement divisions (STAD): Applications to the social studies classroom. In R. J. Stahl (Ed.), *Cooperative learning in social studies: A handbook for teachers* (pp. 189–211). Menlo Park, CA: Addison-Wesley.

Shaftel, F. R., & Shaftel, G. (1982). *Role playing for social values*. Englewood Cliffs, NJ: Prentice Hall.

Slavin, R. E. (1990). *Cooperative learning: Theory, research, and practice*. Englewood Cliffs, NJ: Prentice Hall.

Stahl, R. J., Meyer, J. R., & Stahl, N. N. (1994). Co-op C-op: A student interest-based cooperative study/learning strategy. In R. J. Stahl (Ed.), *Cooperative learning in social studies: A handbook for teachers* (pp. 277–305). Menlo Park, CA: Addison-Wesley.

Steinbrink, J. E., & Stahl, R. J. (1994). Jigsaw III = Jigsaw II + cooperative test review: Application to the social studies classroom. In R. J. Stahl (Ed.), *Cooperative learning in social studies: A handbook for teachers* (pp. 133–153). Menlo Park, CA: Addison-Wesley.

Stone, J. M., & Kagan, S. (1994). Social studies and the structural approach to cooperative learning. In R. J. Stahl (Ed.), *Cooperative learning in social studies: A handbook for teachers* (pp. 78–90). Menlo Park, CA: Addison-Wesley.

VanSickle, R. L. (1994). Jigsaw II: Cooperative learning with "expert group" specialization. In R. J. Stahl (Ed.), *Cooperative learning in social studies: A handbook for teachers* (pp. 98–132). Menlo Park, CA: Addison-Wesley.

Webb, N. W., Nemer, K. M., Chizhik, A. W., & Sugrue, B. (1998). Equity issues in collaborative group assessment: Group composition and performance. *American Educational Research Journal, 35,* 607–651.

■ WEB SITES ■

Cooperative Learning Center
www.co-operation.org
Advise and essays on cooperative learning

The Critical Thinking Community
www.criticalthinking.org
Lesson plans to develop critical thinking skills.

MarcoPolo: Internet Content for Your Classroom
http://marcopolo-education.org/
Access lesson plans. Strong on use of technology in classrooms.

Chapter 5

Using Multiple Assessments and Evaluation

In this chapter, we examine the logical extension of looking at standards and objectives and at methods for setting up activities (Chapters 3 and 4). Evidence is needed to see whether students have achieved the objectives for instruction. NAEP and state tests are now mandated. The many types of assessment include performance-based assessment, paper-and-pencil tests, and informal observations. All of these assessments should provide feedback to the students about their progress. Knowing how to design various assessments can help you to diagnose student learning difficulties and then apply corrective measures such as reteaching or using different strategies. Grades and report cards are ways to communicate to the students about how well they have achieved the standards/objectives. The following topics are discussed.

- Perceptions of Evaluation
- NAEP and State Tests
- Assessing Student Learning
- Teacher-Made Paper-and-Pencil Tests
- Performance-Based Assessment
- Grades and Report Cards

■ PERCEPTIONS OF EVALUATION

How students are achieving standards and objectives of instruction is not a matter just between students and teachers. Let us look at the many groups involved and how their perceptions of the process may differ.

SMALL GROUP WORK	YOUR REACTION TO TESTS AND GRADES
5.1	*How do you feel about the tests you encountered when you were an elementary student? A high school student? A college/university student? Were they fair? Did you get feedback on how to improve your writing or other skills? Was getting good grades a big concern for you? Do you think your own experiences with testing and grades influence how you will prepare tests for your own students? Tests often evoke an emotional response.*

What makes some students really focus on taking a test?

Students

Testing students can have positive or negative effects. If there is **high-stakes testing** with important consequences for those being tested, some students may not get a school diploma or promotion to high school. If they become too discouraged and quit trying to achieve passing test scores, they may drop out of high school, which will reduce their opportunities in life. Most students, however, concentrate on their grades on their report cards. Grades can be an incentive to students. Given the wide range of students, their perceptions about the social studies grades they receive in school vary widely. A national sample showed that the average social studies grades during the four years in high school were as follows: during their high school years, 10 percent of all students received the grade of A; 31 percent received the grade of B; 36 percent received Cs; 20 percent earned Ds, and 4 percent got an F (Chapin, 2001).

With the exception of As and Fs, it is difficult to assess how the rest of the students felt about their social studies grades. Perhaps most of the students who received grades below an A wanted a higher grade, but it is also possible that some were content or even glad that they received the grade they did. How their peer group and families regard grades, as well as the motivational climate in the school, influences how students evaluate the grades they receive.

However, we can also conclude that for most students, grades were not a matter of indifference. Although some students loudly announce that they don't care, most do want to receive at least passing grades. Grades may affect the courses in which a student is placed. Grades, in effect, are a judgment about the academic progress of a student, and most students have some degree of sensitivity about their grades. Grades affect how students perceive themselves (Covington, 1992) as well as how they are perceived by their friends, parents, and teachers. High school students may also be concerned about grades if they affect their ability or their parents' ability to get lower car insurance policies, as well as, ultimately, their postsecondary options.

Another problem with interpreting social studies grades relates to how important the students think social studies is. In the same national sample, eighth-grade students were asked about the usefulness of four different academic subjects. In their estimation, math was first in importance, followed by English and science. Social studies was in last place, with students seeing it as the least useful of four subject areas. This means that students may care more about getting good grades in math and English because they think their future may be influenced by what they know or do not know in these subjects. This may make them more willing to do homework in these subjects than in social studies. The U.S. Department of Education's report of the International IEA Civic Education Study (Baldi, Perie, Skidmore, & Greenberg, 2001, p. 28) indicated that 60 percent of ninth graders reported that they spend less than one hour a week on social studies homework. Another 26 percent spent one to two hours on social studies homework.

Interestingly, the majority of eighth-grade students looked forward to their social studies class and were not anxious about asking questions in class—but again, they did not see much usefulness in social studies. This highlights a serious problem of civic education, as it appears that most students do not see the relationship of their social studies classes to civic education and everyday life.

Parents and Guardians

Parents and guardians usually see grades and tests as a preview of how successful their students will be after they finish school. Parents are often worried about what is happening to their children and whether their children will thrive out in the real world of technology and the associated necessary skills, such as teamwork and problem solving. In particular, if high-stakes testing is required for graduation or promotion, parents and guardians want their children to pass because they realize that the lack of a high school diploma will not improve the economic well-being of their youngsters. With more students attending postsecondary institutions, grades are important because they help to determine what type of institution students may attend.

If students pass AP examinations with high scores while in high school, they may be able to reduce their time at and the expenses of college or university.

To help their daughters and sons achieve their expectations, parents want teachers to give their children as much attention as possible and see each of them as individuals with strengths. They want special help if their child is struggling. Parents do not always want teachers to apply the rules too stringently to their children, instead citing exceptional circumstances to explain their children's behavior. Some parents want *more* homework assigned, whereas other parents think too much homework is already being given.

Teachers

If social studies is tested at the state level, teachers may worry about how well their classes will do. Teachers are now being held accountable for their students' performance. In some states there is incredible pressure on teachers to improve test scores, particularly in schools with low achievement scores. The instructional quality of teachers' classes is being judged by their students' performance on state and district tests. Social studies teachers may also feel more pressure to do more on reading instruction, as the whole school tries to improve the reading scores of their students.

Since the implementation of state tests, a few teachers have actually resorted to explicit cheating. This usually has occurred in low-performing classes. There have even been cases in which teachers have changed their students' test marks on state tests. These teachers have not been aware that computer programs can successfully identify classes in which students miss the easy questions but answer all of the difficult questions correctly. This is a red flag for further investigation and can result in a retest of the whole class as well as severe penalties for the teachers who have not been honest. Cheating of this type, if not caught, could also penalize the next year's teacher(s): The students had high test scores last year and now this year they appear to be declining and not learning. To help prevent cheating, in some districts an independent proctor (often a volunteer parent) monitors the classroom during the testing period.

Many teachers regard giving grades as a necessary but onerous chore. Teachers also bear the heat and anger of students who receive lower grades than they expected or wanted. At times, parents also join the chorus of complaints about student grades, resulting in some interviews that have left teachers exhausted and emotionally distressed.

Teachers also vary on how they evaluate students. Almost everyone in the whole school knows which teachers are regarded as tough or hard graders and which teachers have the reputation of being easy graders. In addition, teachers may feel some pressure from administrators not to fail too many students, especially if the students are from certain racial or ethnic groups. At times teachers are so busy that they cannot take the time to think out how test scores could lead to improvement in planning the curriculum or helping individual students. Yet a *focus on student work* is essential because assessment is one of the teacher's most important responsibilities.

Administrators

In this age of testing, with school scores on the Internet and published as headline news, administrators are more worried than ever before about how their school is performing on state and district tests. These concerns about test scores apply to everyone from the superintendent on down to every single administrator. If principals do not have tenure, their position is at stake if the school consistently scores lower than expected. In the worst possible case, the school could be taken over by the state if, after several years of efforts, school test scores have not improved. Feeling this pressure, administrators want teachers to improve test scores. At the same time, they may not want teachers to give too many low grades because of parental reaction.

A few administrators have been accused of manipulating test data by moving students to different schools. Educational triage practices have been used by both teachers and administrators in some states to give more resources to students who are just below passing—those students whom educators believe to be capable of improving. One-to-one instruction or small group instruction is typically used, sometimes using a resource teacher. This strategy is based on the assumption that there is a greater payoff in improved test scores by helping those students who need just a little more assistance. In contrast, trying to get the lowest-performing students to pass or do better on tests is regarded as a "lost cause." This practice targets some students with additional resources at the expense of others. Parents of gifted and above average students also are annoyed, because little attention is given to their children, who can safely pass tests. However, No Child Left Behind (NCLB) mandates that every individual student, including those with disabilities, be given the best education possible. It appears that some states are currently not aligned with this NCLB requirement.

Administrators in failing schools also have the responsibility to give parents information about supplemental services and the option for their children to change schools. Administrators should appraise the qualifications of the providers of supplemental services because this is a task that is difficult for most parents to make. In addition, administrators need to monitor the providers' success. A real problem has been the erratic attendance of students in after-school programs, as well as lack of space for those students who wish to transfer out of their failing schools.

Principals often set goals with their staff for integrating assessment into instruction and assist teachers to achieve these goals. They plan and present workshops that contribute to the use of sound assessment. And most important, the principal has to communicate effectively with members of the community to interpret the test results and their relationship to the instruction going on in the school. In talking to the public, the principal should compare the school with others that educate the equivalent student populations—students with disabilities, ELLs, race/ethnic groups, and so forth—because administrators are now required to sort test results by various categories.

The Community

Communities want to have good schools, and they partly judge the effectiveness of the schools by released test scores. Real estate agents report that the quality of the schools affects property values. Homeowners do not want the value of their homes to decrease, but this may occur if the local schools are perceived to be poor. Employers want a skilled labor force. The support for public schools is based on how well the community's schools are believed to be doing. Poor test scores discredit the public schools. The community may look with more favor on charter schools, vouchers, and home schooling if it thinks the community's schools are not up to par and not improving.

Stakeholders

Looking at all of these perceptions of evaluations, you can easily see how critical this topic is. Everyone gains if the process of assessment and evaluation is fair and clearly thought out and students are given feedback on their progress. There is value to testing because students are more likely to retain what they have learned if they are tested on it (Nungester & Duchastel, 1982). But remember that a grade or evaluation is not an end in itself. Tests should be a crucial factor in curriculum planning. What should be done to help students learn? If students do stumble on tests, what intervention and support services should be offered? What can be done to help teachers to teach more effectively? Tests and evaluation should be used to help improve instruction and to help individual students. Yet, as we know, too often the grade or the test score becomes paramount in the eyes of all stakeholders involved in evaluation. Grades, rather than learning, become the high priority for students and their parents. Learning becomes earning a grade.

Definitions

Terms such as *evaluation, assessment,* and *grades* are often used indiscriminately. To be more precise, a **test** is a procedure for gathering data to determine whether learning objectives have been achieved. A test is a way of getting a sample (and thus a limited amount) of information about what a student knows or is able to do in a given subject or area. In many cases, tests are also used to make comparisons between the students taking the test. Tests might further be characterized as (a) *informal, teacher-made,* or *standardized* and made by specialists; (b) *oral* or *written;* (c) *mastery of basic knowledge and skills* or *diagnostic of specific disabilities;* (d) *verbal, nonverbal,* or *performance.*

Assessments are the many ways we use to check whether students have achieved certain objectives of instruction. Sometimes the term *assessment* is carelessly used for *evaluation.* Assessment is the systematic appraisal of an individual's ability and performance. The best assessment tools synthesize a variety of data, because students ought to be assessed in multiple ways that allow them to show what they have learned. Assessments include:

- Teacher-made tests
- State tests
- Classroom assignments
- Homework
- Collected course work
- Samples of other student work such as reports
- Projects, student presentations, and portfolios
- Teacher observations and interviews with students

Evaluations, using the data from the assessments, are the judgments and interpretations made about students, teachers, and schools as to how well they are achieving standards and objectives. Evaluations are the process by which both quantitative and qualitative data are processed to arrive at a judgment of value, worth, merit, or effectiveness. There are two types of evaluation strategies. First is **formative,** checking on student progress during instruction. Second is **summative** evaluation, the formal evaluation at the end of the unit and an important component of the student's grade. Both strategies are needed for improving student learning and teacher effectiveness. Students and the teacher will not be surprised by the results of a summative evaluation if the teacher has employed many formative appraisals as the class proceeded.

Evaluations by the teacher, because of their importance, should be made on the best possible information so as not to devastate students. **Grades** are the familiar way of communicating evaluation of individual students, normally a letter grade at the middle and high school level. More schools, however, are using proficiency levels instead of grades of A, B, C, D, or similar marks.

■ NAEP AND STATE TESTS

Important Test Principles

Before starting a discussion of tests in the social studies, let us look at three important principles.

1. **What gets tested, gets taught.** Priority usually is given to subject areas covered by state tests. If social studies is not tested, resources may be focused mainly on the tested areas. Particularly for high-stakes testing, tests may dictate the degree of emphasis on what is taught and what students tend to learn. This is more likely to be done in schools with minority and poor students who have low achievement scores. Because of these factors, a state needs to research both the positive and negative effects of the state's testing program.

2. **Socioeconomic status and the family may account for about 50 percent of students' achievement.** Other researchers believe socioeconomic status and the family count for about one-third of a student's achievement, showing the disagreement on this issue. This does not mean that teachers do not count and cannot make a difference. In fact, it points out the vital need to have well-qualified, effective teachers in low-achieving schools, because teaching quality is the most important in-service factor for improving student achievement. It also implies that more attention should be given to working cooperatively with parents and the community to reduce the troubling achievement gap between white or Asian American students and students in other racial or ethnic groups. Adequate resources and the opportunity to learn must be provided for all students.

3. **Use multiple measures.** Organizations such as the American Psychological Association, the American Educational Research Association, and the National Research Council warn that it is dangerous to make individual decisions about students on the basis of just one test score. Other relevant information should be taken into account so that alternative acceptable means are provided to demonstrate attainment of the tested standards. The college or university entrance process is given as a model.

Besides test scores on the SATs and other standardized tests, admissions officers usually take grades into consideration. At elite higher education institutions, essays, letters of recommendation, and interviews also are used in making a decision to admit a given student. As a minimum for fairness, for high-stakes decisions on passing or getting a diploma, students must be afforded multiple opportunities to pass the test.

4. **Use standards to improve instruction.** Using multiple assessments to determine whether standards and objectives have been met should not focus only on the one annual test. Instead, teachers need to monitor student progress throughout the year. Teachers should use **formative** evaluations, checking constantly on progress during instruction. Constant and multiple kinds of assessments can be used to make curriculum decisions and to help individual students (Popham, 2004). Immediate feedback during the year can be given to students about their strengths and weaknesses.

5. **Ask the following questions when looking at student assessment data:**
   a. Did I teach the content assessed by the item? Sometimes the knowledge and skills have not been taught.
   b. Did the students perform as well as I expected? If not, why am I surprised?
   c. What do I need to do to improve students' performance? Review, reteach with different methods. When will I do this?

In this process of assessment and evaluation, hanging over everyone is the concern for fairness and equity. Are some types of assessment more fair than others? What adaptations, if any, will be made for students with disabilities or different language backgrounds?

SMALL GROUP WORK	**FAMILY AND SOCIAL CLASS**
5.2	*Some critics believe we have gone too far in attacking the idea that poor children can't learn by replacing it with the idea that family and social class no longer matter in education. Should schools with largely poor populations be held to the same standards as schools in wealthier areas?*

NAEP

In 1969, as mandated by Congress, the **National Assessment of Educational Progress (NAEP)** became the nation's report card by assessing the academic performance of fourth, eighth, and twelfth graders in a range of subjects including U.S. history, geography, and civics. In 2006, economics was first tested in the twelfth grade, and world history will be tested in 2010. NAEP's national sample allows the results to be generalized to the whole nation. NAEP is designed to show the strengths and weaknesses of U.S. students' achievement.

NAEP has been criticized for promoting a pessimistic view of the achievement of U.S. students. NAEP tests now go far beyond multiple-choice items. In general, the

NAEP tests are considered to be "harder" than state tests, which may be aligned with a specific state's own standards and curriculum. In particular, too few students are judged to be "Advanced." Because the individual students taking NAEP tests see no personal ramifications, their motivation may not be as strong, possibly resulting in somewhat lower NAEP test scores. The state tests may also be geared to more basic skills, whereas the NAEP tests may focus more on thinking skills. NAEP scores, however, were mandated by Congress (in 2001) to confirm states' achievement gains by 2005–2006. NAEP scores will become more important if state NAEP scores are released in such subject areas as U.S. history, geography, and civics, which currently are released only at the national level. To give an idea about the U.S. History, civics, and geography questions that are on these tests, questions from a past NAEP survey are available online at http://nces.ed.gov/nationsreportcard/ITMRLS/intro.shtml.

No Child Left Behind

No Child Left Behind mandated that each state have an accountability system that includes four requirements: (1) state standards; (2) assessments; (3) annual progress goals; and (4) incentives. This is a test-based accountability system, as tests scores under NCLB determine whether students are proficient in reading, math, science, and other subjects. Test results are to act as incentives. Those schools making adequate progress are praised, whereas failing schools have strong incentives to try to improve. If schools are not improving, parents have choices of supplemental services and transfers out of the failing schools. Failing schools also risk being taken over (Thomas, 2005).

States have flexibility in the standards they use, the particular type of assessment, comparing results of tests to targets (the annual progress goals), and the rewards and punishments (incentives) to achieve these goals. Although almost everyone approves of the *goals* of NCLB, critics see NCLB as a disaster. Here are some of the long list of complaints about NCLB:

1. Federal funding is not high enough to justify the state's costs of trying to bring all students up to par.
2. The results of testing can demoralize students, teachers, and administrators, especially as comparisons are made between schools.
3. Instruction time in nontested subject areas has been reduced because of a narrow curriculum and too much time spent on worksheets and test-prep materials.
4. The annual progress goals are unrealistic and too many schools are labeled as failing.
5. The federal government has usurped state and local control of public schools.
6. Relying on test scores uses the wrong indicators for judging a school's success.
7. The rules for testing students with disabilities are not fair.
8. Just because one group in the school is not making progress, the whole school should not be labeled as failing.
9. NCLB has not raised educational achievement but has undermined reform efforts.

In turn, the U.S. Department of Education has strongly supported all provisions of the federal law and refutes all criticism. Others also agree that even given the limitations of testing, standardized testing can be defended (Phelps, 2005). The Department of Education cites evidence, such as NAEP scores, that student achievement is improving and that it would be a serious error not to ensure that every student—low-income, minority, ELL, disabled, and the like—has the right to the appropriate knowledge, skills, and values necessary for successful adulthood. However, in light of the continued friction between the states and the Department of Education, some of the Department of Education's rules may be interpreted more leniently.

Let us now look at the tests the states are using for NCLB, because tests are the linchpin of the reform efforts to improve student learning.

States differ greatly on what they emphasize in social studies tests. Some states have more questions designed for higher-level thinking and more open-ended written responses from students. What proportion of the test is objective multiple-choice questions and other formats is another variation. Of course, states also depart from one another on how often tests are given at the different grade levels. But judgment about the state social studies tests is limited if the test items are not released. Some states release the test items every year because they use different test items every year. These results usually can be found on the state's web site. Other states are using the same questions year after year and the test items are not released.

In the final analysis, most states pay attention to costs and practical issues. For cost effectiveness, the tests must be simple to administer and relatively easy to grade. Sometimes these constraints limit the test to that portion of the curriculum that is easiest to measure, such as objective test items versus students' writing short answer questions or essays. Open-ended questions can measure high levels of skills and knowledge, but they are more expensive to grade. Although somewhat controversial, computer technology can be used to grade essay questions quickly for elements such as grammar and spelling. Computer-graded essays may become more common in the future, as well as using computers to adjust test items to each student's ability level. A routing test initially determines each student's approximate skill level. If the student appears advanced, a lot of the easy questions are skipped. If the student appears to be challenged, the test starts with the easier questions. Not testing out-of-level knowledge reduces frustration.

Norm-Referenced Tests

Most state tests are **norm-referenced tests.** Here an individual's performance is compared with the performance of others in the group (Popham, 1995). Norm-referenced tests are specifically designed so that most students will miss a number of questions—and some students will fail. Students are graded with reference to the normal curve. The results are expressed as a percentile, which is easily interpreted by students and their parents. Maria was at the 81st percentile, whereas David was at the 48th percentile. A problem is "the Lake Wobegon syndrome," whereby everyone wants all the children to be above average or above the 50th percentile. Norms are typically determined every seven years, when test makers give exams, to a representative sampling of students. It should be noted that standards *cannot* be assessed with norm-referenced exams, because they test how students compare with others, not how much of the standards students know.

Criterion-Based Testing

In contrast to norm-referenced testing is **criterion-based testing.** Now more and more states are creating state exams based on standards or other criteria. This system measures student performance based on standards, and the test items are tied to specific standards or objectives. It is sometimes called the mastery learning approach. This means the variability of scores is of little consequence and there is no "curve." Everyone, theoretically, can be proficient. Each student is graded on the basis of his or her performance relative to the standard(s), regardless of the performance of other students. Emphasis is on an individual's performance relative to an a priori criterion instead of relative to the performance of other people. Scores are reported as levels: Not proficient, Basic, Proficient, Advanced. This is the familiar pattern used by NAEP in reporting their scores. It is also used on Prospective Teacher examinations, in which applicants have to get a certain score to pass. Note that a judgment, ideally made by experts and members of the community, is needed for the cutoff scores that define performance categories such as Proficient or Expert. In some cases, the cutoffs are set after looking at the test scores to see how many will fail, instead of looking at how well students achieved the standards.

Because of standards, most test publishers of nationally normed tests now offer to report test results in terms of "standards." This means that they have defined cut scores for categories such as Proficient or Advanced. In a similar manner, now many states and districts treat the 50th percentile as the defining standard for accomplishment. Then they report norm-referenced scores in terms of those who "meet" the standard.

Over time, the controversy and anxiety about state test scores may diminish as students, teachers, and parents become more comfortable with state tests. New teachers seem more accepting of standards-based testing. However, if more students have to attend summer school or repeat grades, or if there is an increase in the number of school dropouts, the public will put pressure on states and districts to make the tests easier to pass, most likely by changing the cutoff scores for passing.

Teachers Need to Research Their State Test

If your state has a social studies test, you need to become familiar with both the standards and the format of the test. As you look at the standards from your state, you will notice the huge number of content standards, usually for each grade level. Your second reaction, given the time available, will be, How can I teach all of the content standards? There are just too many! The sheer number of standards also means that with the current state testing situation, the state test cannot possibly measure all of the standards. This has left teachers confused and uncertain about what they should emphasize. This points to the desirability of states revisiting their standards to determine which standards should be the high priority. If your state has not done this, you and your department should establish priorities among the many standards.

First, teachers in a school or department usually examine whether all of the state standards are included in the present curriculum. Usually, if you and your department colleagues look at the standards and the tests carefully, you will find there are curriculum gaps and redundancy. Changes are therefore needed to ensure even coverage.

In addition, what is the proportion of history, geography, economics, and political science in the test? There are wide variations here.

What are the essential key concepts for each standard? In what courses or grade levels will certain standards be emphasized? Taking these steps can ensure that the curriculum is challenging and rigorous and meets the state standards. One positive effect of the standards movement is that it has forced isolated teachers to talk more with one another. One possible negative to social studies teaching is that teachers may cut down on discussions of current events because that material, although of extreme importance in relating the past to the present, is unlikely to appear on the test.

Second, in what formats are the test items and what are the demands of the test? What kinds of questions are asked? Multiple-choice and open-response questions? Approximately how many questions involve timelines, maps, analyzing political cartoons, or reading charts and graphs? Are primary sources used? How much time is allowed? Will there be a written task? Given the format of the test, what instructional goals and materials are needed? Analyzing the most recent student test data showing students' strengths and weaknesses is helpful. Finding out as much as possible about the test is valuable, and communicating these insights to students is essential. In many states, this information plus sample and released questions are found on your state department of education web site.

Knowing the standards and the testing format does not preclude creativity in teaching. The standards and the tests need not result in a rigid, narrow curriculum. Students are cheated if mere memorization is thought to be the best way to learn something. Instead, teachers should maintain the best teaching practices all year while preparing their students for state tests. Instead of cramming a few weeks before the test, it is best to incorporate the various types of learning and assessment in the ongoing social studies program. The focus should be on the knowledge and skills necessary for success rather than solely on test-taking skills. In fact, students who receive assignments that require more challenging intellectual work achieve higher scores on standardized tests. Improved thinking skills have a direct bearing on successful test taking.

You, as a teacher, need to assess all students in many different ways that allow them to show what they have learned. Use multiple types of assessment for a complete report on their progress toward meeting the standards. Check to see that all evidence of achievement addresses all of the standards.

The test should not be regarded as a one-shot effort; rather, there should be continuous growth in learning, along its assessment, throughout the year. You should communicate to students that they can be successful in test taking if they learn what you are teaching and that success does not depend only on luck. It is especially important for students to attend classes daily. **Attendance**—just showing up for school on a regular basis—is one of the biggest keys to school success. Research indicates that in many low-achieving high schools the difference on passing a test is simply related to a student's attendance. In summary, to achieve better results on tests requires that everyone involved buy into the idea that all students can learn and be successful. Administrators, teachers, students, parents, and community—all are stakeholders in the evaluation process.

SMALL GROUP WORK	**WHAT IS HAPPENING IN TESTING IN YOUR STATE?**
5.3	*From newspapers and other media, is testing a hot topic in your state? What are the concerns? Are any changes suggested?*

■ ASSESSING STUDENT LEARNING

Types of Assessment

In thinking about how to assess student learning, we have to decide which student **product(s)** and **performance(s)** will provide evidence of student learning. These can be divided into three main categories: written, oral, and visual. In actual practice, the categories may overlap, as when the student makes an advertisement poster (Table 5.1). Note the many interesting methods of assessment. These can be used daily as teachers collect data on students' progress. Classroom assessment should not be considered something done only at the end of a unit but instead should be used as constant feedback to both the students and teacher on how learning is being supported. Assessment should be an ongoing, dynamic process integrated with learning. It should include challenging tasks to elicit

TABLE 5.1 Designing Assessment Tasks

Written	Oral	Visual
Advertisement	Advertisement	Advertisement
Biography	Debate	Banner
Book report	Dialogue	Cartoon
Character portrait	Discussion	Chart
Diary	Dramatization	Collage
Editorial	Interview	Computer graphic
Essay	Newscast	Data table
Journal	Oral presentation	Drawing
Letter	Oral report	Graph
Note-taking	Role play	Map
Poster	Skit	Outline
Questionnaire	Speech	Photograph
Readers' Theater	Teach a lesson	Poster
Research report		Timeline
Script		Venn diagram
Story		Webbing
Test		

Source: Adapted from Porter, P. H. (2000, March). "Show What You Know: Linking Assessment with Standards." California Council for the Social Studies Annual Conference.

higher-order thinking and not just memorization of basic facts. Use assessments to fo-cus on the learning of individual students, especially those who are **underperforming.** Assessments can help generate methods to shape instruction to meet students' varied learning needs. Remember that the main purpose of the many assessment tools is to determine whether *students have achieved the standards or objectives.*

Performance Assessment

In recent years, **authentic assessment** and **performance assessment** have received more attention as a new perspective on assessment (Nickell, 1999). *Authentic* means con-nected to real-life problems and concerns. The outstanding characteristic of authen-tic assessment is that the particular tasks that students tackle are worthwhile, significant, and meaningful—in other words, authentic. They are real instances of learning instead of indirect estimates of learning. However, some observers (Ter-williger, 1997) are worried that the proponents of authentic assessment see such as-sessments as superior to more conventional assessments and that the emphasis on authentic assessment may denigrate the role of knowledge.

Performance means what students are able to do. In practice, the two terms *au-thentic assessment* and *performance assessment* are often carelessly treated as being interchangeable. *Performance* is the term used in the rest of this chapter. Performance assessment arose in the 1980s and 1990s, partly as a reaction to paper-and-pencil ob-jective test measures that were being used primarily for testing of factual knowledge in the schools (Darling-Hammond & Ancess, 1995; Grady, 1992; Herman, Ash-bacher, & Winters, 1992; Perrone, 1991; Wiggins, 1999).

This form of assessment is more in tune with the constructivist approach to teaching and learning, as students get feedback to help them understand what they are learning. Learning activities become assessment practices as students debate, write editorials, role play, or make a timeline. In performance assessment, students create an answer or product and do not simply answer paper-and-pencil tests. Al-though it is true that some subject areas such as physical education, art, and music have always relied heavily on performance-based assessment, social studies teachers normally have been only moderate users of performance assessment.

Performance assessment ranges from the simplest student-constructed responses to collections of a large amount of work over time. Writing is the largest category of per-formance assessment. In contrast to a multiple-choice test, in which the student must identify the correct spelling, grammar, or usage, when writing students can demonstrate skills in stating ideas as well as their knowledge of language, grammar, and syntax. The advantage of writing is that it can test higher levels of thinking because a student has to organize and analyze material to produce a good essay answer. In other words, performance-based writing is a more open-ended response.

Portfolios

Portfolios are a form of long-term performance assessment. Portfolios are usually files or folders that contain collections of a student's work. Portfolios have been used more in language arts classes than in social studies classes. They furnish a broad portrait of individual performance assembled over time and allow monitoring of a student's progress. By including the actual products, they give more insight than the teacher's gradebook alone does. As students assemble and review their portfolios, they decide what to include, often reflecting on their work. Ideally, students should evaluate their own work by commenting on why they selected particular pieces and how their work shows progress. Student evaluation and taking the responsibility for improving their own work are the goals of performance assessment.

However, in practice, we are seeing mixed portfolios in which teacher-corrected tests and teacher comments are included. This is because portfolios are usually reviewed by parents, who, without seeing the work of other students in the class or knowing the standards, may assume that all is well with their child's performance when instead there may be serious problems for the student in terms of learning the objectives of the course.

Probably the main deterrent to using portfolios is the heavy time demands placed on the teacher to evaluate the portfolios. However, a few states such as Nebraska have statewide writing assessment. The time demands have limited portfolios' adoption by teachers. Teachers may also be concerned about ELL students and students with disabilities if writing is one of the main assessment tools. Typically for these students, writing is their weakest skill.

Anticipating Problems with Testing

Let us first examine the category of the paper-and-pencil tests that are typically used at the end of the unit, because in many social studies classrooms this is what the students and teacher value most. Assessment should not be viewed as occurring only at the end of the unit but as an ongoing process, integrated with instruction and with students well aware of what they are to learn. However, too often teachers conscientiously mark daily assignments but fail to give guidance on how students can improve. For students who are unsuccessful, this oversight increases their sense of failure.

Tests or assessments are not usually either a teacher's or the students' favorite activities and for that reason often do not receive the attention they deserve. Nevertheless, they are necessary to determine whether the standards and objectives have been met. There is evidence that frequent in-class tests help students to learn, so they should not be eliminated. Part of the value of frequent testing is the feedback to students such as discussing correct answers after the quiz or activity. Frequent testing enables students to monitor their progress, focuses on what is important, and may help raise student interest.

However, tests need to be designed with care because one of the most common student complaints about their teachers is that their "tests are not fair." To avoid this perception on the part of your students, make your tests fair, challenging, and as creative as possible. Refrain from "setting yourself up" for complaining students who argue with you about their grades and poison the relationship between you as a teacher and your students. After the "teachers don't care" catchphrase, students' complaints about unfair tests are one of the most common criticisms about their teachers.

SMALL GROUP WORK	**WHAT WERE GOOD OR BAD TESTS?**
5.4	*What in your school experience made a test fair or unfair (good or bad)?*

The Timing of Tests

Day by day, activities in the classroom should be giving you and your students information on how they are achieving the standards and objectives in the unit. Some teachers also ask that students record their own scores on daily activities to alert students as to how they are doing. However, the end of the unit is a natural breaking point for a more formal, summative type of test. This is the point at which most teachers think about evaluation, although day-to-day evaluation is also necessary. By this stage of their educational careers, students have been socialized to expect a test—although a test need not be given for a unit if a project or some other work has been substituted. The ideal time to plan *when* you will test is at the beginning of the semester when you block out the units you are planning to teach.

To avoid student discontent, it is essential that your students know the date of the test. Announce and **write** the date well in advance. Many teachers spend part of the time the day before the test reviewing the unit so that students have a better idea of the content and skills likely to be covered in the test. In some schools, giving tests also has to be coordinated with other departments so that students do not have tests in all their classes on Friday. In these schools, for example, social studies tests can only be given on Wednesdays and math tests can only be given on Thursdays. Also look over the school calendar to see how your test dates fit in with social and athletic events of schoolwide importance. Especially for juniors and seniors, be aware of national examinations such as SATs that your students may be taking. After setting a date for the test, try not to be pressured by students to delay giving the test. This is a constant and common student tactic. Changing the date for the testing does not reward the students who have planned and studied with the date of the test in mind.

In planning the timing of a test, also consider your teaching and grading load, especially if the test does not consist of objective test items only. Remember that it is best to return tests as quickly as possible both for students to learn how to correct their misconceptions and for you to do any necessary reteaching. Stale tests returned two weeks later do little to encourage students to improve relearning or take advantage of necessary reteaching. This is also true of any activity: *immediate feedback* helps students know how they are doing. Nevertheless, do not create impossible burdens for yourself. If possible, stagger your workload by not giving tests to all your classes on the same day. Still, many teachers believe that giving all their classes a test the last day before a holiday may pay off in terms of avoiding classroom management and discipline problems and students' forgetting content over the holidays.

In planning the time of the test, you have to consider what type of test items you will use. The advantages and disadvantages of different test questions are discussed later. However, the widespread popularity of objective test items, often multiple-choice items, is related to the ease with which teachers can correct them, especially if there is a "mark sense" machine available. In most high schools, equipment is readily available for marking objective answer sheets. This essentially means that the teacher only has to record or enter the student grades. Software is also available to grade tests electronically. Using a handheld device, teachers can give multiple-choice and short-answer tests that are automatically graded and downloaded into their grade books. Observational data also can be recorded.

Most social studies tests for middle school and high school students are taken in class. An in-class test forces students to read, to think, and to write material rapidly under time pressure. It rewards students who can form their thoughts quickly and write rapidly. The alternative to an in-class test is a take-home test. A take-home test is most often done if the test consists of an essay question(s). It is not common in most social studies middle and high school classes, because having essay questions for a social studies test takes time for the teacher to correct. In addition, there is the model of the AP history/social sciences national examination in which essays count for about two-thirds of the students' AP score. However, the essay part of the AP test is timed, so the best way for students to practice writing essays for their AP exam will be in a classroom, not during an untimed period of writing at home.

A further reason for not having take-home tests is that students often receive unauthorized help. It is almost impossible for a teacher to monitor any assistance a student might receive at home and how much time is spent on the test. Still, the advantage of a take-home test is that it is easier for the teacher to read because it is more likely to be typed and better thought out. For that reason, it may be worth trying on occasion.

Handling Missed Tests

A problem always arises as to what to do about students who missed taking the unit test. Probably some of the reasons for missing the tests are legitimate, such as illness. But a given student may want to take advantage of learning more about the questions on the test to get a higher grade. Therefore, some teachers choose a time for make-up tests that requires a certain amount of inconvenience on the part of the student— such as before school, after school, or during lunch. However, first check to see whether your school or the social studies department has a rule about how to take care of students who have missed tests.

In addition, do not give the same test that was already given, because many of the questions may have been "leaked" to the absent member of the class. This problem is not unique to absent members of the class. You can probably remember from your own school experience that the divulging of questions is common if the same examination is given on the same day to three U.S. history classes scheduled at different time periods. The last period class often has the highest scores! For makeup tests, you can substitute an essay question for a series of multiple-choice or short-answer questions. If you had an essay question(s), reword it a little to change the focus. This process of changing the makeup test makes it fairer to all students.

Avoiding Cheating on Tests

Most students are honest, but you need to be alert to the possibility of cheating on tests. Some disturbing surveys show that many high school students admitted to cheating on a test at least once in the past year. Multiple-choice items are the easiest format for students to cheat on because all they have to do is look at their neighbor's answer sheet. For this reason, some teachers give alternative sets of multiple-choice questions. These have the same questions but in a different order. Using word processing, it is easy to scramble the test items to create tests with different patterns of answers. Avoid having your head lowered as you correct papers at your desk. Being in the back of the classroom and walking around with widespread visibility is helpful. Also, revise the test before you give it again. Be aware that high-tech cheating using cell phones and PDAs can also be a problem.

SMALL GROUP WORK	WHAT CAN BE DONE TO DISCOURAGE CHEATING ON TESTS?
5.5	*What do students think about cheating? What can be done to discourage cheating?*

Keep Grades Confidential

In recent years there have been more concerns about respecting the privacy of student grades. It is best if you return the tests yourself; do not have a student pass out the tests to the rest of the class. Students can retrieve their own tests if the marks are on the inside and not visible on the front page and if the tests are in alphabetical order so a given student does not have to plow through a whole set of papers. In addition, try not to allow other students to overhear when you are discussing grades with a particular student. Avoid leaving your grade book or graded papers out in the open for other students to see. Do not publicly ask students to report their scores. All these techniques are designed to ensure that grades are kept as confidential as possible to avoid any possibility of lawsuits.

■ TEACHER-MADE PAPER-AND-PENCIL TESTS

Objective or paper-and-pencil tests are the most common assessment found in social studies classes. Their popularity is due to their coverage of a lot of material, their ease of scoring, and their easy translation into points for a quarterly or semester grade. In thinking about testing, remember to use a short **pretest** before starting a unit. Often this will point out the wide range of your students' knowledge and what you may need to emphasize more. Let us first look at the most difficult objective questions to write, multiple-choice items. This type may be the most valuable of objective test items.

Multiple-Choice Test Questions

Multiple-choice questions have such a bad reputation that some publishers now call them "selected response questions." The criticism has been that too often teachers or

What type of thinking do you think is encouraged by most tests?

the publishers' test items have stressed isolated factual information, with little attention given to higher-level thinking. Students get the impression that there is only one right answer. Multiple-choice test items and other objective test items also neglect writing skills. They are also not useful for showing that students can apply skills and knowledge.

As you know, the major publishers all have objective test items that match the content of their textbooks. These prepared **commercial tests** are a lifesaver in terms of teacher time. In many instances, the publisher's prepared test items may be better thought out than those a harried teacher could produce. Nonetheless, if you wish to use the publisher's tests, make sure that the content and activities you have been teaching match the coverage of the textbook. Sometimes it is best to use some of the commercial publisher's test items and to write some of your own. This requires work, versus having a test ready to go that only needs to be copied for your number of students. If you use the publisher's test items, remember to keep the commercial tests in a secure place. Some teachers keep the publisher's test booklet at home to prevent students from getting a copy of the test. In the future, more and more teachers are likely to use the Internet to find assessment items. Again, you always have to make sure that test items are aligned with your curriculum and suitable for your students.

One advantage of multiple-choice questions is that they can assess a broad range of your unit's content and your students' skills. Twenty multiple-choice questions can often better gauge a student's understanding of the unit than one essay question on a narrow topic. Multiple-choice items can also give poor writers such as ELLs and students with disabilities a better way of showing you what they know. Indeed, with care, multiple-choice questions can test the ability of students to think. In addition, multiple-choice questions are easy to grade and reliable in scoring.

A multiple-choice question consists of a *stem,* which is the body of the question. A stem should contain a subject and a verb. In some examples, cartoons, tables, and graphs are included as the stem. Then there are incorrect responses (sometimes called *distractors*) and the correct answer (also known as the *key*).

It is important to use clear language and not place a heavy burden on student reading. Avoid double negatives and "all of the above" or "none of the above" choices. Have the same number of responses, if possible five but at least three. This means that if there are five responses there is only one-fifth chance of guessing correctly. Try to have all of the responses approximately the same length. It is not uncommon for the correct answer, the key, to be longer than the rest. Emphasize important ideas, events, or individuals, not trivia. Look at the following test items that were used by NAEP in their history assessment. For the first item, 78 percent of a national sample of students responded with the correct answer, B. For the second item, 80 percent of the students responded with the correct answer, B. For the third question, 56 percent of the students responded with the correct answer, D.

Grade 8, Number 1

Between 1960 and 1990, what invention most changed the way people in the United States worked?

    A   The typewriter
    B   The computer
    C   The superconductor
    D   The radio

Grade 8, Number 2

> O Freedom!
> O Freedom!
> O Freedom over me!
> And before I'd be a slave
> I'd be buried in my grave,
> And go home to my Lord and be free!

This song was associated with

    A   the temperance movement.
    B   the civil rights movement.
    C   pioneers on the Oregon Trail.
    D   farmers in the Dust Bowl during the Great Depression.

Grade 12, Number 3

The Great Awakening of the 1730's was important because it led people in the American colonies to

    A   increase toleration for Roman Catholics.
    B   examine the different positions of men and women in society.
    C   reaffirm that God gave kings the right to rule.
    D   question the authority of church and government leaders.

ON YOUR OWN	**EXAMINE THE QUALITY OF QUESTIONS**
5.1	*Look at these three multiple choice items. Are they examining important U.S. history content? Is the reading level appropriate? Do you like them?*

Other Paper-and-Pencil Test Items

In **true/false** items, students are asked if the statement is true or false. True/false items have such a poor reputation that many experts do not recommend they ever be used, because they allow guessing and there is a higher probability of being correct than with any other type of test item. Some teachers ask students to correct false statements, but this increases the time needed to correct these test items.

To be good test items, true/false items must be very carefully written in simple language. Always state only one idea as clearly and concisely as possible and make sure that the items are clearly true or false. Remember, often there are exceptions! If you do use them, be careful to avoid specific determiners such as *always, all, never, only;* these are clues that the statement is false. Also avoid *may, generally,* and *should,* which usually make the statement true.

Matching

Matching test items in social studies typically evaluate students' ability to make associations between persons and their achievements or words and definitions. They have also been used to match dates (1776, 1914, and the like) with events. Matching items usually are testing only recall and identification, as shown in the following example.

Directions: Match the people in Column A with their inventions in Column B.

Column A

_____ 1. Alexander Graham Bell
_____ 2. Thomas Edison
_____ 3. Elias Howe
_____ 4. Samuel F. B. Morse
_____ 5. Elisha G. Otis

Column B

a. Electric lightbulb
b. First commercial telegraph message
c. Safety elevator
d. Sewing machine
e. Steel plow
f. Telephone
g. Typewriter

Notice the format of this matching test item: Column B has more choices than prompts in Column A, to cut down on guessing; the items in the columns are in alphabetical order so that students do not waste time rereading to find the answer; the category A is not long (a good rule of thumb is to have five to seven prompts); also, the category is not mixed with explorers or political leaders but contains only inventors.

Sometimes you see **fill-in-the-blank** items. Here a student supplies a word or a phrase. These are less common because they require a teacher to correct, and for that reason they are not used for standardized tests. The classic example of a poor fill-in-the-blank test item is "_____ invented _____ in _____." Such sentences are vague because they eliminate so many words and can have many answers. Ideally, there should be only one correct response for this type of item. Better is "The inventor of the cotton gin was _____," putting the one blank at the end of the sentence.

Furthermore, in designing a test with objective test items, put easier questions at the beginning of the test and the more difficult items at the end so that students do not panic and give up.

SMALL GROUP WORK	**WILL YOU USE OBJECTIVE QUESTIONS?**
5.6	*Given your subject area, how much of your assessment will be objective questions? Why?*

■ PERFORMANCE-BASED ASSESSMENT

Essay Questions

Although essays have long been used to assess a student's understanding of a subject, they are classified as a performance-based assessment. In an essay, the student writes a description, analysis, explanation, or summary in one or more paragraphs. An essay asks students to develop a thesis and support it with data. The essay ends with a summary of the thesis and the main points. An essay question can be a valuable challenge to get students to engage in higher-level thinking. A good essay question does not stress memorization of facts. Instead it asks students to develop their own interpretation or response using the information they have studied in class.

Teach the Five-Paragraph Essay Format?

Should you teach your students the five-paragraph formula for answering an essay question? This format is as follows:

- First paragraph: introduction, restate the thesis
- Second to fourth paragraphs: three fitting examples that support/contradict, evidence
- Fifth paragraph: conclusion that restates the thesis

Teachers who object to the five-paragraph essay believe it kills creativity and does not allow students to think. Those in favor of using the formula feel it especially helps low-proficiency writers. These teachers maintain that students are better off using the formula than trying to write without it. Other teachers believe in a balance. There is a place for creative writing (which plays with conventions), but students must first master the essentials of organization and evaluation. Then students can move beyond the five-paragraph formula.

Constructing Essay Questions

Avoid using verbs such as *describe* or *discuss*. Usually the student responses from these verbs will elicit little analysis, and that content can be better tested by multiple-choice test items. The same rules that apply to asking higher-level questions also apply here. Do not ask "who, what, when, and where" essay questions.

Instead, for essay questions use verbs such as *analyze, compare, contrast,* and *evaluate*. This should produce a wider range of responses, tapping higher levels of thinking. You can ask students to respond to a short statement or quotation. You can make up your statement if you think the real quotation is too hard to read. Furthermore, try to estimate how long it will take students to answer the essay question. A frequent problem is that not enough time is allocated. In addition, some experts deplore giving just one long essay question because of the limited sample of content covered. It is generally better to have three short questions than one long essay question.

Document-Based Question

For many years, Advanced Placement essay tests have used a **document-based question (DBQ)**. In this, several primary sources (such as documents, political cartoons, quotations, and the like) that are related to a single topic are used as the student prompt to answer the given essay question. These questions are typically scored on the basis of points: certain points for an acceptable thesis, points for synthesis of the majority of documents, and so on. In the past, few teachers, other than those teaching AP courses, used this particular format of essay question. However, a few states (such as New York) are now using document-based questions for their state social studies examinations. If the state examination includes this type of question, some teachers will respond by also using document-based questions, especially those used as sample models, so that their students will be familiar with this format before taking an important test.

A Choice

Should students have a choice of which essay question to answer? Many test experts reply that ideally all students should have the same task so that grading can be fair. It is almost impossible to have all the essay questions be of the same difficulty level. With many choices, the student will choose the one essay question he or she feels the most comfortable and knowledgeable about answering. Perhaps two choices should be the limit rather than a choice between five or six essay questions.

Grading Essay Questions

One disadvantage of using essay questions is the subjectivity process of grading them. There are horror stories about different teachers giving widely different grades to the same essay question. In one study, the same teachers graded a set of essay questions and then six weeks later graded them again. There were wildly divergent scores by the same teacher looking at the essay six weeks later. To reduce these problems, set the criteria ahead of time: the point value and approximate time limit for each essay question. This also means it is important to establish a set of standards or criteria or a rubric so that you can grade fairly.

Using Rubrics with Essay Questions

The use of rubrics in grading (Figure 5.1) is increasing in popularity and is highly recommended as part of the authentic assessment movement. A **rubric** is a scoring tool that lists the criteria of work or what counts in a grade. Notice that in Figure 5.1 there are four different levels that could correspond to the grades of A, B, C, and D. If a student did not attempt to answer the question or only wrote a sentence or two, the grade equivalent would probably be an F.

A rubric thus provides specific criteria for describing student performance at different levels. Do you think the rubric in Figure 5.1 would be helpful? Notice that it could be divided into more categories (Table 5.2), and the range of scores could be expanded into more than two categories.

FIGURE 5.1 Scoring Rubric for a History Essay Question

Distinguished or Advanced Level
- Thesis well developed
- Clear, accurate, and well structured with a beginning, middle, and end
- Shows understanding of the historical time period by use of many important historical facts and reasons
- Weighs multiple perspectives

Proficient Level
- Is organized
- Uses some important facts and reasons to support ideas
- Presents two perspectives or viewpoints

Apprentice Level
- Does not have a beginning, middle, and end
- Indicates little understanding of facts
- Supports a position without reason

Novice Level
- Poorly structured
- Very few facts and shows little knowledge of history
- Inconsistent statements or unrelated to the test question

TABLE 5.2 Possible Categories to Use in a Rubric

Scoring Categories	Highest Score	Lowest Score
Point of view	Very clear	Erratic
Organization of information	Skillful	Erratic
Historical knowledge	Detailed	Little/often tangential
Degree of significance of issues	Most significant	Little/often tangential
Reasons, evidence	Appropriate	Generalizations
Examples	Relevant	Limited
Primary source materials	Well represented	Rarely
Cause and effect	Complex analysis	May sequence
Compare/contrast events, people	Thoughtful	May name a few
Various other points of view	Carefully considered and incorporated	Sometimes considered
Links to the present	Accurately and insightfully	Not attempted
Geographic knowledge	Detailed and accurate	No mention of places
Historical/factual	Few or no errors	Extreme errors
Communication	Clear and effective	Mostly incomprehensible

Source: Adapted from Leary, D. (1999). "Grade 8 History–Social Science Abbreviated Scoring Guide" in "Using the New History–Social Science Content Standards as an Opportunity for Teachers." *Social Studies Review, 38,* 52.

Rubrics are used mostly for written work, but they are sometimes applied to oral presentations, discussions, and projects. As mentioned in the examination of small discussion groups (Chapter 4), using a rubric, a teacher or a student could mark how often the student participated and how often she or he made encouraging remarks, as well as more complex behavior such as resolution of a value conflict. Rubrics are typically used in state writing assignments, AP examinations, and other important examinations so that the graders can give a more uniform set of grades or increase the reliability of the scores.

When rubrics are used, points are often given to students for fulfilling the criteria of the assignment. For example, for a homework assignment on a political campaign, students will get ten points for an accurate portrayal of the candidate, ten points for the development of ideas on why they would support or not support the candidate, and five points for grammar and the use of language. This is a more detailed format of the old practice of giving two grades on an essay: one for content and the other for format such as grammar and spelling.

Rubrics used by teachers vary in the amount of detail. In some cases, they are very detailed: A student will get an A for writing a 500-word paper that cites five sources and supports its theme with at least two arguments. However, a C paper is 250 words with two sources and one argument. The grade of F is usually reserved for students who did not hand in the work or produced only a few paragraphs.

One rationale for the use of rubrics is that they are a powerful tool to help students clearly see what they need to do. The proponents of rubrics believe that rubrics are a great improvement over the "good old days" when students did not know what was expected and a teacher's bias was perceived as not subject to control. A rubric makes a teacher's expectations clear. In the past (as you probably have experienced yourself), essays often had unexplained or vague criteria. In contrast, rubrics are supposed to give students the reasons for the evaluations they receive. Students, in turn, are supposed to perceive the evaluations as being less subjective on the part of the teacher. Rubrics can help make students more thoughtful judges of their own and others' work. Have students fill out a rubric with the headings shown in Figure 5.2. You can have them put the categories underneath, such as "Various Points of View" or "Supporting Details." If students mark 0, 1, or 2, they need to edit their work before handing it in to the teacher.

Rubrics can also be beneficial if a parent complains of harsh grading on an essay because the student's political views were different from those of the teacher or the community. As the teacher explains to a parent how the essay was graded on the basis of a list of required elements, charges of unfairness can be diffused. Teachers who cannot explain their grades on essay tests annoy students, parents, and administrators. However, it should be noted that although a rubric reduces subjectivity, the teacher is still making interpretations as she or he evaluates the essay.

Do rubrics work? As with all methods, rubrics can be helpful and useful to both the teacher and the student when properly used. Developing a rubric is initially difficult. The assignment first must be broken down into its vital parts. Some teachers invite their students to help set the criteria. The published rubrics available in journals and other sources typically must be modified to reflect your own curriculum and what you consider to be important. Students also need to understand what each term in the criteria means. What does *organize* mean? What benchmarks show good organization?

FIGURE 5.2 Feedback Rubric

	Not Evident (edit work before handing in)			Very Evident	
	0	1	2	3	4
Various Points of View					
Supporting Details					

But the more important issue is that teachers vary on how they approach grading essay questions. One teacher may feel more comfortable judging holistically, whereas other teachers break the essay question into points. Teachers who grade holistically do not appreciate using a rubric that judges by points. In many cases, these teachers are looking for a beginning (stating a thesis), a middle (citing relevant evidence), and an end (a summary or conclusion) without going into detail about points for different criteria. In addition to this concern, critics of rubrics believe that rubrics drive out creativity and limit the imagination of students in their writing. Defenders of the use of rubrics think if this is so, it is because the rubric is too detailed. They also believe that for students with writing difficulties, rubrics can be very helpful. Some students do not have a clue about what to do without a rubric.

ON YOUR OWN	**YOUR USE OF ESSAY QUESTIONS**
5.2	*How do you think you would use essay questions in your assessment of students? Would you consider the use of rubrics for grading essays? Why or why not? Would you approve of computer grading of essays? Why or why not?*

Other Hints for Grading Essays

Timing also makes a difference when a teacher sits down to grade essays. It has been noted that in the beginning of the scoring process, teachers are less lenient; then, as they get a feel for what is more or less average, they become less strict. The standards for evaluation change after the teacher reads more. To control for this problem, it is a good idea to skim several exams so you can get a feel for what an average essay looks like and what grades are appropriate for what level of performance. This is called *range finding*. Furthermore, after looking at two "A" essays, a teacher will tend to mark down the next response whose quality is not as good. In a similar manner, after grading two lower-scored essays, the next better one gets a higher grade. For these reasons, one recommendation is to tentatively mark in pencil and put the essays into piles, perhaps the five grades from A to F, or three piles of above average, average, and below average. Then go over the essays again to see that you are marking fairly.

It is also recommended that for more than one essay question, read all of the number one questions first, and then read all of the number two questions second. This avoids the "halo" effect. Thus, if a teacher sees a good response on the first essay question, he or she does not automatically give a higher grade on the second question. Likewise, a poorer response in question number one will not automatically cast a negative light on the second question. Also watch for fatigue. Try to give yourself breaks so that your mood is not affecting how you mark.

Short-Answer Questions (Open-Response or Constructed-Response)

The *short-answer question* is a good compromise between the essay and multiple-choice questions. Sometimes it is called an open-response or constructed-response question. This type of question can allow you to test for factual knowledge and critical thinking without placing undue burdens of writing on the students and an onerous grading burden on you. It can be an ideal situation, used in combination with many multiple-choice questions. In a short-answer question, the student is required to produce an answer to a question. The question may have just one correct answer or may be more open-ended, allowing a range of responses. The form can vary, as in writing short answers (Figure 5.3) or drawing a map. Often the number of lines provided after each question gives students a clue to the length of the expected response.

Typically the following short-answer questions are used in the social studies:

- *Identifications* normally require that students provide, in a few sentences, a brief synopsis of a person, event, or development. Make sure that they describe why the person, event, or idea is significant.
- *Clusters* generally are a list of events. Students are asked to place the material in the proper order and explain why the sequence makes sense. If you are having them give the time sequence for such events as the signing of the Declaration of Independence, Lexington and Concord, Bunker Hill, and so on, use this format in an objective question. The clusters should ask students to explain relationships.
- *Source-based questions* present students with a written chart, graph, primary source, cartoon, news headline, or photograph and ask students to explain a perspective or interpretation that can be made. Sometimes this is called an *open-response question* to distinguish it from an essay, which has a thesis. In state tests, open-response question responses are often limited to one page or less.

FIGURE 5.3 Question and Rubric on U.S. History Test Item

Name two kinds of work women do today that they could not do 100 years ago.

1. _____

_____

2. _____

_____

Explain why the kinds of work women do today are different from the kinds of work women did 100 years ago.

_____

_____

_____

Responses are scored according to a three-level rubric as 1) Inappropriate, 2) Partial, and 3) Appropriate.

Source: Beatty, A., Reese, C., Persky, H., & Carr, P. (1996). *NAEP 1994 U.S. History Report Card* (p. 101). Washington, DC: U.S. Department of Education, National Center for Education Statistics.

Other Written Assessments

Besides essays and written projects, writing is often assessed in day-to-day assignments. For students to be able to write, they must have had activities that have given them an abundance of ideas. These writing assignments could take a variety of formats: newspaper articles, dialogues between two historical figures, song lyrics, diaries, advertisements, speeches, poems, letters to family members, and eulogies. In a diary format, for example, they might write what was happening to a struggling sharecropper family or to a member of the nobility during the French or Russian Revolution. These various formats can be more motivating and exciting than doing a research-type written assignment, and they usually can be done in less time.

Often students need help organizing their ideas; having students put their ideas into a web or an outline can be beneficial. Teachers can insist on a first draft even if the first draft is not corrected by the teacher. Give time in class for students to get feedback from their peer group. Some teachers have another student read the written work and sign off on it. This greatly helps the teacher's time commitment in grading the final copy and at the present time does not appear to be an invasion of student privacy.

Oral Assessments

Typically assessments of discussions and role playing are made on the spot by the teacher or shortly after the activity by the group. On more formal presentations such as debates and reports, the assessment is likely to include the use of a rubric.

SAMPLE CLASSROOM EPISODE

STUDENTS WHO FAIL TO COMPLETE ASSIGNMENTS

Ethan, a high school government teacher, looked over his computer grade book. Ethan's philosophy is that no student who comes to class and does the assignments will fail his class. If they walk in the door and try, he can help them. But he had a few students who almost always failed to hand in assignments done both in class and for homework. Ethan had checked and for three of them—two boys and one girl—there was no problem with ability to read or to comprehend the textbook or what is said in class. They were not low-skilled students. Yet by not handing in assignments, these three students who were getting a grade of zero for not handing in assignments were risking failure for the entire semester. In Ethan's grading system, 30 percent of the grade is earned by completing assignments and only 30 percent comes from tests. Ethan knows that compared to other teachers, a much lower percentage of a student's grade is due to test scores. He counts 10 percent for a community service project and 30 percent for class participation.

(continued)

Ethan seemed to remember something about how in a 100-point grading system, normally even a grade of D is 60 points and F is 50 points. Giving a zero really lowers the overall grade average. Should he designate a grade of A 4 points, B 3 points, C 2 points, and D 1 point, and then give zero points for assignments not turned in? That did not seem to lower the average as much. Of course, the real solution would be to motivate the students to complete the assignments. Alas, no success so far. Or should these three students learn that there are consequences to not handing in their assignments? Should Ethan schedule time to talk to each student individually to show what the missing assignments were doing to the final grade? Ethan was annoyed that these students were not trying.

What mark should Ethan give for students who do not hand in assignments? What can be done to encourage students to hand in assignments and homework? Do you like Ethan's philosophy on grading?

■ GRADES AND REPORT CARDS

Effort

The most common form of feedback that teachers give to their students is a letter grade on a report card. Usually teachers have a wide range of freedom over what components they will use to determine individual student grades (Brookhart, 1993). Will you give any consideration to **effort**? What grade do you give a student who does all the homework, listens in class, but averages a D on tests? Should she or he be given a D or a C? Teachers are divided on this point, but there is now more pressure to keep "effort" out of the calculation of grades, which, according to this view, should measure only academic achievement. Advocates of keeping "effort" out of grades say that too often the high school grading system allows students to slide through school. They pick up their diplomas without learning much. Teachers give credit without holding the students accountable or applying the assessment criteria. In contrast, defenders of "effort" believe that it can motivate students, especially low-skilled students. Effort often includes attendance, punctuality, work habits, and cooperation.

Or will you give attention to **individual improvement,** how much a student has gained since the start of the semester? Consideration of effort and individual improvement is typically used by the teacher to encourage students, especially students having difficulty with the course. Sometimes these two characteristics are subsumed into a category called "participation" or "citizenship." The teacher gives a certain percentage of the grade, perhaps 20 percent, to participation. Social studies teachers are less likely to include portfolio items in their grade because portfolios are rarely used. Be careful not to grade too much for effort and yet have students who fail high-stakes tests. This is very confusing to students, parents, and administrators. In addition, some experts (Airasian, 1994) state that these two attributes—participation and effort—are difficult for teachers to really assess.

Other Grading Models

Other teachers go strictly by the grades in their grade book or in their computer grade book. Here grades are accumulated from a series of objective tests and then averaged. Points are also given for assignments, including homework, reports, projects, and student presentations. In some classrooms, points are given daily for coming to class on time, bringing materials, being positive and respectful, and completing assignments in class.

Many high school social studies teachers go by the amount of points a student has accumulated over the grading period and then have to determine the cutoff points between A, B, C, D, and F. Here, using computer grade book software is certainly a time-saver. In some districts, parents can access their child's grades, but privacy protection is essential. It is wise, after recording a set of grades, for the teacher to make a copy at that point. Some students reportedly have been successful in hacking into the system to change their grades—but your copy, made at the point of entry, provides supportive evidence if any question of such activity arises.

Students should more or less know what grade they can expect to receive by the constant posting of their grades in their notebook evaluation sheet. Ideally there should not be any big surprises if students keep track of their grades on assignments and tests. Do not keep students guessing what their grades may be. It is helpful to have students do a **self-assessment** of their program by filling out a form assessing their progress. Regardless of what grade is given, students should be left with the idea that they can improve their grades. This is one purpose of grades. Often this may involve better attendance in class and handing in all of their classroom assignments. The teacher has to probe why students are not doing the assignments. Special tutoring may have to be arranged.

Standards-Based Report Cards

In addition, communication to both students and parents, especially if there is a state or district test, needs to be as accurate as possible and not misleading or misinformed. This is especially true if mandatory summer school attendance or a lack of a diploma are possible consequences for not achieving the standards.

Some districts now have a Standards-Based Report Card indicating whether the standards and the state test have been met. More middle schools are using this format. With the Report Card, the standards are listed and the student's progress toward the standard is identified. There are usually three or four choices or levels, as indicated in the following levels used by three districts in their report cards:

Standard: Understands the key elements and results of World War II

District A	District B	District C
Below Basic or Standard	Incomplete	Beginning
Basic	Limited	Progressing
Proficient	Partial	Adequate
Advanced	Thorough	Exemplary

This poses a comprehension problem for some parents. Most appear to associate Advanced and Exemplary with the grade of A, Proficient with the grade of B, Basic with the grade of C (average), and Below Basic with a D. Parents tend to make judgments based on how their child is doing compared to others in the class instead of on how well their child has met a particular standard. Honest information about grades and honest communication are essential for both students and parents, but information needs to be presented with a focus on possible improvement if grades are not high. Parents, even of older high school students, want to know what can be done to help their daughter or son. In some communities, report cards also have to be translated into different languages.

SMALL GROUP WORK	**WHAT TO DO ABOUT GRADING?**
5.7	*What would you do about a student(s) in your class who is clearly unable to achieve at what you consider to be a minimal level? About ELL students?*

LARGE CLASS DISCUSSION	**CONTROVERSIAL ISSUE**
	As you are aware, the No Child Left Behind Act is controversial. Do you think students are learning more due to the test-based accountability system implemented by the NCLB Act? For evidence, you may wish to go online to check the data that your local school district, state, and NAEP publish about their test scores. What changes, if any, would you recommend to NCLB?

■ **SUMMARY**

Together, assessment and evaluation are one of the three components of teaching. State tests in the social studies are very important in some schools. But the state test is only one test given during the whole year. Teachers spend a lot more time on their own assessments given throughout the school year. Use a wide range of assessments, including both informal assessment of daily activities and unit tests or some form of performance-based assessment. Performance assessment, especially the use of essay questions, is being encouraged. Remember, students need feedback so that they know their strengths and weaknesses. Self-assessment by students should be encouraged. Try to show students how they can improve. The assessments can also help teachers to evaluate and to refine their own teacher practices and to modify the curriculum. The grading system needs to be thought out carefully and explained to students; it also needs to be understandable to parents.

■ REFERENCES ■

Airasian, P. W. (1994). *Classroom assessment* (2nd ed.) New York: McGraw-Hill.

Baldi, S., Perie, M., Skidmore, D., & Greenberg, E. (2001). *What democracy means to ninth-graders: U.S. results from the International IEA Civic Education Study* (NCES 2001-096). Washington, DC: U.S. Department of Education, National Center for Education Statistics.

Beatty, A., Reese, C., Persky, H., & Carr, P. (1996). *NAEP 1994 U.S. history report card.* Washington, DC: U.S. Department of Education, National Center for Education Statistics.

Brookhart, S. (1993). Teachers' grading practices: Meaning and values. *Journal of Educational Measurement, 30*(2), 123–142.

Chapin, J. R. (2001). From eighth grade social studies to young adulthood voting and community service: National longitudinal study of 1988 eighth graders. *The International Social Studies Forum, 1*(1), 33–44.

Covington, M. V. (1992). *Making the grade: A self-worth perspective on motivation and school reform.* Cambridge: Cambridge University Press.

Darling-Hammond, L., & Ancess, J. (1995). Authentic assessment and school development. In J. B. Baron & D. P. Wolf (Eds.), *Performance-based student assessment: Challenges and possibilities* (pp. 52–83). Chicago: National Society for the Study of Education.

Grady, E. (1992). *The portfolio approach to assessment* (Fastback series). Bloomington, IN: Phi Delta Kappa Educational Foundation.

Herman, J. L., Ashbacher, P. R., & Winters, L. (1992). *A practical guide to alternative assessment.* Alexandria, VA: Association for Supervision and Curriculum Development.

Nickell, P. (1999). Authentic sssessment in social studies. Issue with twelve articles in Nickell (Ed.), *Social Education, 63,* 326–381.

Nungester, R., & Duchastel, P. (1982). Testing versus review: Effects on retention. *Journal of Educational Psychology, 74,* 18–22.

Perrone, V. (1991). *Expanding student assessment.* Alexandria, VA: Association for Supervision and Curriculum Development.

Phelps, R. P. (Ed.) (2005). *Defending standardized testing.* Mahwah, NJ: Lawrence Erlbaum.

Popham, W. J. (1995). *Classroom assessment: What teachers need to know.* Boston: Allyn and Bacon.

Popham, W. J. (2004). *America's "failing" schools: How parents and teachers can cope with No Child Left Behind.* New York: Routledge/Falmer.

Terwilliger, J. (1997.) Semantics, psychometrics, and assessment reform: A close look at "authentic" assessments. *Educational Researcher, 26,* 24–27.

Thomas, R. M. (2005). *High-stakes testing: Coping with collateral damage.* Mahwah, NJ: Lawrence Erlbaum.

Wiggins, G. (1999). *Educative assessment: Designing assessments to inform and to improve student performance.* San Francisco: Jossey-Bass.

■ WEB SITES ■

Educational Testing Service
www.ets.org
Information on their tests.

National Assessment of Educational Progress
http://nces.ed.gov/naep
The nation's report card.

No Child Left Behind
www.ed.gov/legislation/esea02
Links to the full text of the law.

Testing: The Need and Dangers
www.civilrightsproject.harvard.edu/resources
Civil rights group concerned with education.

Chapter 6

Teaching History

In this chapter, we focus on the dominant role of history in the social studies program, the controversies in history over standards, and methods and resources that can be used in teaching history. The following topics are covered.

- The Predominance of History in the Social Studies Curriculum
- Controversies over What History Should Be Taught
- Methods and Resources for Historical Understandings
- Methods and Resources for Historical Thinking Skills

■ THE PREDOMINANCE OF HISTORY IN THE SOCIAL STUDIES CURRICULUM

Central Place of History

The teaching of history is the academic subject within the social studies curriculum that receives far more attention than all the other social sciences. History truly has the central place in the social studies curriculum. In many middle school social studies classes, the three years from the sixth to eighth grades are mainly devoted to history. In the high school, typically two more years concentrate on U.S. history and world history. From transcript analysis, 95 percent of all high school students take a one-year U.S. history course and over 60 percent a one-year world history course; this figure would be even higher if global and area studies were included. World history is more likely to be taken by college-bound students and is regarded as a course for those in an academic program versus a vocational program.

Yet, as with math and science, for all the years that students spend learning history, the results are scarcely impressive. NAEP results (Lapp, Grigg, & Tay-Lim, 2002) and state tests show that a large proportion of our students apparently do not have either an adequate knowledge of key figures in our nation's history and the historical evolution of critical developments in our nation's history, or the ability to place significant dates accurately. Furthermore, Saxe (1996) and others maintain that history as presently taught does not foster citizenship goals.

This does not mean students do not know *some* history. From the popular culture available in film, TV, and music, students have images of such events as the Civil War and the Holocaust. In addition, every student is enveloped by the history learned from the family and at holidays. But this history, often social history, is usually not tested. The students' knowledge of history from these informal sources and previous courses points out the importance of **testing prior knowledge** before starting instruction.

In this discussion, it is presumed there will be no major changes in the amount of course time devoted to history. Although some teachers have pleaded for years to implement a two-year world history high school course rather than a one-year course, at the present time it does not seem likely that increases in the amount of course time will occur. Far more likely are changes within the existing course framework, such as a consecutive two-year course of U.S. history or world history. Even here one cannot expect at the present time radical revisions of the social studies curriculum.

Interpretations of History

There are different definitions of **history.** Historians also disagree on why history is important to study and what history should be taught. One definition of history is "the past experiences of society." Another definition may emphasize how history affects our lives, including the lives of students. Still another definition might focus more on the necessity of the cultural transmission of our ideals and heritage.

Currently, a vast outpouring of scholarship is transforming historians' understanding of our memory of the past. There is a frequent and ongoing *rethinking* of the past, ranging from an increased emphasis on the cross-cultural interaction between ancient civilizations, to new interpretations of Abraham Lincoln—even though hundreds of books have already been written about this president. The changes in the interpretations of Lincoln match changing conditions. Lincoln is part of our national memory and a standard of what is valued (Schwartz, 2000). However, some aspects of the past that hold special significance today may well be matters merely of curiosity in years to come. On the other hand, events that may have seemed unimportant at the time, such as the introduction of cell phones, may assume more importance at a later time.

Historians always interpret evidence and construct tentative versions of what has happened. They select what they study because they cannot possibly study everything in the past. History is therefore socially constructed, debated, and revised. This means that *interpretations* of history are constantly changing, with no fixed version of history written in concrete. What is known about history today is not the same as what was known twenty years ago—and what we will know in twenty years, as new research and new perspectives will continue to change the interpretations of history. This points out the necessity for students to engage in two tasks: (1) to make sense of the interpretations of the past and be aware of various perspectives and (2) to use thinking skills and reasoning as a historian would do in looking at evidence, point of view, and interpretation.

In recent years, historians have given more attention to the everyday life of the vast number of people who have inhabited our planet. From this flows more research, with a more inclusive history of race, gender and popular culture. Some historians emphasize that history belongs to everyone and believe that in the past there has been too much silence on the lives and culture of ordinary people. In particular, they feel that women, minority groups, gay and lesbian people, and people with disabilities have been slighted and marginalized in both U.S. history and world history courses at the middle and high school levels. They argue that the breathtaking diversity of human perspectives, values, and belief systems has been ignored.

In other words, history is more than just politics, wars, and rulers. These historians want to re-vision history. They want to widen the array of **voices and viewpoints.** Along with these concerns of inclusion is an ongoing debate about the history of Western civilizations versus that of non-Western civilizations. Some historians cite the limited attention given to non-Western civilizations, perspectives, and voices. They and other critics advocate more emphasis on the global human experience through time (Grant, 1999).

Many of these historians want more attention to global forces and large historical themes such as climatic change, disease, the spread of religions, and the expansion of the market economy and technology. Others want to emphasize the importance of cross-cultural contact in world history and to examine U.S. history from a global perspective. However, not everyone approves of all or some of these newer emphases. Some believe that the newer interpretations focus too much on the dark side of the U.S. past, with a too-critical approach to Western civilization.

In summary, U.S. history textbooks reflect the trends of the time and do change. In the 1950s and 1960s, during the cold war, textbooks emphasized unity (consensus) at the expense of division and dissent. With the upheavals of the 1960s and 1970s, multicultural historians replaced the consensus historians. This period ushered in many detailed local and ethnic histories, often reported from the perspective of the underdog. By the 1990s, more attention was being given to the founding fathers such as Washington, Jefferson, Hamilton, and the Adams family. After September 11, 2001, there was more emphasis by historians on how the global community has always influenced U.S. history, such as during the American Revolution when France and other European nations lined up against England.

Another issue is the relevance of history to the present. Too often students do not see how the past influences the present or understand the conditions that underlie issues and problems today. Teachers often have to make explicit the connections of history to the students' lives by linking the past with the present on topics such as immigration and technology.

■ CONTROVERSIES OVER WHAT HISTORY SHOULD BE TAUGHT

National Center for History in the Schools

These different controversial perspectives on history came to a climax when the National Center for History in the Schools (1994a, 1994b, 1994c) released their national standards in three books on what history should be taught for K–4, U.S. history (5–12), and world history (5–12). Immediately, conservatives and other groups condemned these history standards. Lynne Cheney (1994), former head of the National Endowment for the Humanities, and whose husband became vice president (2000–2008), argued in a *Wall Street Journal* editorial that the U.S. history standards presented too "gloomy" a picture of the United States, one that is too critical of all things white and too uncritical of all things brown, black, and other.

As evidence, Cheney stated in her critique that Senator Joseph McCarthy or McCarthyism was mentioned nineteen times, the Ku Klux Klan seventeen times, the

Seneca Fall women's rights convention nine times, and Harriet Tubman six times. However, male heroes such as Paul Revere, Daniel Webster, Robert E. Lee, Alexander Graham Bell, Thomas Edison, Albert Einstein, Jonas Salk, and the Wright brothers were not mentioned at all. She and other critics felt that not enough attention was being given to the positive aspects of U.S. history in its long struggle for liberty, justice, and equality, and that too much emphasis was placed on the nation's failures.

The media and commentators jumped into this controversy. Headlines in the leading newspapers and magazines had such titles as "The Hijacking of American History," "Instead of Western Civ, It's Multiciv," and "History without Heroes?" In general, critics condemned the standards for left-wing "political correctness" and extravagant multiculturalism, especially in the U.S. history document. They criticized almost all the examples of content that students should achieve for each standard—the bulk of the documents. Showing the widespread lack of support for these history standards, the U.S. Senate passed a resolution condemning the standards by a vote of 99 to 1. Furthermore, neither President Clinton nor any cabinet member spoke out in defense of the standards, although the history project had received federal funding (Chapin, 1995).

Reacting to this intense criticism, the National Center for History in the Schools (1996) dropped examples of content to be achieved by students. Instead, the center condensed the three separate volumes into one that focused only on the standards, because it had been the examples of student achievements that had brought about most of the criticism. Lost in the defense of the standards was the appraisal that the national history standards did not reflect *enough* of the contributions of diverse groups to our nation's development. Muted also were three criticisms from teachers: (1) The standards were too demanding; (2) the performance standards emphasized more what students should "know" at the expense of what they should "do"; and (3) the standards might lead to memorization of facts.

The hot debate over the history standards highlighted an important point: The teaching of these subjects is inherently controversial. What should be taught? In general, liberals advocated including more multiculturalism, presenting the experiences of all Americans and expanding the traditional Eurocentric perspective. In contrast, conservatives saw "extreme" multiculturalism as a fragmentation of U.S. society and a rejection of the core values and cultural heritage of Western culture. Conservatives perceived an erosion of national heroes and heroines, with each racial or ethnic group supporting its own heroes and heroines.

Your own political values influence how you think about this issue. An important point to remember is that history rests in the eye of the beholder. Every work of history has to omit far more than it includes, and this is certainly true of history textbooks for students. Historians always have to decide what was significant, and this always leads to discussions on what is incomplete and whether there is lopsidedness and lack of balance. In addition, historians' backgrounds affect their attitudes toward their work, and social, religious, racial, ethnic, and gender differences contribute to varying points of view. Ideology is one of the greatest sources of disagreement among historians. Therefore, whether certain individuals, groups, events, movements, religions, and turning points are getting enough attention in standards, textbooks, and programs is frequently debated. The story is always incomplete, partly due to the complexity of history. Almost no group is completely satisfied with what is emphasized or included in standards, textbooks, and programs.

The issue is further complicated by the fact that different classroom teachers and students within the same class also have formed their own perceptions from studying U.S. or world history. Previous knowledge, experiences, and their background—gender, racial or ethnic group, and the political orientation and social class of their family—also influence their perspectives on history and what counts as "knowing" history and its significance.

ON YOUR OWN	**CHECKING TEXTBOOKS**
6.1	*Most social studies experts (Banks, 2001) cite the need to balance diversity and unity. Find some recent history textbooks and evaluate how much attention they give to women and minority groups. Do you think the textbooks are encouraging and respecting diversity? Are texts sufficiently emphasizing our nation's core values and ideals? Do they maintain the balance of the complex heritage of e pluribus unum?*

State History Standards

The partisan firestorm that hit the proposed National History Standards in 1994 and 1995 ended any possibility of a national consensus on the history curriculum in K–12 schools. This meant it was up to the states to try to make sense of history standards, and they produced a wide range of history standards. More than ten states essentially gave up on the attempt to formulate history standards and created very broad history standards almost without any history content. Other states, such as Virginia, produced detailed history content standards with specific people and events to be taught. In a report sponsored by the Thomas B. Fordham Foundation, Saxe (1998) did a critical appraisal of history standards in thirty-seven states and the District of Columbia and concluded that most states do not have "good" history standards based on five criteria—clarity, organization, historical soundness, historical content, and absence of manipulation. Virginia, California, Texas, and Massachusetts were judged to have the best history standards at that time. However, since then some states have revised their history and social studies standards.

Rationale for Teaching History

Despite all the controversy, no state has eliminated history from the social studies curriculum. There was—and is—little debate on the need for students to know history. Here is the rationale for teaching history in the schools:

1. **Historical Understandings.** All students need to know about the history of their nation and of the world. These understandings of human beings and their activity

come from the following areas: social, political, scientific and technological, and cultural—which includes religions, arts, and philosophies (National Center for History in the Schools, 1996). Therefore, history draws on the visual arts, literature, and music as well as the more traditional sources.

Related to historical understandings, some historians state that all students need a **sense of history,** of both the United States and the world. A sense of history means more than learning facts and dates. A sense of history allows students to view time from a larger perspective, tackling such great questions as why political and social conflict erupts and how it is resolved. A sense of history should help citizens when they face policy decisions.

2. **Historical Thinking Skills.** These skills include chronological thinking, historical analysis and interpretation, and historical research capabilities. These skills allow students to use the methods of historians to identify and analyze current problems facing us today.

Historical thinking skills are far more demanding to teach than historical understandings. The difficulties are similar to those encountered in inquiry or problem solving (Chapter 4), but the payoffs in such teaching can be enormous. Not everyone has the empathy to look at another perspective or the motivation to detect bias, to weigh evidence, or to evaluate arguments. Raising questions about what we assume to be obvious can be upsetting to some students. However, the skills for evaluating any type of information are gaining in importance as more people acquire information from the Internet, where the challenge is to filter and to evaluate data.

On a broad general level, there is almost no disagreement that students need to know the history of how our nation and the world were formed so that they can fulfill their citizenship rights and responsibilities. Students need to know their historical roots so that they can develop a personal identity and see themselves as members of families, communities, nations, and the global community. They need to visualize what life for different groups was like at different periods of time. It is the details and interpretations of coverage that cause the controversy, because there is an infinite amount of historical data and different perspectives.

Importance of Better-Quality History Instruction

In the following suggestions for teaching history, one must never forget that *students must be engaged in learning*. Unfortunately, for many students motivation decreases as they get older. Teachers face a real challenge in large classes, standards, and inadequate materials and resources. Teachers must build confidence in students that they can improve their understanding of and skills in history. As much as possible, teachers also need to connect the past to the present, helping students see the relationships.

Remember that history is for girls too. Traditional history texts have been male dominated both in people and types of history, political and military. More recent textbooks do include more about the contributions of women. The National Women's History Project (www.nwhp.org) offers numerous ideas for lessons and activities. A supportive and friendly classroom environment is also important for all students, and activities should include topics of interest for all students, including girls.

SMALL GROUP WORK	AN EMPHASIS ON HOPE AND TOLERANCE?
6.1	*Should a teacher convey optimism about the course of history? What emphasis should be given to the dark side of history?*

■ METHODS AND RESOURCES FOR HISTORICAL UNDERSTANDINGS

The following methods and resources should not be restricted to teaching history. Instead, consider all the methods and resources as possibilities as you teach geography, economics, and history.

Traditional Methods: The Textbook and Its Supplementary Materials

The principal resource for all history classes is the textbook. Teachers have to decide how they are going to use the textbook that has already been purchased for the class. The typical social studies textbook has moved away from two dull columns of text. There are literary inserts, ties with geography, interdisciplinary connections, vocabulary and terms at the beginning of chapters, timelines, skill activities, and a wide variety of colorful photos, maps, and graphs.

The biggest change in textbooks in recent years is the attention given to reading and, to a lesser extent, writing. Vocabulary and "Focus on Reading" questions are becoming more extensive. Reading during class is recommended so that the teacher can engage the students, monitor understanding, explicitly teach vocabulary, and integrate reading and writing. Writing is seen as a vehicle for clarifying historical understanding.

Are you going to use most of the chapter? Supplement it with other sources of information? An additional factor is that each publisher has a wide array of supplementary materials to correlate with the text. The most likely to be in a teacher's hands is the teacher's edition. The second most likely resource for teachers is assessment activities: section quizzes and chapter and unit tests. Sometimes there are two forms of the test; this is helpful for giving the alternative version to the students who were absent for the original test.

Then there is the wide assortment of workbooks for reinforcement of content and skills, outline maps, software and CD-ROMS, DVDs, videos, transparencies, simulations, Internet activities with "safe" web sites, posters, and student books imaged on DVDs with audio narration and other features. In addition, materials can include ready-made PowerPoint visuals, and more increasingly include English language learner resources, especially in Spanish. Publishers claim that if teachers have the supplementary resources available, they are more likely to use them and teach with greater success. The cost of these supplemental activities is probably the greatest barrier to their implementation because otherwise most teachers welcome as much help as possible. Be sure to ask if some of these resources are available from other teachers, or are available in the school or in the district or county resource center.

History textbooks now have colorful graphics, but critics call them dull and boring. A common complaint is that history textbooks are bland and devoid of controversy so that they can avoid offending special interest groups or being labeled as racist, sexist, or ageist. The Thomas B. Fordham Foundation (www.edexcellence .net/institute/publication) published *A Consumer's Guide to High School History Textbooks* by Diane Ravitch, for which a panel of experts in U.S. history evaluated six widely used high school U.S. history texts and six world history texts. The reviewers complained that the texts tried to cover far too much material in the space available. This was especially true of the world history textbooks, in which everything is touched on but nothing is explained.

An important decision is whether to assign the text readings before you introduce a topic. In many classes, the good readers are the only ones to read the text, and they dominate class discussion (or any other activity) because they are the only ones who have some knowledge of the topic. On the other hand, assigning the text after a lecture or discussion activity on the content may not motivate the students. If the text is assigned after the lecture or activity, it is best to be specific, asking students to use the text to find a different perspective or specific details that were not covered during the class.

Other teachers, despairing that most students do not or cannot read the text outside of class, use the last part of the class period for students to read the text, usually with some follow-up questions to answer. Although this uses up valuable teaching time, more students may become familiar with the content. For some, it may be their only reading of the text. In summary, each teacher has to decide what role the textbook will play in the teaching of the social studies and how to explicitly teach vocabulary.

Making History Alive

Through the years and more recently with the explosion of Internet use, a wide variety of methods and strategies have been recommended to increase students' knowledge and understanding of history. The following categories will be examined: Using Exciting Information, The Promise of the Internet, Analysis of Photos or Artwork, Media, The Arts and Music, Artifacts and Virtual Museums, Posters, Simulations, History as Narrative, Organizing Content around Key Ideas and Themes, and Teaching Social Issues in History.

In the following discussion about teaching history, an artificial distinction is made between (1) teaching historical understanding and knowledge and (2) teaching historical thinking skills and the methods of a historian. In fact, as students use the methods of a historian, they are also learning history content, although usually fewer topics are covered in detail. In practice, many good lessons include both knowledge and skills.

Using Exciting Information

For years, teachers have been trying to make history exciting for students so they do not hear the chorus of students' voices saying "history is boring." Too frequently, students think history is deadly because the class is the same from day to day and does not capture their interest. In many cases—and this is especially true of U.S. history in high school—nothing is new for students because the same pattern of instruction—listening and reading—and the same content is repeated from the eighth grade. Although content and skills *do* need to be revisited, if the repeated instruction is at a low level with little or no development in terms of complexity, students gain little. Furthermore, teachers often do not build on what students already know from their families and the media. Paradoxically, it appears that more adults today are interested in history—as evidenced by the popularity of reading histories and biographies and viewing historical TV programs, films, documentaries, and docudramas. Local historical societies are also thriving, and genealogy for all age groups is booming.

Experienced teachers enliven history by collecting interesting and surprising information about presidents, such as John Quincy Adams swimming in the nude in the Potomac River with a female newspaper reporter sitting on his clothes wanting her questions to be answered. Or they bring in worthwhile information about the influenza epidemic that broke out in the last months of World War I and probably killed more people than the military campaigns but is not usually covered in textbooks (Richburg, 1999). Teachers often pose questions to challenge students and stimulate their curiosity by showing discrepant data about African Americans or Native Americans. Often teachers "ham up" their presentations so students will not think history is boring.

Books of anecdotes from U.S. history that are suitable for independent reading or teacher use are available. These books include colorful historical stories, curious quotations, and other odd facts designed to intrigue students. An example is *Unsolved Mysteries of American History* by Paul Aron, in which the author probes thirty classic dilemmas such as the following: What happened to the Lost Colony of Roanoke? What destroyed the *Maine*? Who kidnapped the Lindbergh baby? Were the Rosenbergs guilty? Who killed JFK? With David Gerwin and Jack Zevin's *Teaching U.S. History as Mystery,* students will have fun playing the role of detectives looking at cases such as the relationship between Thomas Jefferson and Sally Hemings and at the role of women in the Old West.

The Promise of the Internet

Compared to previous ways teachers had of finding material to make history interesting, the greatest change is now the wider use of the **Internet** to find primary sources, lesson plans, and resources such as historical archives and art and historical museums. Stimulating material for the teaching of history can be found and continues to grow on the Internet. One of the most convenient sources is the web site maintained by the California Department of Education on resources and thousands of history and social science lessons organized by grade level: http://score.rims.k12.ca.us. The resources and activities are organized for the California history/social studies standards, which are more or less typical for the nation. The resources cross-link with other sites and include brief comments on the value and difficulty for students. This web site is a boon to teachers and is very user-friendly. Many other states also have excellent web sites with lessons and resources.

A treasure trove of free U.S. history primary sources is "Our Documents," 100 milestone documents from the National Archives (www.ourdocuments.gov). It also contains a Teacher Sourcebook with an annotated timeline, key themes, guidelines to primary sources, and lesson plans. These documents range from the familiar Bill of Rights, Emancipation Proclamation, and the like to the more unfamiliar such as the Chinese Exclusion Act and the Boulder Canyon Project Act.

The superb Library of Congress web site (www.loc.gov) has links to the *American Memory Historical Collections* (http://memory.loc.gov) and *America's Story* from America's Library (www.americaslibrary.gov). These offer a huge online museum of historical collections featuring films, manuscripts, prints, photographs, maps, and sound recordings that tell the American story. This is an outstanding resource, with materials ranging from "Baseball Cards, 1877–1914" to "First-Person Narratives of the American South 1860–1920." The Library of Congress also has a Getting Started section (memory.loc.gov/learn/start/index.html) for orientation to the Learning Page (http://learning.loc.gov/learn).

Although at first glance teachers may think that many primary unedited source documents have too high a reading level for their students, not all collections are printed. *The Northern Great Plains 1880–1920* contains 900 photographs of rural and small-town life at the turn of the century. Photographs of child labor, selected Civil War images, and the Great Depression, just to name a few, can make more of an impact than the written primary source documents and can be used in any classroom.

Analysis of Photos or Artwork

Let us look at how to analyze a photo or artwork from the Library of Congress Memory Collection. Teachers often make copies of the photo, preparing a set for each student pair or group along with questions to stimulate their thinking. Here are some questions and typical answers relating to the photo, on page 164, of the two boys eating ice-cream cones.

1. **I see . . .**
   Two boys eating ice cream cones
   The boys are seated on a feed sack or gunny sack.
   The pickup truck is scratched and dented.
   The cars in the background are "old."

2. **The photo/picture suggests to me that . . .**
   The boys are healthy.
   It is summertime.
   The boys live on a farm.
   The photo was taken **many** years ago (1941).

Farm boys eating ice-cream cones. Washington, Indiana, July 1941.

3. I wonder if . . .

The family is poor.

The ice-cream cones are a rare treat for the boys.

The boys were surprised that someone was taking their picture.

The boys come into town infrequently.

After the pairs or small groups finish considering the photos, they meet as a whole class to discuss their findings.

Again using photo analysis, let us look at two photos taken from the Hine Collection (page 165) and possible student responses to a worksheet.

1. I see . . .

A girl standing in a textile factory (photo A)

Girls working with machinery at a textile factory (photo B)

2. **The photo suggests to me . . .**

The girl is about 10 years old (photo A)

The environment is very dusty.

Standing up at machinery for a long time is tiring.

Photos were taken a long time ago (dress and hairstyles).

3. I wonder if . . .

The workers have many accidents with the machinery.

Working in a factory is not good for the girls' health and education.

(A)   (B)

(A) "Mills seem full of youngsters." Newberry, South Carolina, 1908. (B) "Girls at weaving machines." Lincoln Cotton Mills, Evansville, Indiana, 1908.

These photos also raise the question of bias. A child labor reformer, Hine, took these photos. How might the owners have taken photos of their factories? Would they include children? Emphasize more the products produced?

Also valuable are presidential libraries (www.nara.gov/nara/president/address .html) and the regional records centers of the National Archives and Records Administration (www.nara.gov/regional/nrmenu.html). Because of the enormous amount of materials, many teachers prefer to go to web sites that have already organized the materials for teacher use. Commercial sites also hold promise, such as the popular History Channel (www.historychannel.com) and some publishers who have maps that can be downloaded free. In using primary documents, focus on the processes used by historians and different perspectives, not just on the use of primary sources for content.

Media

What is the most interesting activity for students in social studies classrooms? Most students say what they like best is to watch videos. There is an enormous range of video topics, from turning points in history to biographies of both U.S. and world history figures. Increasingly, more teachers will be using CD-ROMs and DVDs, which can contain even more images and narratives, primary source documents, activities, and assessment items. Cost is probably the major deterrent to even wider use.

The Arts and Music

Some teachers bring into the classroom the visual arts and music of the time period and culture to increase both interest and understanding. Hearing music and seeing artworks give students clues as to what the people at that time thought was important and enjoyable. It also shows the wide diversity of the various art and music forms throughout the world and in different time periods. Sometimes the teacher can work cooperatively with art and music teachers in the building, who may have resources readily on hand. But increasingly, teachers will turn to the Internet and CD-ROMs for thousands of images and audio clips of folk songs and music of different time periods. In a few classes, students in the middle school have used the Constitutional Convention or the Lewis and Clark expedition to dramatize historical events. Students have learned their lines and even set their lines to music.

Artifacts and Virtual Field Trips

Some teachers collect and bring in **artifacts** of historical interest. They may comb the countryside and garage sales to find old tools or household items such as nonelectrical irons, straight razors for shaving, or vintage clothing. They may bring in old school yearbooks showing the different hairstyles and clothing of students many years ago. In addition, teachers bring travel souvenirs, such as saris from India or boomerangs from Australia, into the classroom to add to the realism of the ideas on the printed page. War relics, too, are sometimes available.

More students have the opportunity to see artifacts now through **virtual field trips** or a **virtual tour.** Instead of the teacher having to deal with the difficulties of arranging a field trip or overseas travel, students can visit historic sites and museums using web sites. From their computers, students can tour the Egyptian pyramids or view African art. The National Park Service has a web site, Teaching with Historic Places (www.cr.nps.gov/nr/twhp), with lesson plans by location, theme, and time period. The lessons examine African American history, women's history, and U.S. presidents.

Some web sites are more specific, such as Plimoth on the Web (www.plimoth.org/index.html), where you can access biographies and information about this settlement. The J. Paul Getty Museum (www.getty.edu/museum) in Los Angeles has lesson plans relating to its outstanding art collection. The National Museum of American History (http://americanhistory.si.edu/) collects items for the whole country, with more than 18 million objects. The online version allows viewers to look at topics such as The First Ladies, or From Wood to Plastic. Teachers have to do some lesson planning for effective use of the web sites, but many historic sites offer real possibilities for students both to visualize and to question the data.

Simulations

Typically, the simulations used for history enable students to imagine how it was to be North American Indians, pioneers, farmers, workers, labor leaders, immigrants, and the like during certain time periods. Other simulations focus on great American confrontations, such as "New Deal on Trial: 1939." In this mock trail of the New Deal policies of President Franklin D. Roosevelt, students take on the roles of famous and average Americans who debate the worth of FDR's diverse federal programs. Another simulation is of a congressional committee during 1943 at the site of a Japanese American relocation camp in Poston, Arizona, that is investigating charges of false imprisonment, prejudice, and war hysteria. Although the greatest number of simulations are in U.S. history, there are also simulations for world history on topics such as the warlords of Japan, Vikings, and Islam.

History as Narrative

History has a storytelling structure. A story well told helps improve student historical understanding, a characteristic that is often not found in textbooks. Advocates of using adolescent literature (Levstik 1989; Levstik & Barton, 2000) point out that good stories usually have a much higher level of interest and appeal for students than textbooks. However, more textbooks now have literature inserts. As you saw in a classroom episode in Chapter 2, a middle school student teacher decided to use four novels to teach the American Revolution because a good novel is more personalized, focuses on young people making decisions, and is less abstract than a textbook. From the reading of these novels, students may gain a better understanding of loyalists, not just as enemies but as people with a different viewpoint about the American Revolution. A novel also gives more detail about the everyday life of people of the time. Certain periods, such as the Civil War or World War II—especially the Holocaust—offer many choices of adolescent novels. Most teachers are familiar with the powerful narrative *Diary of Anne Frank*.

As mentioned in Chapter 2, some experts fear that using the narrative or literary approach to social studies may focus on trivial aspects of the main topic or devote excessive time to literature at the expense of history content and important social studies goals. Others warn that students might accept the story as true and not ask questions about the accuracy of what they are reading. However, including alternative points of view to the narrative or novel can be a wonderful correction, moving students toward a higher level of thinking about history. Comparing two different perspectives pushes students to realize that history is an interpretation, which is an understanding they may not get if they read the novel alone or if they simply learn interesting historical information. So that novels will not take up too much time, some teachers have students read only excerpts from well-known literature. Books are available that arrange excerpts of literature in chronological order, with background information for each excerpt.

Organizing Content around Key Ideas and Themes

Numerous experts (Rossi, 2000) advocate that a more explicit framework is needed to focus on the key ideas to be developed in a history unit or course. Otherwise, history may be a dry-as-dust succession of endless facts, from the terms of the Mayflower Compact to the meaning of the alphabetical agencies in the 1930s. Thus, instead of using the textbook as the structure of a course, the teacher builds her or his own structure—key ideas, questions, or a theme—for a unit or a topic. This could be organized around conflict, change, success or failure, the role of the individual in a culture, cultural values, religious beliefs, the American dream, and the like. Or for U.S. history, the ideas could be sectionalism, the quest for social justice, the American sense of mission, and so on. This nontextbook structure is also advocated by the critics of textbooks who believe that textbooks cover too much information without sufficient depth, or that information about women and minority groups is inadequate.

In this approach, the teacher looks at a topic or theme and tries to find the most important elements to use as an organizing structure. This requires that the teacher have a good background in the topic. For example, "How did the hierarchical structures give people of the Middle Ages their identity?" can prompt and motivate students to activate what they know about the social class organization in many other societies they have studied, such as India and China. Using the issues approach (see next section), this focus question may invite students to think about the following issues: Will there always be inequality and social classes? How should wealth and income be distributed in the United States? Should talented people (rock stars, sports figures, computer creators) be allowed to reap sizable material rewards for their performances?

Or a theme for a unit could be "Learning from Mistakes in History." Here the teacher could use a variety of examples of different time periods and cultures. It would necessitate having a wide variety of materials for each example, certainly not the typical textbook approach. However, there could be increased student interest and payoff, with big dividends in student learning. The teacher, in turn, might feel very proud of the unit.

The advantage of organizing content around key ideas and key questions is that without a clear structure, the facts typically learned in history do not hang together and are quickly forgotten. This is partly because the theme of the textbook unit is often not explicit or is lost in the minds of the students (and even the teacher) after a few days into the unit. Ideally, the main question(s) should center on universal themes and dilemmas, call into play students' own experiences, and trigger their thinking. The question should be open-ended with multiple answers, and it should relate to the present. These important questions might include the following powerful and useful social studies concepts: authority, revolution, capitalism and labor, the frontier, immigration, the Industrial Revolution, reform, and the city. Notice that these are all key social studies concepts.

This approach moves students into a more active role in thinking, an area in which many students lack both the confidence and the skills to perform successfully. Students may not want to think more, preferring instead to be passive receivers of information, only memorizing the material. A certain type of classroom climate is necessary for encouraging students to think; otherwise, they may balk at examining major historical questions and ideas. Remember that these were the same concerns for students doing inquiry and problem solving and therefore are not unique to an approach that promotes thinking in history.

Teaching history does not mean a choice between a narrow approach or broad coverage. The two approaches can be united. For example, in a world history class the key idea could be "The People on the Globe," taught broadly with students then examining in depth the various regions of the world. Combining broad coverage with in-depth study can promote learning by allowing students to compare societies in different regions or areas. Or, students could explore the general reasons for the collapse of civilizations by looking at specific examples.

Teaching Social Issues in History

The **issues approach** has a diversity of definitions. Sometimes it is called the *social issues approach* or the *issues-centered curriculum*. From these names, you can see that the issues approach examines persistent, controversial questions that confront citizens. Its purpose is for students to develop skills (improve thinking, research, discussion, and the like) and to make important decisions about public issues that are relevant today. Thus, its ultimate goal is to emphasize the skills and dispositions necessary for participating in a democratic society.

To achieve these important goals of the issues approach, the teacher must raise provocative, controversial, persisting, and relevant questions and teach students to offer defensible, intellectual, well-grounded answers to these questions (Evans, Newmann, & Saxe, 1994). To answer these questions and to reach a decision, students should examine an assortment of evidence, competing values, and alternative outcomes. This approach has been in use for many years, from Dewey (1933), Hunt and Metcalf (1955), Oliver and Shaver (1966), Newmann and Oliver (1970), to Engle and Ochoa (1988), among others, but currently it is not widely used in classrooms and schools.

The social issues approach is not unique to the teaching of history but can be (and is) used in teaching geography, global studies, and the social sciences. Far more than many of the other history approaches, the issues approach aims to *directly and strongly link the past with the present*. This way, history courses are not just about the distant past but are related to the lives of the students. Compared to the previous approach of organizing content around important ideas and questions, the issues approach is far more political. But it is one that can be used by both liberal and conservative teachers because it does not aim to provide the right answers but puts its emphasis on skills and developing a commitment to democratic participation in our society. It is an approach that tries to tie the subject matter, whether that be history or any of the other social sciences, to improving citizenship education. An issue is raised, such as race relationships or poverty. But a "topic" does not equal an "issue," because an issue includes many points of view.

What are the other characteristics of the issues approach? Promoting knowledge for its own sake is *not* a goal. However, it does call for challenging content from various disciplines, using a variety of sources, and providing practice in thinking. These are shown in oral and written work as students search and explore for information and clarify their responses. In effect, this approach leads to a more in-depth understanding of content, often called "postholing," instead of a superficial coverage. In addition, the issues approach makes extensive use of interaction strategies as the teacher and students discuss and try out ideas.

Selection of the Problem

The importance of selecting the issue is paramount. The issue can come from the teacher or the students as a result of learning activities set up by the teacher. For example, an issue could be the study of government authority and protest against it. When and how should citizens challenge constituted authority? Examples covered could be the American Revolution, the Whiskey Rebellion, the Alien and Sedition Acts, the Civil War, the Pullman Strike, the civil rights movement, or any other protest movement that has occurred in the history of the United States. The issues approach in the teaching of history may move history away from a strict chronological order by starting from a present-day issue and using a flashback approach, hitting only certain time periods of U.S. history.

Or the question could be, How should we evaluate the U.S. participation in World War II, especially the dropping of the atomic bomb on Japan in 1945? As the *Enola Gay* controversy connected with the exhibit at the Smithsonian Institution indicated, there was (and is) a heated debate among both historians and the public about why American leaders approved the dropping of the bomb as well as whether we should view the Japanese as victims. Other more global issues investigated by students might be population growth, human rights, gender issues, conflicts among nations, globalism, terrorism, and science and technology. Issues could also come from the local community, such as environmental problems or decisions on land usage.

Implementation

After selecting the issue, frequently the teacher puts students in small teams to first conduct research on the question and then write out their reasoned responses, often orally presenting them to the rest of the class. Typically, each small group will take just one piece of an issue such as the Whiskey Rebellion and give their response as to whether government authority in the particular case was legitimate. Other students may challenge the facts, definitions, values, or interpretations given by different groups. Students may formulate a position or course of action on the issue.

Why are so few teachers using this approach? The issues approach puts both students and teachers in the inquiry mode, which is more demanding on both students and the teacher. However, the effort put forth by both the teacher and the students is well worthwhile. In addition, a new teacher may hesitate to bring controversial issues into the classroom and fear that it reduces time that should be spent on content. For this reason, some teachers believe that this approach only works with average and above-average older adolescents. Furthermore, student groups may research their projects unevenly, causing gaps and frustrations. Others feel that this approach distracts from students developing a sense of historical perspective such as understanding chronology and change. But its strengths are teaching skills for the analysis of political issues and (hopefully) promoting citizenship. For those who need more convincing of the merits of the issues approach and its implementation, the NCSS *Handbook on Teaching Social Issues* (Evans & Saxe, 1996) is most helpful, with about 400 pages of suggestions. Perhaps most teachers would want to start using the issues approach with only one unit.

In summary, having an exciting storehouse of information, artifacts, the arts, music, simulations, and posters that goes beyond the textbook is valuable when you are teaching history. Computer resources also offer much promise—both as data sources and for organizing materials by key questions and teaching to social issues. Teachers always have to be on the alert for new information, media, and computer resources. To do this, the teacher needs a strong background in history and a commitment to continuing to learn about content in history through resources such as *The History Teacher, Magazine of History, Social Education,* and *The Social Studies.* Teachers need access to social studies catalogs, such as *Social Studies School Service* (http://socialstudies .com), and to conferences where they can learn about the more exciting and worthwhile materials.

However, right now in some states, teachers do not use some of these methods described to teach an understanding of history, especially those approaches involving treating history in depth, because they feel obliged to cover all the details in the history standards, regardless of student apathy. In addition, many social studies teachers' belief systems and experiences reinforce their idea that their main job is to transmit information and not to stress that history is an interpretation.

ON YOUR OWN	MAKING A WISH LIST
6.2	*Collect catalogs from* Social Studies School Service *and other publishers. Glance over the various offerings. What would be the most helpful to you? Most teachers spend their own funds for some of their materials because school budgets are not adequate for materials needed. What would you select for the department and what would you buy for yourself?*

■ METHODS AND RESOURCES FOR HISTORICAL THINKING SKILLS

To foster the understanding that history is an interpretation, teachers now encourage students to use historical inquiry or historical methods to evaluate documents of the past and to "do" history by doing historical research and publishing their results online (www.ncsu.edu/midlink). Doing history becomes an active activity in which students examine multiple perspectives and critically examine historical sources. It may encourage students to develop historical empathy (Foster & Yeager, 1998).

Primary Sources

Use of primary sources or **document-based instruction** (Gagnon & Bradley Commission, 1989; National Center for History in the Schools, 1996; Seixas, 1993) is now strongly advocated. Right now the distinction between a **"primary"** and a **"secondary"** source is becoming a little blurred, as current styles of communication complicate the issue—as when a president or an official signs letters but has not written the letters. A documentary film is also hard to classify. Whether a source is considered primary or secondary also depends on how it is used as evidence. If there is a study on how newspapers treated 9/11, newspapers, usually a secondary source, become a primary source. The terms—*primary sources, source documents,* and *document-based instruction*—are often used interchangeably, although the source and document-based instructions could include both primary and secondary source materials.

The recommendations for using source documents are in spirit with the increased emphasis on seeing how actual participants viewed a situation—whether that involves workers during a strike or one of the first doctors reporting that he had administered ether to perform an operation. Primary sources can capture the spirit of both the great and more average people and therefore may have an inherent human interest. Primary source documents are particularly helpful for showing multiple perspectives, especially the views of unpopular people or ideas and proposals that were unsuccessful. Primary source documents can also stimulate thoughtful analysis and an appreciation of the problems and preconceptions of others. They can encourage a sense of the conditions of people who lived long ago as well as developing historical skills.

Typically, we think of primary source documents as the written official documents. Primary source documents include a wide range of written materials: editorials, propaganda leaflets, quotations, newspapers, advertisements, public debates, personal letters, diaries, eyewitness accounts, autobiographies, congressional testimony, speeches, court decisions, and the like. Source documents can be about an individual, events, other people, and groups or organizations. Having a wide variety of these sources on a CD-ROM or in a book or booklets organized by topics certainly is a time-saver for teachers. Jackdaws, a commercial provider (www.jackdaw.com) of primary sources, has an extensive collection of U.S. history and world history kits, ranging from the Incas to the bombing of Pearl Harbor. Other primary sources are artifacts such as clothing, tools, and food. Oral primary sources include music, stories, and folklore. Visual sources include paintings, photographs, videos, and movies. Overlooked as a primary source are historical places, sites of significant events, and local architecture.

Methods

In using primary sources, realize that they are not an end in themselves, but one means of promoting historical understanding and historical thinking skills. Sometimes it is better simply to tell students that the United States purchased Alaska than to have students read the original documents. *Remember that the document should have a connection to students' prior knowledge and interests.* Primary sources should be carefully selected.

Good teacher questions (see Chapter 3) are essential in using primary sources. Here are some of the questions that might be used. Although the word *document* is used, remember that the questions could also refer to an artifact, a cartoon, a poster, a film, or any other type of primary source.

- What type of document is this?
- What is the date of the document?
- Who created the document? What audience or person was the document written for?
- What was the author's perspective?
- What does the document say about American life in this era?

What methods can be used to integrate primary sources into the classroom? *Social Education,* the journal of the National Council for the Social Studies, devoted an entire issue (November/December, 2003) to teaching U.S. history with primary sources. Here were some of the ideas presented:

- Focus activity to start day's topic; document on overhead projector or given to students
- Visualization exercise to learn about another time or culture
- Writing activity by having students respond to the document
- Small group activity prompted by asking them "what if" the document had never existed
- Assessment through a document-based essay question

It is helpful to number the lines of a text so that reference can be easily made to a certain part of the text. Having the source double spaced also helps readers. Students should look at more than one primary source on an event or particular period so they can see the many possible interpretations that can be made of a historical event or era. One method is for students to write a letter based on source documents showing support for or opposition to certain events or policies, because most primary sources reflect their author's particular point of view. Students can also create and perform historical scenarios based on source documents. These could be Northern young men in 1863 discussing the draft, the Sioux at Wounded Knee, or two people standing in a food line during the Great Depression.

Only in a few cases are students using primary sources to research and then to write their conclusions. These students may be participating in **Annual History Day,** with competitions at the county, state, and national levels. The categories for History Day include traditional written papers as well as dramatic performances, posters, documentaries, exhibits, and historic web sites.

Problems

What are the problems with using source documents? See Sample Classroom Episode on Primary Sources: The Latest Fad. Number one is that for written documents the reading level is far beyond the level of many members in the class. This is especially a problem with older source documents. The writing style may be one the teacher considers quaint but that students, especially poorer readers and ELLs, consider almost a foreign language. For this reason, many teachers use only a few sentences or a paragraph from the source document, or they rewrite the document, use small amounts, or use a graphic organizer. It is crucial that the document be put into historical context so that the reader is better prepared to tackle the main arguments or to understand the reactions of the writer.

SAMPLE CLASSROOM EPISODE

PRIMARY SOURCES: THE LATEST FAD?

Let us zoom in on a department meeting at Roseville High School.

Ms. Annabelle: Although I think all of our students should be familiar with key documents such as the Declaration of Independence and Martin Luther King's "I Have a Dream" speech, I think all the present emphasis on primary sources is just the latest fad.

Ms. Mia: But my U.S. history class really got excited by looking at some pages of an early (1890s) Sears catalog. It conveyed to them what clothing women were wearing and women's roles at the time better than anything the textbook or I could have said.

Mr. Liam: That worked because there was not too much reading. Just try having a class read a written source document. Only good readers can really understand diaries, letters, and the like, and that lets out half of my class. Source documents can tell something about how people lived in the past, but it is not worth the time or effort to include them except in Advanced Placement classes.

Mr. Jack: I agree that Advanced Placement classes need to become familiar with document-based sources to respond to the essay questions. But even there, students must be familiar with enough background to adequately answer the essay questions. You just can't teach isolated primary source documents.

Ms. Ava: True, piecemeal analysis is not always helpful.

Ms. Isabella: I think it is an inflated idea that using primary source documents gives students a sense of historical inquiry. A real historian selects his or her own sources. We are the ones selecting the documents, not the students.

Mr. Bob: I disagree. Source documents can help students recognize bias.

Mr. Jack: Let me play my cynical role again. Do you really think we can change or influence students' perspectives on history? I am constantly aware that gender, race, and socioeconomic status influence how my students interpret what content I present to them, whether through primary source documents or textbooks. Students already come to us with perspectives on slavery, the civil rights movement, Vietnam, Native Americans, and so on.

Bell rings: No consensus.

Which views expressed do you agree with? Why?

In using source documents, the teacher needs to ask more general questions, such as, What was going on during that time period? Are the documents primary or secondary sources? How do you know? How reliable is the account for historical accuracy? What bias can the writer or artist bring to the work? Then more specific questions relating to the document(s) are needed so that students can focus on interpretations.

To avoid the daunting reading problems caused by older written source documents, more teachers engage students by using visual images—photographs, political cartoons, and propaganda posters. An example would be using the photographs by Lewis W. Hine about child labor that were discussed earlier. Students can view photographs of children working in factories and mines, selling newspapers, and picking fruit. From their viewing, they can answer questions about the working conditions, the risks involved, and the impact on the children's education. As assessment, they might be asked to write letters to local and state groups asking for plans to protect children from working too long hours and in unsafe conditions.

However, in this example and for other uses of source documents, ideally students should also see other perspectives, even if almost everyone agrees that the children were working in dreadful conditions and that their health and well-being were certainly not being protected. Hearing what the factory owners or parents thought about the situation would also provide insight into why child labor is a complex problem, difficult to solve in the past as well as today. Examining multiple perspectives should be encouraged when using any type of source document. As a result of studying a source document, students could gain more insight than if they read about it in a textbook or other written materials. However, now more textbooks contain colorful visual material and excerpts of source documents.

In using source documents, some teachers divide students into groups, with each group looking at a different written document or photograph. Using the Jigsaw II method, each group writes out their answers to the questions and then teaches others about their source documents so that the whole class learns about several documents. By this means, more source documents are analyzed.

You can certainly locate source documents from the Internet. Another source is the National Center for History in the Schools, with many units (for a fee) that include primary source documents along with reproducible worksheets. In addition, there are CD-ROMs and DVDs containing hundreds of historical documents with explanatory text to accompany each document, placing it in its proper historical context. These CD-ROMs also have audio clips of period music and speeches, along with teacher's guides and assessment items. For teachers whose departments cannot afford a primary source CD-ROM, there are much cheaper primary source books available, divided by topics or questions. Questions might be "How democratic was Andrew Jackson?" or "The Aztecs: What should history say?" It would appear that with the increased use of the Internet and CD-ROMs, more and more primary source documents will be used in the classroom.

SMALL GROUP WORK	
	WOULD YOU USE PRIMARY SOURCE DOCUMENTS?
6.2	*There is some evidence that teachers who had courses in which they used primary source materials are more likely to use these materials in their own classes. Did you use primary source documents when you were in school? When would you use primary source documents in your teaching?*

Oral History

One exciting way both to interest students in history and to gain some insight on how historians go about their work is **oral history.** Oral history is the recollections and reminiscences of living persons about their past. It is a historical inquiry undertaken by means of interviewing individuals about events they have **personally** experienced. Oral history is used not only with famous and well-known persons, but also to see how ordinary people viewed certain events and historical periods. You can use the American Memory Project of the Library of Congress to obtain oral histories on topics ranging from slave narratives to dancing as a form of recreation. Or students can gain data from local informants on how they viewed certain events, satisfying part of the emphasis that historians place on how everyday people experienced certain events in the past. An oral history project can illustrate the problems of working with **data** and of interrogating historical data to judge its reliability and bias.

Topic

The first step is the selection of the historical topic. This could be how local residents reacted to the rigors of the Great Depression, their experiences in World War II, the Cuban missile crisis, the Vietnam War, the civil rights movement, or the assassinations of John F. Kennedy or Martin Luther King, Jr. The topic also could be a local event such as a strike or a flood, or a more cultural topic such as "Games I Played as a Child." The choice of the topic determines the age range of the respondents, an important consideration in terms of reliability of the data.

Often, if available, students will interview a family member (a grandparent or even a great-grandparent), and this helps to tie students personally to the broad abstractions of the past through people they know. Using a family member also usually solves the problem if the respondent does not have English fluency. It gives life to what are a few pages in the textbook. Students also may look at their elderly relatives in a different way as they learn how these individuals had to face certain problems and to overcome obstacles. It is especially stimulating for minority group students to discover, when interviewing family members, that U.S. history includes their lives too, and that history is made by ordinary people they know and care about. Oral history can also be assigned using students as respondents, as when students relate their experiences of why and how they came to the United States or experiences of students who moved to their current state from somewhere else.

Questions

However, before going out to interview someone, students need a guide on what questions to ask. This means that *students have to understand the historical period* before formulating the interview questions. It is best to try out the questions first with a pilot study, to reveal confusing or ambiguous questions. Students also have to decide if they will use video or audiotape to record the responses to the questions, or write down the answers in front of the person. If they do neither, it is essential that they jot down the responses as quickly as possible after the interview.

In addition to the written interview form, role playing the interview process will help students feel more comfortable and excite their interest. An interview form with the written questions is then given to each student with a lot of space for students to write down the responses. Students should always be courteous and tactful and respect the confidentiality of the data. The interviewee should also sign a release form giving the class the right to publish the interview if this is the intent. Students need to thank the interviewee for his or her time and follow up with a note of thanks.

For example, if the interview is on the World War II period 1941–1945, helpful background information is needed. First, the name of the interviewer and the relationship to the interviewer should be noted. This might include the following:

1. Age: How old were you during the period of 1941–1945? (An easier question is, What year were you born?)
2. Gender
3. Where did you live? Did you move during this time period?

Then there are more general questions on how the individual recalls the particular time period.

1. Were you in military service during this time period? Where were you stationed? What happened to you?
2. Did you have a job? What did you do? Did you like your job? Did you receive a good salary? If you were too young to work, what work did your parent(s) do?
3. What war event or events do you recall the most vividly?
4. What changes occurred on the home front? (Prompts: Gas rationing? Rationing coupons for food? Victory gardens? Buying war bonds? More women working?)
5. What changes did the war make in your life and that of your family?
6. Did you keep a diary or letters?

Another popular focus for high school students has been interviewing Vietnam veterans. More veterans' organizations have been encouraging teachers to invite former members of the military to classrooms to share their wartime experiences. The aging survivors of the Holocaust are also in demand, especially in states that have mandated the teaching of the Holocaust. Have students ask interviewees if they can take a picture of the respondent to include with the written responses.

If all of the members of the class use the same questions, the class later can pool the responses from the interviews. Students are often eager to share their results. The first thing the class will probably notice is the wide diversity of experiences from their sample. For many of those interviewed, World War II was the single most important event in their lives as they married, achieved better economic well-being, or had painful experiences. They may tell powerful stories, stating, "It was not a pretty sight," or "I felt mighty good when I got my first paycheck." Besides possibly improving relationships with family members, the real payoff of doing oral history is realizing the problems that historians have in trying to make sense of an enormous amount of data and evidence.

Can the data be quantified? Using categories such as gender, are there any patterns discernible? Realizing that perspectives may vary on what took place, how can the class check for accuracy and reliability of the responses? Do the data confirm the general picture of what was happening during World War II? Have some of those interviewed exaggerated or forgotten essential experiences? Checking standard reference books and textbooks is one way to check the responses of those interviewed.

Results

After students have finished their interviews, they have many options. Some classes have made a video from parts of the interview, or a book with selections from the interviews. A local paper might run selected interviews. Or the project can be put on a web site. If loaded onto a web site, be careful not to include identifiable pictures or personal information. Parent consent for displaying student work is also necessary. Part of the difficulty in doing this is that both individuals as well as professional historians disagree on what is most significant, or what should be included as history. What gets left out of history is an important decision by both professional historians and students. Students can better appreciate this problem after they select what they consider the most interesting experience of their respondents.

Other examples of oral histories can be a field trip interview. Or a pair of students could interview a person, although too large of a group may be intimating for the respondent. Groups of students, however, can interview a guest speaker. Students can interview government officials or community leaders.

In summary, doing oral history can be both an in-depth and a more personalized way of learning for students. It places local history in the overall context of U.S. history. It also provides an encounter with the problems and promises of doing historical research. Students can increase their questioning, listening, writing, and organizational skills. In addition, the community is enriched by having a record of its residents' memories and experiences.

Doing History

Besides oral history interviews, another long-standing recommendation for the teaching of history is for students to actually "do history" by investigating a historical problem. This involves a process similar to inquiry, in that the historical question or problem must be defined, a hypothesis developed, research procedures employed (such as locating and analyzing sources), the historical data interrogated, and then findings and conclusions formulated based on a sound historical interpretation. Part of the reason students can do this task of being a historian is that there is no essential difference between a "professional" and an "amateur" historian because, in a certain sense, we are all historians of our own life. The great advantage of the professional historian is that he or she has tried to thoroughly read everything on the topic and has written clearly about it.

Students need skills to do historical research: reading, thinking, and writing come into the foreground as well as finding information. Students must be able to comprehend what the source says. In addition, they must differentiate between historical facts and historical interpretations as they read. Complicating the situation even more, students encounter and need to evaluate competing historical narratives. In effect, the students are doing **historical analysis and interpretation.**

In writing, students must construct a sound historical interpretation. One problem, hard for beginners to appreciate, is that some of the material they have spent so much time finding may not be used. These skill requirements on the part of the students have caused teachers to limit having students "do" history. However, if they never have the opportunity, students may never learn how historians do their work. Students now have more opportunities to publish their work on the Internet, a motivation to write.

Biographies and Term Papers

With increased pressure to improve student writing, some school districts are demanding that all students write a junior paper, often between three to five pages long. Typically all the research components are completed in the U.S. history class. A supervised rough draft is completed in the English class, with final copies turned in to both the history and the English teachers. Students generally have a full semester to write this paper. The process is often broken down into several steps: selection of researchable question, research, documentation of sources, revisions, and the like.

Because of the required length of the paper, most students choose to write biographies. Biographies are the written life of a real person, and writing them can help students develop more complex historical research skills as well as become better communicators. In addition, in doing a biography, the student becomes familiar with the context and chronology in which the individual lived, which helps prevent "presentmindedness," or judging the past solely in terms of today's values.

Local History

For a topic, local history is right in one's own backyard, and studying it avoids problems such as trying to find and use international sources that might cause possible language difficulties. Local history may also be more relevant to students than something that happened far away. Students might make use of the local historical societies and visit historical homes, cemeteries, industrial mills, and other sites. Usually the broad question is how the community has changed from a certain decade to the present and how these changes were related to what was happening on the national and international scenes. This often involves a comparison of key people and events in the community in the past with the present. It is usually best to narrow the search to about ten years, because too much information is available if a period of fifty or so years is used.

Typically, students are assigned to small groups with each group investigating one area, such as changes in population, land usage, transportation, business and industry, education, recreation, and community organizations. Students may be asked to make a timeline of the period showing, on the top line, events on the national and international arenas, with the local events below the line. Students are often encouraged to use primary sources such as pictures, photographs, and the like.

Focusing on local history requires the teacher to be familiar with the community and to know what local sources are available in order to anticipate many of the problems that students might encounter. The following list of general sources is suggestive:

- School library and then the local library for city and county histories already published, as well as reference materials
- Historical societies
- City directories, business directories, telephone books
- City clerk or city historian
- Local newspapers
- Long-time residents of the community
- Internet, using sites such as the U.S. Census Bureau for past data

More specialized sources include census records, older as well as more recent maps of streets in the area, lithographs, prints, photographs, diaries and genealogies, memorabilia, public school records and yearbooks, calendars of local events, city archives, public transportation agencies, Chamber of Commerce materials, business histories and anniversary booklets, and many other sources.

Students often are fascinated by how much the community has changed when a comparison is made of a certain decade to the present. However, you can see that this project will involve students being able to go to where resources are located. In other words, the work usually cannot be done within the school walls. This requires some thinking about what transportation will be involved for students, as well as their time commitments. For this reason, sometimes "doing history" is an optional activity for students, as the necessary ability level is high and time is needed to produce a good history. Thus some schools participate in History Day, but not all students take part.

Probably the most common history project for students to do on their own is "Exploring Family Roots." This is often undertaken in conjunction with a unit on immigration and varies on the detail required. A teacher needs to be aware that investigating biological parents and relatives can be a sensitive area for students.

Individual projects for students in large cities have been to locate a historical monument in a park or public place. They then try to find out what groups wanted the monument or statue erected and why, some background on the honored person or event, and how the person or event is perceived today. Or students investigate the names of certain streets, parks, schools, buildings, and landmarks in the community. This also requires some consideration of transportation and time. Cemeteries have been used for history projects, as students look at the average age of death and gain other information about life in the past. More projects are now going onto web sites for use by other classes.

Teaching Chronological Thinking

In history we study the memories of the past, but what is the **past**? The present is only an instant and quickly melds into the past. The future is our projection of what our past knowledge thinks it will be. **Time** is an attempt to quantify the past and the future. Yet there is a subjectivity about the past and time. We all know that when we are waiting in an anxiety-provoking situation such as at a job interview or in an emergency room, time can appear to drag, yet when we are enjoying ourselves, we say that time flies. Objectively, we know that time is being measured in increasingly exact, tiny increments due to the latest technologies.

To make sense of the world, it is essential to acquire **chronology,** a clear sense of the order in which events occurred. To foster chronological thinking, the first step is for students to distinguish between past, present, and future time. Generally, as students mature, they develop more sophisticated views on chronology, but there are not fixed Piagetian patterns of development for this understanding. When they have reached middle and high school, almost all students have mastered this task of distinguishing past, present, and future in their own lives.

In reading literature such as autobiographies, biographies, and narratives, able readers usually comprehend the order of events in terms of a beginning, middle, or end in what has happened to the main characters. Reading a wide variety of literature helps to reinforce chronology skills. But have most students developed this sense of chronology in history? Evidence suggests that too many do not know when the Civil War occurred or whether the Constitution was written before or after the Declaration of Independence. Yet they can describe these historical events. In effect, they have not been able to group important events in American history into time periods or eras.

To help develop chronology, students need to see and understand the time structure as they read a textbook or a historical narrative. The teacher can help by making frequent references to the year of the event and writing it on the board to avoid having students think of events as flowing by without any pattern. Chronology involves more than just putting dates into chronological order, an important first step but not the last step. Ideally students should have visual images of what society was like during the American Civil War or the Italian Renaissance. Often students use the type of transportation and communication or the particular type of clothing people wore as clues to the main characteristics of the society at a given period.

Timelines

To help in establishing this temporal sense, events presented in timelines are most helpful for seeing the sequential order. Multiple-tier timelines of social, economic, and political factors help students see what was occurring on various fronts at the same time. Furthermore, making timelines of their own lives, their families, and their communities may foster chronological thinking in students, as well as enrich the timelines found in the textbook. Students often forget about the timeline on the first page of the chapter unless it is pointed out and reinforced during a unit. Commercial timelines, some colorful and laminated, can be purchased for bulletin board or wall display. Software is also available for students and the teacher to make their own timelines (see Sample Classroom Lesson).

SAMPLE CLASSROOM LESSON

A COLD WAR TIMELINE

Objective
Students will identify the key political, social, and economic effects as they relate to the cold war era from 1945 to 1970.

Assignment: Students will make an illustrated annotative cold war timeline.

1. The timeline must have a *minimum* of ten events for each category: political, social, and economic.
2. Create illustrations for ten of the events you place on your timeline.
3. Compile a bibliography of the sources you used to construct your timeline.

Calendars

To do chronological thinking, students must also understand calendar time. Calendar time is culturally determined, as indicated by the many different solar and lunar calendars used throughout the world. For example, some individuals have a desk calendar with two calendar times: a Western Gregorian calendar that measures time from a fixed point relative to Christ's birth and a Muslim calendar that starts with the Hegira. However, international standardization is now the trend. Regardless of type, calendars are important because they give meaning to our lives, marking the important dates such as birthdays, vacations, and holidays. Students (and their teachers) often are counting the days before school ends. Students need to learn the meaning and understanding of terms such as *decades, centuries,* and the *millennia*. They also have to understand what time period constitutes the nineteenth century or the fifth century B.C.

Two problems associated with time are that most students in middle school have difficulty understanding the difference between the commonly found B.C. and A.D. time or the increasing use of the alternative B.C.E and C.E. In effect, they do not see the B.C. time as a negative number that they must add to the number of years in the A.D. sequence of years. Going over many dates such as the death of Socrates and using math to figure out how many years ago it was is essential for chronological understanding of B.C. Likewise, our calendar does not have a true zero, making it seem that terms such as *first century* are 100 years off.

LARGE CLASS DISCUSSION

CONTROVERSIAL ISSUE

The most significant controversy in the teaching of history is whose history should be taught. What do you think should be the emphases in U.S. history? World history?

■ SUMMARY

History *can* be taught creatively and thoughtfully so that students will acquire the necessary knowledge, skills, and values to participate as active citizens in our society and the global community. Many strategies can be used to make history interesting and more understandable: use of the Internet, media, arts and music, artifacts, simulations, and history as a narrative. Some experts want teachers to concentrate on selecting and organizing historical content around enduring ideas, patterns, and universal historical themes and dilemmas. Still others insist that history must show the vital connections between the present and the past and be issue oriented.

More attention is also being given to whether students use and understand historical thinking skills. Oral history, doing a historical report, and the teaching of chronology are used for this purpose.

■ REFERENCES ■

Banks, J. A. (2001). Citizenship education and diversity. *Journal of Teacher Education, 52,* 6–17.

Chapin, J. R. (1995). *The controversy on national standards for history.* Paper presented at the annual meeting of the National Council for the Social Studies, Chicago. ERIC EJ589039.

Cheney, L. V. (1994, Oct. 20). The end of history. *Wall Street Journal,* pp. A26(W), A22(E).

Dewey, J. (1933). *How we think.* New York: D. C. Heath.

Engle, S., & Ochoa, A. (1988). *Education for democratic citizenship: Decision making in the social studies.* New York: Teachers College Press.

Evans, R. W., Newmann, F. M., & Saxe, D. W. (1994). Defining issues-centered education. In R. W. Evans & D. W. Saxe (Eds.), *Handbook on teaching social issues.* Bulletin #93. Washington, DC: National Council for the Social Studies.

Evans, R. W., & Saxe, D. W. (Eds.). (1996). *Handbook on teaching social issues.* Bulletin #93. Washington, DC: National Council for the Social Studies.

Foster, S. J., & Yeager, E. A. (1998). The role of empathy in the development of historical understanding. *The International Journal of Social Education, 13*(1), 1–7.

Gagnon, P., & Bradley Commision on History in the Schools. (1989). *Historical literacy: The case for history in American education.* New York: Macmillan.

Grant, C. A. (1999). The California history–social science standards: Multicultural education and habits of the mind. *Social Studies Review, 38,* 22–25.

Hunt, M. P., & Metcalf, L. E. (1955). *Teaching high school social studies: Problems in reflective thinking and social understanding.* New York: Harper & Row.

Lapp, M. S., Grigg, W. S., & Tay-Lim, B. (2002). *The nation's report card U.S. History 2001* (NCES 2002-483). Washington, DC: U.S. Department of Education.

Levstik, L. S. (1989). Historical narrative and the young reader. *Theory into Practice, 28,* 114–119.

Levstik, L. S., & Barton, K. C. (2005). *Doing history: Investigating with children in elementary and middle school* (2nd ed.). Mahwah, NJ: Lawrence Erlbaum.

National Center for History in the Schools. (1994a). *National standards for history: Expanding children's world in time and space (K–4).* Los Angeles: Author.

National Center for History in the Schools. (1994b). *National standards for United States history: Exploring the American Experience (5–12).* Los Angeles: Author.

National Center for History in the Schools. (1994c). *National standards for world history: Exploring paths to the present (5–12).* Los Angeles: Author.

National Center for History in the Schools. (1996). *National history standards: Basic edition.* Los Angeles: Author.

Newmann, F. N., & Oliver, D. W. (1970). *Clarifying public controversy: An approach to social studies.* Boston: Little, Brown.

Oliver, D. W., & Shaver, J. P. (1966). *Teaching public issues in high school.* Boston: Houghton Mifflin.

Richburg, R. (1999). Surprise! The world isn't always the way students think it is. *Social Studies Review, 38,* 65–69.

Rossi, J. (2000). At play with curriculum development in history. In S. W. Bednarz & R. S. Bednarz (Eds.), *Social science on the frontier: New horizons in history and geography* (pp. 52–66). Boulder, CO: Social Science Education Consortium.

Saxe, D. W. (1996). Using issues in the teaching of American history. In R. W. Evans & D. W. Saxe (Eds.), *Handbook on teaching social issues.* Bulletin #93. Washington, DC: National Council for the Social Studies.

Saxe, D. W. (1998). *State history standards.* Washington, DC: Thomas Fordham Foundation.

Schwartz, B. (2000). *Abraham Lincoln and the forge of national memory.* Chicago: University of Chicago Press.

Seixas, P. (1993). The community of inquiry as a basis for knowledge and learning: The case of history. *American Educational Research Journal, 30,* 305–324.

■ WEB SITES ■

American Historical Association
www.historians.org
Prime organization for historians.

The History Channel
www.historychannel.com
Popular source.

History Matters
www.historymatters.gmu.edu
Web site annotations and primary source documents, interactive exercises.

HistoryTeacher.Net
www.HistoryTeacher.net
Good on primary sources and European history

National Archives and Records Administration
www.archives.gov
Provides materials from the National Archives and methods for teaching with primary sources.

National Council for History Education
www.history.org/nche
Both professional historians and K–12 participate in group's activities; has links to many other sites.

National Park Service Links to the Past
www.cr.nps.gov
List of sites of people, places, objects and events

Smithsonian Institution
www.smithsonianeducation.org
Manuscripts, photographs, music, art, movies with good search engines, some types of transcriptions with manuscripts, and linked to teacher-created lesson plans.

U.S. History
http://members.aol.com/MrDonnHistory/American.html
Collection of lesson plans for most areas of U.S. history.

World History
http://members.aol.com/MrDonnHistory/World.html
Lesson plans and resources from ancient through modern day.

Chapter 7

Teaching Geography, Economics, and the Behavioral Sciences

In this chapter, we focus first on the important role and status of geography as a discipline, its place in the social studies program, geography standards, geography skills, and methods and resources used to teach geography. Then we examine the status of economics in the schools and the teaching of economics. Last, the behavioral sciences—psychology, sociology, and anthropology—are addressed. The topics of this chapter are listed below.

- The Status of Geography in the Schools
- Geography Standards and the Teaching of Geography
- The Status of Economics in the Schools
- National Economics Frameworks and Standards
- The Teaching of Economics
- Behavioral Sciences: Psychology, Sociology, and Anthropology

■ THE STATUS OF GEOGRAPHY IN THE SCHOOLS

Status of the Discipline

What images come to mind when you hear the word *geography?* Do you envision where Estonia and Namibia are located on a world map? Or do you think of map skills such as filling in a blank outline map with names of the nations and their capitals of South America? This is probably how most students and their teachers think of geography. And for some students, traditional geography activities such as learning the state capitals have actually been enjoyable. Students feel a sense of accomplishment and satisfaction in doing these fact-based activities, and for that reason, many report liking geography better than history. Geography is also about people, and students like learning about different cultures in faraway places. The only geography requirement for many students has been to memorize facts, with the result that even lower-ability students can feel successful. The stereotypic components of "old" geography teaching can be summarized as follows:

- Place location memorization
- Textbook-driven, with recall of information a prime goal
- Limited problem solving and skill development
- Fact-based objective testing
- Hooray! It's Field Trip Day!

Why did this happened? One reason is that so much information is now available on cultures and places that it is easy to overemphasize facts instead of concepts. Some memorization is helpful, especially if it is not likely to change. However, learning to find and to evaluate information is assuming even more importance as a skill in the twenty-first century.

But **geography** as a discipline is broader than place locations, map skills, or a collection of arcane information for a quiz show contestant. Geographers want the underlying principles of the discipline and their way of thinking emphasized rather than mere lists of facts. For geographers, geography organizes both the human and the physical dimensions of the information about the world so that people better understand its nature. Geography is the science of space and place on Earth's surface. In the area of *human culture,* geography looks at the relationships between people and environment. On the *physical* side, geography examines our planet's varying surface and the processes that shape it, such as mountains, plains, and volcanoes. In effect, geography is a bridge between the social and physical sciences, uniting the physical and cultural world in the study of people, places, and environments (Geography Education Standards Project, 1994). Geography points out how "the local" affects "the global" and vice versa.

Geography, like history, is constantly changing, with new emphases and new knowledge resulting in changing interpretations. One dramatic change in interpretation is the questioning of the usefulness of one of the most important geography concepts, regions (Riebsame, 2000). In the United States, is Los Angeles part of the "West"? In what region does Los Angeles really belong? Where are the boundaries of the "South"? Do you ignore the variations within a region? This changing view of regions is a major shift in thinking.

Geography is thus not a static field with a set of permanent facts. In particular, geographers have presently moved heavily into *environmental studies* as people worry about global change, species loss, and other threats such as the cutbacks of farmlands with commuters moving into outlying areas and creating urban sprawl. At some departments of geography, the main specialty is now environmental studies, another big change from the past. In addition, in cartography, new satellite images and other technological innovations show with increasing clarity the whole planet with all of its variety.

Geography in the K–12 Grades

Test Results

Geography tests of both K–12 students and U.S. adults in an International Gallup Survey have certainly not been encouraging. The NAEP Geography Report Card (Persky, Reese, O'Sullivan, Lazer, Moore, & Shakrani, 1996) for students at the fourth, eighth, and twelfth grades used a wide variety of questions. Evaluation included the use of maps, photographs, tables, and charts, along with short-answer and constructed-response questions that went beyond memorization of geography facts. More questions were based on a conceptual understanding of geography.

The results indicated that many students found the assessment difficult. Using only three categories, Basic, Proficient, and Advanced, approximately 70 percent of the students were at the Basic level, reflecting only partial mastery of prerequisite knowledge and skills that are fundamental for proficient work at each grade level. About 25 percent were judged to be Proficient, representing solid academic performance that included subject matter knowledge, application of such knowledge to real-world situations, and using analytical skills. This left only about 5 percent in the Advanced category.

Correlating with past educational research, White and Asian American students did better than Hispanic and African American students. However, unlike results in reading and writing, male students outperformed female students on all three grade levels, reinforcing the common observation that males, on the average, are better than females in geography, probably due to their higher spatial skills. Research has also shown that geographic awareness among students is influenced more by travel experience than by any other factor. Obviously not everyone can take trips around the United States and the world, and it is up to the schools to promote geography education.

The geography questions used in this older NAEP assessment are available online. Teachers will find the test questions with charts, photographs, and maps especially helpful for teaching these skills to students (http://nces.ed.gov/nationsreportcard/ITMRLS/intro.shtml). The 2001 NAEPs assessment concentrated on three areas: space and place, environment and society, and spatial dynamics and connections—reflecting the recent trends in geography away from memorization.

Difficulties

Geographic education in the schools is inadequate but it can be improved. There are two main difficulties in improving geography teaching in the schools: first, many teachers have not taken formal geography courses while at college or university, although with current certification changes more new social studies teachers do have some courses in geography; and second, there are few geography courses offered at the middle school and high schools. Physical geography may be taught in science courses such as Earth Science. Also, the life sciences with their topics of biodiversity and the need for fresh water are also covering geographical topics. Furthermore, math courses teach how to understand data in graphs.

However, for the human side of geography, typically there are no separate geography courses, so geography has to find its place among the required history courses such as in U.S. history and world history. The exception is that some schools offer a World Cultures course, usually with a global geographic orientation, found at the ninth- or tenth-grade level. This course is usually divided into widely based subdivisions such as "the Middle East." This course has been criticized as being "four weeks on Asia and then three weeks on Africa," isolating one world region from another despite their interconnectedness. On the positive side, this course has been more popular with students of average and below-average ability. But this course is changing, as, for example, in New York State, where the ninth- and tenth-grade World

Culture course has been changed to a World History and Geography course using a chronological approach.

Some critics have asserted that geography had almost *disappeared* from the curriculum, but this is an exaggeration. Probably about one-fourth of all high school students have had at least a one-semester geography course, a limited number compared to the total student population. A few seniors are taking the newly offered AP Human Geography Course. From these data, you can understand that the advocates of geography certainly want a more prominent place for it in the curriculum, with a greater number of students learning about geography.

Importance

At the same time, geography, if anything, is assuming a more important role as the global economy becomes more interconnected and our physical environment becomes more of a concern. Students need to understand global and environmental issues as our planet becomes more crowded and our physical environment more threatened. We are all part of the global community in both the economic realm and the political world. The consequences of the interaction of humans and the environment invite careful analysis to determine the impacts. Some human environment interactions have been harmful, whereas others have led to an improvement in the quality of life. There are key issues regarding the appropriate basis for government and private-sector environmental policies on global warming and ozone layer depletion.

Furthermore, you cannot understand the news today from all parts of the globe without at least some background in where the event is occurring and why it is happening there. Some teachers frequently use news items and then ask their students to answer a series of questions. Where did the event happen? What was the effect on people? On the environment?

■ GEOGRAPHY STANDARDS AND THE TEACHING OF GEOGRAPHY

The Five Themes

In the mid-1980s, the National Geographical Society, the largest nongovernmental geographical organization in the world, worked hard to improve both the quality and the quantity of geography taught in the schools. "Think Geographically" is their motto to reduce geographic illiteracy. In 1984 the following short five themes of geography were published in the *Guidelines in Geographic Education K–12*. Sample questions by the author are illustrated for the five themes.

1. **Location.** Position on the Earth surface
   - How does the location of _____ affect its economy?
   - Why are cities and towns in _____ located where they are?

2. **Place.** The physical, human, and observed characteristics that distinguish one place from another (see Sample Lesson Plan.)
   - What landforms are characteristic of this place?
   - What is the population density? Ethnic makeup?
   - Where are the residential areas? Commercial areas?

SAMPLE LESSON PLAN

THEME OF PLACE

Standard/Objective: Identify examples that characterize your school and neighborhood. This lesson can be helpful for new students (first-year students, ELLs, etc.) as they enter school.

Activities for School

1. Where is your school located? (Address, street intersections, latitude–longitude, relation to other places)
2. List three attractive features of your school or around the school.
3. Secure a map of your school. Are any features not included? Athletic fields? Staff parking? If your school does not have a map, make one. Show the physical elements. Mark each room number. Circle the classrooms where you need to go. Is your map oriented toward the north?
4. Describe the human elements of your school. Who is there? What ages are they? What ehnic/racial groups can you identify?

Activities for the Local Neighborhood around the School

1. List three attractive features of your school neighborhood.
2. Secure local maps of your neighborhood. If not listed on the map, place community facilities such as the library, fire station, police station, and the like on the map.
3. Do a neighborhood survey. Write from memory or actually observe the neighborhood (after school).
   a. Kinds of buildings
   b. Kinds of plants
   c. People (ethnic groups, religious groups, languages spoken, age levels)
   d. Transportation
   e. Businesses—just list types
   f. Topography and natural features
4. Compare your local neighborhood with living conditions in ancient Greece, Mayan civilization, Philadelphia during the Constitutional Convention (or other areas you have studied).
5. Writing
   a. How are lives affected by the geography characteristics of the neighborhood?
   b. Should anything be changed in the neighborhood? How could this be accomplished?

Source: Modified from M. Miller & E. Hipolito. (2005). *A sense of place.* Presentation at the California Council for the Social Studies." Burlingame, California.

3. **Relationships within places.** How people have modified or adapted to natural settings
   • How have people used their resources?

- What are the advantages of irrigation? Disadvantages?
- What is happening to forested areas in _____?

4. **Movement.** Movement of people, ideas, and materials
   - Why did people emigrate from Ireland to other parts of the world? (See Sample Unit Plan.)
   - What transportation systems are used in _____?

5. **Regions.** Areas that display unity; way of organizing and subdividing people and places
   - Where is the Middle East?
   - Where is the "Corn Belt"?

SAMPLE UNIT PLAN

THEME OF MOVEMENT TIED INTO IRISH IMMIGRATION HISTORY UNIT

Standard: List the reasons for the wave of immigration from northern Europe to the United States and describe the growth in the number, size, and spatial arrangements of cities. In particular, studying Irish immigration is a standard in many states.

Activities

1. Explain what is meant by "push/pull" factors that encouraged emigration. Ask or use small groups of students to tell why their families came to the United States. From what places did they come, how did they travel (transportation system), and to what places did their families/ancestors originally settle? Use world and U.S. maps. Graph results.
2. Brainstorm in small groups the factors that pulled people to the United States in the 1840s. Small groups report to the whole class and check with the text and other resources for accuracy.
3. Show a video of the Great Hunger (many are available about the Irish famine).
4. Map where the Irish immigrants settled. Why did large numbers not settle in the South? On farms? What jobs did men, women, and children have? Compare these occupations with what they previously had in Ireland.
5. Read in textbook or other sources the reactions in the United States to the Irish immigrants. Here is an Irish American folksong. A *spalpeen* is a rascal.

   I'm a decent boy just landed from the town of Ballyfad;
   I want a situation, and I want it very bad.
   I seen employment advertised, "It's just the thing," says I,
   But the dirty spalpeen ended with "No Irish need apply."

   What reasons were given for the dislike of and hostility toward the Irish?
6. Write a letter to family members in Ireland describing your efforts to establish yourself in a new homeland.

7. Extension: For a "research trip," students pick a country their families/ancestors came from or that they find interesting. Among other requirements of the report, students research the locations, landforms, and climates in their country of origin (or interest) and the effect of these elements on the social, political, and economic development of that particular country. Students then compare the locations, landforms, and climates with the place they presently live.

In the 1980s, Geographic Alliances were established to improve the teaching of geography at a grassroots level, and they are thriving in many states, where thousands of teachers have received in-service training and materials. Later the National Geographic Society gave the Geographic Alliances support. The "Five Themes" were popular and regarded as teacher-friendly, especially among elementary teachers who used these themes as they studied any nation, state, city, or community. Organizing topics could be as follows: the given area's climate; physical features; cultural background of the people; where most people live; how they have changed their environment; the consequences of the change; the major exports and imports; major roads, airports, and ports; how similar is the area to its neighbors in government, culture, and religions.

As an application of the Five Themes, students can study China. They could use or fill out a series of maps, including China's neighbors, rivers, elevation, precipitation, population, political divisions, and crops grown. Each would be a separate map to avoid putting too much data on a given map. Then from maps and photographs, small groups of students could tackle such questions as, Why do people live where they live? How does where you live determine what you eat? How do food resources get to the population? and Why would a person prefer to live in the country or the city?

SMALL GROUP WORK	THE FIVE GEOGRAPHY THEMES
7.1	*Were you familiar with the five geography themes while you were in school? How could they be useful in your teaching?*

Standards

After making progress with the incorporation of the Five Themes in the curriculum, the national standards movement for all subject areas further galvanized the American Geographical Society, the Association of American Geographers, the National Council for Geographic Education, and the well-known National Geographic

Society to assemble geographers and geography educators to formulate geography standards for the field. The geographers who were critical of the Five Themes advocated that more attention be paid to the physical character of geography, which they thought had been neglected. In a very colorful, attractive book, *Geography for Life: National Geography Standards 1994*, eighteen standards under six main categories outlined in detail what students should be able to know and to do at the end of the fourth grade, eighth grade, and twelfth grade.

State Geography Standards

States had a difficult time when they looked at the new national geography standards, although, unlike the national history standards, there was no national controversy about them. States were overwhelmed by the 260-page geography standards book. The states found the *Geography for Life* standards confusing and difficult to use, and many educators liked the old Five Themes standards as being easier to adopt. Working out the relationship between the old Five Themes and the new national geography standards was a real chore. To help educators better understand the standards, the National Geographic Society (Salter, Hobbs, & Salter, 1995) published a brief key to the national geography standards and related geography themes. Later, they published a scope and sequence guide to K–12 geography (Geography Scope and Sequence Project, 2000). However, these documents did not gain much publicity. In 2001 the National Geographic Society distilled the eighteen elements into six essential elements (Figure 7.1).

Furthermore, often the states had no geography courses in place at the middle and high school levels. However, the states had an easier time incorporating the geography standards into the elementary grades, where they concentrated on two main standards: (1) using maps and other geographic tools; and (2) the interaction of natural and human characteristics in the development of their communities and their state. Even here more educators wanted a scope and sequence chart for each grade. The middle and high school geography standards were more difficult to implement because geography was not taught as a separate course. Thus, most states had their own frameworks labeled, for example, History and Geography for U.S. History, or World History and Geography, but the geography was to be integrated with the history and not taught as a separate subject.

Geographers, however, did not feel that this really covered the concepts, skills, and perspective that a more rigorously taught, separate geography course could give—and that was needed by all students. The geographers' perspective, the differences between the Five Themes and the *Geography for Life* standards, and teachers' views on concentrating on location and map skills led to many state geography standards not being clear as to what the student really needs to learn and to do (Munroe & Smith, 1998). Some state geography standards are so broadly stated that practically any content could be justified, and their usefulness as standards is doubtful. However, the National Council for Geographic Education does have a web site for help in implementation of the geography standards (http://ncge.org).

FIGURE 7.1 Six Core Geographic Elements

1. **The World in Spatial Terms (Location).** The spatial relationships between people, places, and environments; expressed by means of a grid (absolute) or in relation (relative) to the position of other places; map, globe, and atlas use.

2. **Places and Regions.** Concept of physical and human features, changes in places and regions over time, regional interaction, political and historical characteristics of regions.

3. **Physical Systems.** Components of the Earth's physical systems (e.g., landforms, water, climate and weather, erosion and deposition), ecosystems, natural hazards.

4. **Human Systems.** The human imprint on the physical environment as created and modified by people, land use, population distribution and dynamics, human migration, transportation, patterns of commerce and economic development.

5. **Environment and Society.** Earth's natural resources, human modification of the physical environment, resource management, conservation, environmental issues (e.g., global warming, energy consumption, pollution).

6. **The Uses of Geography.** Descriptions of places in past times, environmental analysis; interaction of physical and human systems on current and future conditions; role of multiple points of view in contemporary geographic issues; influence of geography on world history.

Source: National Geographic Society. (2001). *Path toward world literacy: A standards-based guide to K–12 geography.* Washington, DC: Author.

Integrating Geography with History

Given the time constraints faced by social studies teachers who are unlikely to set aside days or weeks for geography, the easiest practical approach is to integrate geography with history. According to this view, geography and history can be regarded as complementary subjects best taught together within a social studies framework (Bednarz, 1997; Rossi, 2000). For everything is somewhere! In history, geographic context (or, What was it like in a particular place at a particular time?) is essential, and the teacher needs to be alert to see where geographical concepts can be easily incorporated into the history course. For U.S. history, these places might include what the Americas were like before 1492, the land features of the various European claims in the New World, land of the thirteen colonies, what the land was like in further exploration and settlement of "the West," transportation difficulties linked to geographic features, and the growth of cities. Typically, for world history, particularly in the study of ancient civilizations and civilizations in the Americas, attention is given to geographic features. People of the first known civilizations had to consider many geographic features, such as the amount of rain, bodies of fresh water, natural resources, and the type of weather at different times of the year. Organizing questions/instructions for the unit might include the following:

1. Why are rivers and oceans important to people who want to settle?
2. What is unique about the natural landscape and resources of Mesopotamia? Egypt? Other ancient civilizations?
3. Compare the geographic background of the three great civilizations of the Americas: the Mayan, the Aztec, and the Incan. Each occupied a different environmental setting.

A learning activity might be to assume that you are a real-estate agent selling plots of land. Create a poster and a map to attract buyers to settle in your particular region.

The many conflicts of nations and empires over acquiring and retaining territory also relate to geography. Why were certain areas considered to be desirable to control? The largest category of maps in a textbook is that of historical maps that show boundaries of nations.

Let us examine how geography could be taught with a unit called the "Growth of Islam." The Sample Unit Plan is a world history unit typically taught at the seventh or tenth grades. Often, establishing a sense of place as well as time is done in the first few days of a history unit.

SAMPLE UNIT PLAN

GEOGRAPHY LESSONS INTEGRATED INTO A HISTORY UNIT

Partial List of Unit Objectives and Standards on a Growth of Islam Unit

Goals

1. To understand the geography of the ancient Middle East
2. To identify the geographic and economic significance of early trade routes

Day 1

Objective: To compare trade routes around A.D. 570 with present trade routes

1. Given the environment of Arabia, students brainstorm by making a list of items necessary at that time period for survival along trade routes (water, some form of transportation, etc.).
2. Why would oases become trading centers? Students draw the most important trade routes around A.D. 570. Using the textbook maps and atlases, students check each of these first Arabian towns for a water supply.
3. Bringing up to the present. Students check a current map showing the transportation systems in this area. How are they similar? Different? What are the most common characteristics of where cities are located?

Day 2
Objective: Students will identify the reasons for the establishment of Baghdad.

1. Should Caliph al-Mansur (754–775) establish a new city as his capital? Using a map showing the established cities at that time (Damascus, Jerusalem, Mecca, and so on), students look at the two options: Use an existing city within the domain or start a new city.
2. Working in groups of two, students list the advantages and disadvantages of each option.
3. Class discussion on the geographic factors that support either option. Economic or military factors? Only at the end of the discussion report that a new city, Baghdad, was established.

Source: Adapted from 1994 Course Module, "Growth of Islam," in *Course Models for the History–Social Science Framework, Grade Seven—World History and Geography: Medieval and Early Modern Times.* Sacramento: California Department of Education.

SMALL GROUP WORK	EVALUATING THE INCLUSION OF GEOGRAPHY INTO HISTORY UNITS
7.2	*From the two brief lessons, do you think geography can be successfully incorporated into history units? Does the geography content go beyond key place names such as physical features (Arabian Desert, Euphrates River) and major cities (Medina, Samarkand)?*

Map and Related Geography Skills

Map and related geography skills of finding and interpreting data need to be taught because not everyone learns map and graphic skills in the elementary grades. In particular, some students are confused by legends and too much data on a map, table, or graph, especially crowded data.

How can this teaching be done? Quickly teach the skill to the whole class and model carefully what to do. Using questions, show how you give attention to the title, legend, and scale and what the graphic material is trying to convey. Ask questions such as What year is the data covering? What does the map show? Some teachers use a map analysis worksheet (Figure 7.2). Then put students in a mixed-ability pair with a new exercise. Each pair can work together on the activity and help to correct each other's work. Then debrief the activity, often using an overhead projector, showing possible correct responses. These skill activities need to take place frequently, for students often forget if they are done only once a semester.

Either a U.S. history or world history textbook can easily contain more than 100 maps. These maps certainly are valuable, for each historical event has both time and space dimensions. Wall maps also can be used but are declining in popularity because

FIGURE 7.2 Map Analysis Worksheet or Teacher's Questions

1. What type of map? (Political, weather, military, satellite, etc.)

2. List three things in this map that you think are important.

   A.

   B.

   C.

3. What information does the map add to the textbook's account of this event?

Why is using maps important when studying history?

FIGURE 7.3 Components of the New Geography

- Emphasis on spatial relationships
- Encourages problem solving
- Connected to critical thinking skills
- Depth replaces breadth
- Collaborative learning strategies
- Research-based
- Adaptable to the new technology
- Observation through fieldwork
- Emphasis on human/environmental interaction
- Framework or standards-driven

Source: Based on Marran, J. F. (1994). Discovering innovative curriculum models for school geography. *Journal of Geography, 93,* 9.

teachers are able to download maps from the Internet without cost. Remember to incorporate the practical applications of skills, because apparently one-third of U.S. adults cannot use a map to determine direction or find a given location and are not able to calculate distance to a given point.

"New Geography"

Many geographers maintain that the incorporation of geography into history courses does not get to the true spirit of geographic skills and perspectives. For them, geography skills first start with *asking geographic questions.* This is followed by acquiring geographic information, organizing and analyzing it, and then answering geographic questions. To do this, students use and enjoy geographic tools, incorporating the newer technologies with satellite-produced images and with the use of a spatial database and a geographic information system (GIS) to help answer a question. You can probably recognize this as a variation of the inquiry, problem-solving, critical thinking, issues-centered model that has been advocated in history and all of the disciplines of the social studies curriculum. The key elements of the new geography skills are found in Figure 7.3.

For example, classes have surveyed residents and mapped what residents wanted to be preserved as special historic places. This is an example of asking geographic questions, using geographic resources, exploring and analyzing geographic data, and acting on the results of inquiry. Water quality assessments, natural resources and other topics could also be investigated.

Environmental issues are now probably the most popular geography problem-solving issue studied in the schools. The following topics are just a few that could be studied with data from students' own local community, the United States, or a global perspective: health issues, environmental hazards, land use issues, urban revitalization, migration, transportation, cultural diffusion, pollution, urban planning, population patterns, energy issues, the green revolution in agriculture, future energy development, climate, deforestation, and groundwater resources. Indeed, there is no shortage of possible questions to investigate. Note that many of the topics could have a global education emphasis or a science component. In the minds of many teachers, environmental and global education are intertwined. For example, look at the global decisions that are made about Antarctica. Should there be exploration for natural resources in Antarctica? Access to the fish, shrimp, and whales in the waters off Antarctica? Should the activities of tourists be more tightly regulated, or should the number of tour groups increase, especially ecotourism?

In addition, environmental issues are closely related to economics. A criticism has been that environmental education has de-emphasized economic trade-offs. What do we win or lose if we set higher standards for air or water quality? If we put wolves back into their former hunting areas?

After an issue has been identified, the sequence previously described for problem solving/inquiry and issues-based instruction would be used (Chapters 4 and 6). In many cases, cooperative group work could be used for an efficient division of labor among the group members. This might mean producing a newscast about the effect of deforestation, or producing a brochure advocating a certain policy recommendation, or writing a letter to community officials.

SMALL GROUP WORK	ENVIRONMENTAL ISSUES
7.3	*What role, if any, should environmental issues play in a social studies program in the middle school? In high school? Should there be correlation with the science department? If so, on what topics?*

Resources

Thanks to the Internet, teachers now have access to thousands of maps and data for answering geographic questions. National, state, and local governments now produce most of their maps in electronic GIS format. Using GIS software, computer-literate people can call up a growing volume of geographic data and, choosing a certain theme and scale, create their own maps (Environmental Systems Research Institute, Inc., 1999). The main problem is that GIS is complex and requires training. It may be easier for teachers to use the Internet to access GIS sites that offer information and create online maps. Your state and its universities also may have specialized, useful data on water and air quality, earthquake faults (not just a problem for California), and toxic-release inventories. Many valuable web sites are listed at the end of the chapter for extensive data on individual countries and maps. Regarding deforestation and other controversial issues, almost all nongovernmental web sites are not neutral but strongly advocate certain positions. Evaluating the data from these web sites is a necessary and worthwhile experience that students face in using data from the Internet.

To personalize geography, teachers use pen pals (www.epals.com) and interpersonal exchange projects with other schools, using e-mail (www.siec.k12.in.us/) or electronic postcards (www.schoolworld.asn.au/geocard.html) that accurately represent their community. Another popular activity is for a class to follow a group on an expedition as it travels to distant areas. The Census Bureau files (www.census.gov) contain general yet valuable information.

On field trips, more classes are now using **global positioning system (GPS)** units that allow students to make a map as they walk and know their location. More complex is **geocaching,** in which a person hides a cache for others to find. Teachers have played hide-and-seek in their local area or campus to teach about latitude, longitude, and geographic or "mystery" features. Usually students are taught first how to use GPS units, and the teacher provides the coordinates and clues for small groups to find the cache. Parent volunteers have often been invited to help out with this fun activity.

Traditional resources such as guest speakers, literature, music, and art continue to be used to engage students in thinking about geography. For example, literature such as John Steinbeck's *The Grapes of Wrath*, a novel frequently used in high school English classes, can help students understand the physical and human characteristics that defined eastern Oklahoma and California's Central Valley in the 1930s. Teachers have used rap lyrics and henna painting as starting points to connect students with their own and other cultures. Using this type of creative approach, teachers give meaning to abstract concepts such as interdependence, demographic change, and human–environmental interaction.

Certain concepts can involve an emphasis on an interesting **case study,** a collection of data about a *single* individual, a single social unit such as a business, a particular event or decision, or a given issue. Case studies can appeal to human interests. Because of their potential for capturing interest, case studies are often used to set the stage for student analysis of the unit. There may be value conflicts in the case studies, as when a community must decide whether to approve a new industry that will bring jobs but at some cost to the environment, or whether a given nation or community should develop mineral extraction to earn much-needed cash.

In any case, most social studies teachers realize the need to incorporate the teaching of geographic concepts into their curriculum. However, unless it is planned, geography may be neglected in the social studies curriculum.

■ THE STATUS OF ECONOMICS IN THE SCHOOLS

Course Taking

Economics is the study of how human beings choose to use scarce resources to achieve personal and social goals. If resources were not scarce, we would not face issues of who gets goods and services, what gets produced, and how much gets produced. This discipline, like geography, is becoming more important because we live in a complex global economy. Many key issues such as taxation, the federal budget, and the like are fundamentally economic in nature. Students need economic knowledge to improve their ability to make reasoned decisions about many government policies.

Economics has the popular image of being "the dismal science." This negative feeling about economics has colored what social studies teachers, most of whom had history as their major, think about teaching the subject. This has made the inclusion of economics in the social studies curriculum more difficult. In about half of the states, prospective social studies teachers take only one economics course, although certification standards are changing in many states. Increasing the requirements for teachers to have economic training will help teachers to include economics in their classes and to improve their teaching effectiveness. Already, most high school social studies teachers have had an average of two economics courses, and almost 90 percent have had at least one economics course. Many of these courses have been taken as in-service training, since the National Council on Economic Education (NCEE) has established state councils in almost every state with many college and university centers. The more than 200 university centers have focused on credit courses and workshops for teachers and the development of instructional materials. This has given many more teachers a better background for teaching economics.

Typically at the high school level, about 40 percent of students take a one-semester economics course in the twelfth grade. This represents an increase compared to the period before 1980, due to some state- and local district–mandated economics requirements for graduation. If required, the student takes a one-semester course in government followed by the one-semester course in economics in the twelfth grade. In some schools, a government and economics course is combined in the twelfth grade without having separate courses in government and economics. In other schools where economics is not mandated, the economics course is an elective at the twelfth grade, taken mostly by college-bound students. In contrast to the growth of economics courses in the twelfth grade in the past two decades, the number of consumer and business courses that teach some economic concepts has declined. Where established, Junior Achievement programs (www.ja.org), both inside and outside of the school, also teach economic concepts. Their use of volunteers from the community can be effective.

Growing Importance of Economics

Advocates of economics education believe that everyone needs a separate economics course before leaving high school, and they are concerned that about half of all high school students still do not take a separate economics course. Even those students who go on to higher education may not take a college-level economics course. Tests of adults and students also indicate a poor understanding of economics. Proponents of economics cite the negative consequences—both for individuals and as citizens and voters.

Economic education can help students make decisions about their economic lives and future. The world is becoming increasingly complex financially. Just think about all the "newer" ways that now exist to pay bills—debit cards, electronic check conversion, and automatic payment or deposit. This is just one of the many technologies that is changing our financial world. On a personal level, **financial literacy** or **financial education** can prevent young people from making poor decisions that have serious consequences. Should you go to college? How can you afford to go to college?

How do you enter the workforce? Should you use online purchasing of products? How do you protect yourself from identity theft? In addition, as wage earners and consumers, both children and adults are bombarded with economic information and misinformation. All students therefore need a background in economics that will allow them to manage their financial lives as they differentiate among the wide range of products and services that are now available.

Another problem concerns what is taught in the high school economics course. The National Council on Economic Education advocates economic literacy so that students possess economic ways of thinking in order to be responsible consumers, producers, and savers and investors, as well as effective participants in the global economy. This approach does not focus on practical skills such as how to fill out income tax forms or take out a car loan. However, it appears that teachers in the field differ in approach (VanFossen, 2000). The three most common patterns for teaching were preparation for college economics (we teach economics because they need it in college), a practical consumer approach such as balancing a checkbook, and economics as good citizenship. Therefore, it appears that in many cases the goals of economics teachers vary widely from what is advocated by the National Council on Economic Education. These differences can also be seen when comparing the national economics frameworks with some state standards.

If anything, what was called the consumer education approach has gained ground recently, tied into economic principles so that each economic decision involves costs. However, this approach is no longer called "consumer education" but instead "**financial planning.**" Financial planning has moved away from the somewhat moralistic approach of comparing the costs of a can of pineapple in different grocery stores to examples that require students to decide for themselves when they should use credit. Students learn that credit can be their best friend or their worst enemy. With examples, students learn how quickly credit card balances can grow and how to calculate how long it can take to pay them off.

More mandated courses in economics at the present time do not appear likely. **Integration,** especially at the middle school level and in other social studies courses such as U.S. history, world history, geography, and government, is the most practical way for economics to be included in the curriculum. How much integration of economics takes place and the quality of the integration is unknown. Successful integration depends on teachers with some training in economics, good instructional materials, and little dependence on the history textbooks with their inadequate economics coverage. However, not all social studies teachers choose to make a conscious effort to spend time on the teaching of economics in their regular courses.

SMALL GROUP WORK	**HOW COMMITTED ARE YOU ABOUT TEACHING ECONOMICS?**
7.4	*Were you taught economics in high school? Would you like to teach the twelfth-grade economics course? How much of a consumer approach would you use? Will you include economics in your regular courses?*

■ NATIONAL ECONOMICS FRAMEWORKS AND STANDARDS

Frameworks

Teachers need to know what economics should be taught and how economics should be taught. Economists and economics educators have regularly issued reports on what should be the content in economics courses. The most influential report has been the *Framework for Teaching Economics: Basic Concepts* by Hansen, Bach, Calderwood, and Saunders (1977). This was further revised in 1984 and 1995 (Saunders & Gilliard, 1995). The 1995 framework listed twenty-one fundamental economic concepts (Figure 7.4). Furthermore, various economics interest groups have prepared economics instructional materials.

Standards

The national standards movement received a great deal of attention in the 1990s. The National Council on Economic Education, the main source of economic materials for K–12 teachers, produced their *Voluntary National Content Standards in Economics* (1997) with twenty standards or economic principles. These standards are available on their web site (www.economicsamerica.org). As an example, Content Standard 1 is as follows:

> *Students will understand that:*
> Productive resources are limited. Therefore, people cannot have all the goods and services they want; as a result, they must choose some things and give up others.
>
> *Students will be able to use this knowledge to:*
> Identify what they gain and what they give up when they make choices.

As you can see, this standard on scarcity and opportunity cost gives both the content to be learned and what skills are needed to apply the skill. Benchmark targets for grades 4, 8, and 12 were also listed for each standard.

Like the criticism of the geography national standards for being too complex compared to geography's older, familiar Five Themes, the 1997 economic standards drew flak for being more abstract and not as concept-based as were the standards in the earlier document, *Framework for Teaching Economics*. Some critics were worried about the lack of emphasis on an analytical perspective or on thinking about economic issues, because they wanted more emphasis on economic reasoning and skills. In addition, achieving consensus among economists was always a problem because economists do not agree on what should be recommended as economic policy or what should be emphasized in the teaching of economics.

To help overcome some of the confusing and abstract ideas about economics and the standards, experts in the field, along with the National Council on Economic Education, introduced the following simplified economic way of thinking:

1. People **choose**.
2. People's choices involve **costs**.
3. People respond to **incentives** in predictable ways.

FIGURE 7.4 1995 Economics Framework

Fundamental Economic Concepts
 1. Scarcity
 2. Opportunity Costs and Tradeoffs
 3. Productivity
 4. Economic Systems
 5. Economic Institutions and Incentives
 6. Exchange, Money, and Interdependence

Microeconomic Concepts
 7. Markets and Prices
 8. Supply and Demand
 9. Competition and Market Structure
10. Income Distribution
11. Market Failures
12. The Role of Government

Macroeconomic Concepts
13. Gross National Product
14. Aggregate Supply and Aggregate Demand
15. Unemployment
16. Inflation and Deflation
17. Monetary Policy
18. Fiscal Policy

International Economic Concepts
19. Absolute and Comparative Advantage and Barriers to Trade
20. Exchange Rates and Balance of Payments
21. International Aspects of Growth and Stability

In addition, skills in reading tables, charts, and other methods related to economic reasoning were listed, as well as broad social goals such as economic freedom.

Source: Saunders, P., Gilliard, J. (Eds.). (1995). *A framework for teaching the basic concepts with scope and sequence guidelines, K–12.* New York: Joint Council on Economic Education.

 4. People create **economic systems** that influence individual choices and incentives.
 5. People gain when they **trade** voluntarily.
 6. People's choices have consequences that lie in the **future.**

   Like other professionals, economists disagree on policy issues and definitional problems, such as who should be considered "unemployed" or how inflation rates should be figured. The 1997 standards emphasize mainstream economics, and critics with alternative viewpoints felt that their perspective was omitted. Future major changes in the discipline of economics such as behavioral economics will also influence what should be taught in the schools. But almost all economists agree that economics should get more attention in the social studies curriculum.

In turn, the states often used both the 1995 *Framework of Teaching Economics* and the *Voluntary Economic Standards* as they enumerated their own special separate state standards, which varied in detail. It has been popular to emphasize two concepts that pervade all of economics: *scarcity* and *choice*. Students can investigate by looking at opportunity costs and incentives that consider, for example, why some students do not do their homework or why the school lunchroom is always dirty. Or why do some individuals not recycle even with recycling programs in the community?

From the first to the eleventh grades, the only practical way to teach economics is through inclusion or integration of the subject in the social studies curriculum. However, the addition of state economics standards means that for state social studies testing, a few more economics questions, usually testing economic knowledge, can be included in the state test. This has encouraged more attention to economics. The economics standards do create the potential for students to see the past in a new light—for example, the critical role that slavery played in the economy of the Old South. Other subject areas such as government and geography can also benefit from the inclusion of economics.

SMALL GROUP WORK	**LOOKING AT THE ECONOMICS STANDARDS**
7.5	*Get a copy of the economics standards by downloading the file from the web site for the National Council on Economic Education (www.economicsamerica.org). Examine carefully the standards and benchmarks. How useful are the economics standards for you and your group? Are they too ambitious? Would they require a better background in economics for you and most teachers?*

■ THE TEACHING OF ECONOMICS

Economics Textbooks and Materials

Economics textbooks, which continue to be the major resource for teaching the separate economics course, have generally improved in their coverage of economic concepts. Another resource, in addition to their twenty content standards, is the National Council on Economic Education's (1997) nearly 60 pages of Economics America Materials designed to help teachers at all grade levels. Furthermore, in economics there is a wealth of information from various groups, such as the Federal Reserve or stock market firms, interested in having students come to understand their institution or point of view. The quality of such materials often varies and should be carefully evaluated by the teacher.

How important do you think it is for students to learn about the stock market?

Besides the textbook, economics classes have used simulations to try to better understand the workings of the U.S. economy in a global setting. The most popular have been the stock market simulations, but simulations (especially computer simulations) are also available on topics such as managing a business or examining monetary policy. Consumer economics or personal finance courses, mandated in some states, also use role playing, as when a young person or a young couple must develop a spending plan on a budget of $30,000 a year.

The Integration or Infusion Model

The integration or infusion model means that economic concepts need to be woven into the traditional content at the various grade levels. For example, the concept of *incentives* plays an important role in economic analysis. Students can apply this concept to why people came to the United States or the movement of any other group in the world who leave their homeland for another place. Or what incentives exist for an individual to trade? What incentives are there to recycle goods or to reduce garbage or solid waste? How important were monetary and nonmonetary incentives for historical figures such as Abraham Lincoln or Napoleon in making decisions to go to war or to make peace? What incentives are there for students to do well in school?

Typically, in the middle school, economics instruction emphasizes trade, markets, and the evolution of societies. The middle grade world history focus allows for the introduction of markets and illustrating how markets attract resources and lead the way for exploration, colonization, and social and political exchange among different groups. In the eighth grade, students can explore the development of the capitalist economy, economic incentives for westward expansion, economic conflicts such as the controversy over a central bank, the economics of slavery, and the Industrial Revolution.

In the world history/cultures course, the emphasis could be on living and working in a global economy with a concentration on labor markets, international trade, comparative advantage, economic imperialism, and technology. Students are often surprised, for example, when they take an inventory in their homes and discover where all their family's possessions, ranging from clothing to cars, came from in the world. The high school history course could focus on how people make choices and how government policy affects those choices. A consideration of migration could employ benefit/choice analysis. The changing economic roles of women and workers could also be investigated. The Great Depression and contemporary economic problems such as poverty and the environment could be discussed (Charkins, 1999). All these examples show the possible and fruitful inclusion of economics into the social studies curriculum.

Problem-Based Economic Learning

Like other social studies subject areas, economics, which uses either a deductive or an inductive method depending on the topic, can be used to develop students' skills in gathering and evaluating data and making decisions. Problem-based learning is one option. Here the problem establishes the focus for learning; learning is student-centered, often occuring in small student groups; teachers are guides as students acquire problem-solving skills and new information.

Typically, a dilemma is presented to students, the problem is identified, and resources are investigated to determine a solution. A problem can be a "High School Food Court" (Center for Project and Problem Based Learning, 1999), a situation in which students, working in teams, take on the role of the student council to decide what food concessions will be allowed. The concessions are important, as the student council earns 20 percent of the profit. In addition, competing groups of students want different menus, ranging from vegetarian to French cuisine. In this problem, twelve restaurants have applied for the right to operate. Only seven of them are able to earn a profit. Students select and defend their choice of five restaurants that will operate in the new food court.

Through investigation, research, and cooperative learning, students discover the content knowledge that is essential to solving this problem. Students fill out tables on the demand for entrees, cost data, computed total revenue, computed daily costs, and computed daily profit. In the process of solving the problem, the students study several concepts: costs, demand, economic profit, opportunity costs, scarcity, and trade-off. Although this project will take several days, students' involvement in this problem-solving experience would probably be high. Other units such as the President's Dilemma, also produced by the Center for Project and Problem Based Learning, show the difficulties that a government tries to overcome. On the school level, planning a prom or any other school activity can be explored using economic concepts.

The Internet and Media

The Internet offers great promise for the teaching of economics, especially for correcting the data obsolescence found in textbooks that are several years old, and for finding learning activities. On the Internet, one can find recent data on a wide variety of topics such as employment, international finance, and government budgets and debts. One important web site is the National Council on Economic Education's (www.nationalcouncil.org), which has a link to EconEdLink with resources to NetNewsline, CyberTeach, and EconomicsMinute. The second most important web site is EcEdWeb (ecedweb.unomaha.edu). Some of the lesson plans are free and can be downloaded, but others must be purchased. In addition, reliable data can be obtained from government agencies such as the U.S. Census Bureau (www.census.gov) on income and poverty. Labor force information from the Bureau of Labor Statistics is also available (www.bls.gov). Teachers can use media such as the newspaper section on business and television programs, as well as AOL's and other sources' up-to-date information on business and economics. All of these resources can make learning economics a thoughtful and rewarding experience for students.

■ BEHAVIORAL SCIENCES: PSYCHOLOGY, SOCIOLOGY, AND ANTHROPOLOGY

Value of the Behavioral Sciences

Psychology, with its emphasis on the individual, sociology, with its focus on group behavior, and anthropology, with its stress on culture, overlap in looking at human behavior. Advocates of these behavioral sciences all assert that their subject is needed by the many diverse students in the classroom because all students require a more powerful understanding of themselves and others in a rapidly changing world. In addition, the importance of multicultural issues means that students can gain a better understanding of their own and other cultures from knowledge of the behavioral sciences. Advocates also believe that the behavioral sciences can contribute to the solution of society's problems.

However, despite their vital importance, usually only psychology and sociology operate as separate elective subject courses, and usually only at the twelfth grade. Compared to history, geography, economics, and civics, the behavioral sciences are on the margins of the required social studies curriculum. Illustrating their status, until 1999 none of these three fields produced standards for inclusion in the social studies curriculum and now only psychology has standards. However, the NCSS's ten themes, which included "Individual Development and Identity" and "Individuals, Groups, and Institutions," drew on the behavioral sciences. But only a few states incorporated standards from the behavioral sciences. Most states concentrated solely on four subject areas: history, geography, economics, and civics/government. However, all three of the behavioral sciences can be infused or integrated into existing courses. For example, psychological concepts are incorporated as students study historical figures, and the social composition and dynamics of group action is examined when riots and revolutions are studied.

Psychology

Of the three behavioral sciences, it is clear that psychology has the lead in popularity and will probably continue to increase both as an elective and an AP course. It is estimated that 800,000 high school students are enrolled in high school psychology courses, probably partly reflecting both the interest in psychology in the media and the fascination of the American public with psychological topics such as self-help and personal advice. Psychology is also a popular undergraduate major, and college-bound high school students may be interested in exploring possible career opportunities offered by this field.

Support by the American Psychological Association (APA) encourages the teaching of psychology in the high schools. Within the American Psychological Association there is the subgroup Teachers of Psychology in Secondary Schools (TOPSS), with a newsletter and list of relevant publications. In 1999, much later than the other social studies standards, APA published its *National Standards for the Teaching of High School Psychology* (1999). This teacher-friendly document supplemented the standards with helpful sections on course scope and sequence and further resources. Note that the psychology standards, unlike the other social studies standards, were limited to the high school level. The major education publishers have textbooks and auxiliary materials available for teaching the psychology course.

Textbooks vary from those following the AP psychology exam. Those AP-oriented textbooks give the most attention to the biological bases of behavior, sensation and perception, learning, cognition, motivation and emotion, and developmental psychology. In contrast, other psychology textbooks can focus more on the students' experiences; common categories include Your Self, Your Body, Your Mental Health, and the like. For example, students could examine how tobacco marketing exploits "self-concept problems" in young people to create a favorable image of smoking.

So psychology can be taught in many different ways. In some classes, students design or use the publisher's questionnaires to find out more about moral dilemmas facing teenagers or the number of hours most teenagers are sleeping. As in other subject areas of the social studies, controversial issues such as heredity versus environment, myth versus science, psychobabble and biobunk, can also highlight the different theories and approaches in the field (behavioral, cognitive, sociobiological, and the like). In some classes, students have pretended to be Freud or Skinner and have debated their theories. Other classes have replicated experiments such as those on memory, often comparing their results with the original research and thus learning about research methods used in psychology. All of these techniques have tended to make psychology an attractive elective for many high school students. Teachers can also log on to the APA's web pages for its TOPSS program (www.apa.org/ed/topss/) for unit lesson plans and resources.

Sociology

Among the behavioral sciences, sociology is second in popularity in terms of the number of high school courses. The American Sociological Association (ASA) has been piloting teaching an AP sociology course, and when it becomes an AP course, sociology will increase in popularity as a high school elective. The course will most likely emphasize how sociologists collect, assess, and analyze data, both quantitative and qualitative. Students will become familiar with some of the excellent data resources now available on the Internet. The course includes how groups, cliques, and networks form and behave; how social order is maintained or threatened; how gender roles are changing; how race is socially constructed; and how social inequalities influence life outcomes; as well as give attention to the family, religion, education, polity, the economy, and the media. Like the American Psychological Association, the American Sociological Association has a High School Affiliate Program. Membership includes a subscription to *Contexts,* a sociology magazine designed to appeal to high school audiences.

The high school sociology textbooks emphasize how life connections provide analysis of everyday life and experiences in the United States, global connections, then and now, media and technology, things are not what they seem, and diversity.

In many high schools, the same teacher may teach both the psychology and the sociology course because of her or his interest in the behavioral sciences. A few teachers have their classes use sociological research methods such as questionnaires or interviews to find answers to research questions. Using their own classroom, school, or community as a resource allows students to apply and to test what they have learned. In summary, both psychology and sociology classes appear to have a small established role in the social studies high school curriculum.

Anthropology

Meanwhile, anthropology lacks a firm position as an elective in the high school. Only a few public and private high schools offer a separate anthropology course, and there appears to be little on the horizon to change this situation. In general, anthropology usually comes into the social studies curriculum only indirectly, particularly in the elementary school social studies program whose students study cultures such as Native Americans, Japanese, and other groups. Through the years, however, the amount of anthropology in the social studies curriculum has increased as more students study the customs, folklore, myths, and legends of different groups and as textbooks include more multiculturalism. More and better literature, plus other supplementary materials on many groups, is now available to help teachers develop an anthropological perspective from literature and other activities. Global education has also stressed understanding the culture of different groups.

So integration within existing courses appears to be the way anthropology can be incorporated into social studies courses. The trend toward including more about the everyday lives of people living long ago and today also can promote an anthropological perspective, as students learn how people lived in colonial times in Virginia or how individuals lived during California's gold rush period.

As seen from the previous examples, culture has been a major holistic concept in anthropology. However, some anthropologists believe that culture has lost much of its usefulness to describe the wide diversity within society. For example, individuals do not always follow "cultural" rules, and Japanese culture, for example, is not a single unified force. However, the academic discussions among anthropologists on the usefulness of culture as a concept have not yet influenced the K–12 curriculum.

Nevertheless, more states are requiring their teacher candidates to take an anthropology course(s) as part of their credential requirements so that anthropology can be integrated into the social studies curriculum. This also makes sense. In addition to integration into the curriculum, anthropology issues do arise in communities, as when construction crews uncover Native American artifacts or a burial ground. Native Americans do not want the burial ground disturbed, anthropologists want to study the site, and construction workers just want to get back to building a road or houses.

LARGE CLASS DISCUSSION	**CONTROVERSIAL ISSUE**

Some critics believe that teachers do not emphasize enough the role of economics in our society and in policy issues. In other words, government spending and taxation are neglected in discussions of public issues ranging from protecting endangered species to international conflicts. Do you think this is an accurate observation?

■ SUMMARY

Professional associations and educators make a strong case for geography, economics, psychology, sociology, and anthropology being vital to the social studies curriculum. Of these five academic disciplines, economics is the most firmly established in the high school because it is mandated in many states. However, the recommended economic principles and concept-based standards are different from the consumer-education emphasis taught in many economics classes. For geography state standards to be implemented, they will need to be integrated into existing courses. The apparent decline in the World Cultures course may make it more difficult for geography to be taught. The separate high school elective courses in psychology and sociology may be increasing their limited base in the high school. Anthropology is not widely taught as a separate subject. Implementation of all these disciplines into the social studies curriculum is hindered by the fact that many social studies teachers have had few or even no courses in these academic areas.

■ REFERENCES ■

American Psychological Association Task Force for the Development of National High School Psychology Standards. (1999). *National standards for the teaching of high school psychology*. Washington, DC: Author. Available at www.apa.org/ed/natlstandards.html.

Bednarz, S. (1997). Using the geographic perspective to enrich history. *Social Education, 61*(3), 139–145.

Center for Project and Problem Based Learning, Buck Institute for Education. (1999). *Problem-based economics*. Novato, CA: Author.

Charkins, J. (1999). The new approach to economics. *Social Studies Review, 38*(2), 32–35.

Environmental Systems Research Institute, Inc. (1999). *Getting to know arcview GIS: The geographic information system (GIS) for everyone*. Redlands, CA: Author.

Geography Education Standards Project. (1994). *Geography for life: National geography standards 1994*. Washington, DC: Author.

Geography Scope and Sequence Project. (2000). *A path toward world literacy: A standards-based guide to K–12 geography*. Washington, DC: National Geographic Society.

Hansen, W., Bach, G., Calderwood, J., & Saunders, P. (1977). Framework for Teaching Economics: Basic Concepts. New York, N.Y. Joint Council on Economic Education.

Marran, J. (1994). Discovering innovative curriculum models for school geography. *Journal of Geography, 93*, 9.

Munroe, S., & Smith T. (1998). *State geography standards*. Washington, DC: Thomas Fordham Foundation.

National Council on Economic Education. (1997). *Voluntary national content standards in economics*. New York: Author.

Persky, H. R., Reese, C. M., O'Sullivan, C. Y., Lazer, S., Moore, J., & Shakrani, S. (1996). *NAEP 1994 geography report card*. Washington, DC: U.S. Department of Education. National Center for Education Statistics.

Riebsame, W. E. (2000). The topography of geography: Some trends in human geographic thinking. In S. W. Bednarz & R. S. Bednarz (Eds.), *Social science of the frontier: New horizons in history and geography* (pp. 17–35). Boulder, CO: Social Science Education Consortium.

Rossi, J. A. (2000). At play with curriculum development in history. In S. W. Bednarz & R. S. Bednarz (Eds.), *Social science on the frontier: New horizons in history and geography* (pp. 52–66). Boulder, CO: Social Science Education Consortium.

Salter, C. L., Hobbs, G. L., & Salter, C. (1995). *Key to the national geography standards: Geography for Life: National geography standards*. Washington, DC: National Geographic Society.

Saunders, P., & Gilliard, J. (Eds.). (1995). *A framework for teaching the basic concepts with scope and sequence guidelines, K–12*. New York: Joint Council on Economic Education.

VanFossen, P. J. (2000). Teachers' rationales for high school economics. *Theory & Research in Social Education, 28*, 391–410.

■ WEB SITES ■

Country Listing Factbook
www.odci.gov/cia/publications/
The Central Intelligence Agency prepares factbooks on nations of the world.

Environmental Protection Agency
www.epa.gov/epahome/whereyoulive.htm
Good map resources; data on your community zip code.

Mission Geography
http://missiongeography.org
Curriculum materials linking NASA and geography.

National Council for Geographic Education
http://www.ncge.org/standards
Making the standards work for you.

National Geographic Society
www.nationalgeographic.com/resources/ngo/maps
Wide variety of maps.

U.S. Geological Survey
www.usgs.gov
Official government agency for maps.

University of Virginia
http://fisher.lib.virginia.edu
A good source of Geospatial and Statistical Data Center (GeoStat) information at the University of Virginia. Includes Census Information.

■ JOURNALS ■

Journal of Geography

Journal of Economic Education

■ ORGANIZATIONS ■

American Sociological Association
www.asanet.org
Publisher of *Teaching Sociology*

National Council for Geographic Education
www.ncge.org

National Council on Economic Education
www.ncee.net

Teachers of Psychology in Secondary Schools
www.apa.org/ed/topsshomepage.html

Chapter 8

Teaching Civic Education and Global Education

In this chapter, civic education is the main topic. *The Civic Mission of Schools'* six promising approaches to improve civic education are a focus. Viewing citizenship education from a broad perspective, we examine civic education to see if it can be taught better in the classroom, move into the local community with service learning, and finally move out to the global community. Topics in this chapter are listed below.

- Civics Standards
- NAEP 1998 Civics Report Card
- Improving Civic Education in the Classroom and School
- The Community: Local Government and Service Learning
- Global Education and Multicultural/Diversity Education

■ CIVICS STANDARDS

Different Meanings of Citizenship

Civic education is now the more popular term for what was formerly called **citizenship education,** although both terms are used interchangeably. From their earliest days, the public schools have always had as one of their major goals the teaching of citizenship education; today, that means helping *all* young people to become informed, committed citizens dedicated to the values and principles of American democracy. The term *democracy* is used in this discussion, although in some state standards you may see the terms *representative democracy, democratic government,* or *constitutional democracy.*

Citizenship education has many different meanings (Gay, 1997; Gross & Dynneson, 1991; Kaltsounis, 1997; Newmann, 1989; Parker, 1997; Van Sledright & Grant, 1991). This review is related to the previous discussions on the different approaches to civic or citizenship education (Chapter 1). Many questions need to be considered. Are we talking about active versus passive citizenship participation?

Group versus individual action? Liberal versus conservative? Global citizenship versus national citizenship? Should there be an emphasis on higher-order thinking skills so that students will become informed and thoughtful voters? Focus on a respect for and understanding of diversity? Or should students primarily be taught how to examine and respond to social issues?

In a more recent analysis of a spectrum of civic education approaches, Westheimer and Kahne (2002) outline three main conceptions of the "good" citizen: (1) personally responsible citizen—one who has good moral character; (2) participatory citizen—one who is an active member of the community; and (3) justice-oriented citizen—one who critically assesses structures. Each of these conceptions differs in the skills and values students need to become good citizens, although all three conceptions maintain that an active and informed citizenry is vital to democracy.

The need to improve civic education has resulted in more attention by organizations and policymakers (Carnegie Corporation & Circle, 2003). The report titled *The Civic Mission of Schools,* using the best available research, recommends the following six promising approaches to civic education:

1. Classroom instruction in government, history, law, and democracy
2. Discussion of current events
3. Service learning linked to formal curriculum and classroom instruction
4. Extracurricular activities, particularly student government and journalism
5. Student voice in school governance
6. Student simulations of democratic processes and procedures (voting, mock trials, legislative deliberation, diplomacy)

Despite differing perspectives, almost all social studies educators believe that the central aim of the social studies is democratic citizenship education. **Civic education** for democracy involves four main components: (1) civic knowledge; (2) civic skills; (3) civic virtues, civic values, or civic dispositions; and (4) civic participation. From the intersection of these four components comes an informed decision maker who participates in forms of political service (voting and the like) and action such as jury duty.

For our purpose in this textbook, we define citizenship as *multidimensional,* referring to the numerous roles and levels (e.g., local, state) of being an active participating citizen. This allows us to examine how civic behavior can be promoted first in the classroom, then the school, the community, the nation, and finally the world (global citizenship). It also raises the issue of balance of cultural diversity and national and global teaching.

SMALL GROUP WORK	**YOUR VIEWS ON CIVIC EDUCATION**
8.1	*Which of the three conceptions by Westheimer and Kahne (2002) of good citizenship do you support? Why? Think back on your middle school or high school experience. How many of the six promising approaches did you experience as a student?*

Why are active student councils recommended?

The Civics Course and Infusion into Other Courses

Civic education focuses on the idea that, although all students need to fulfill the duties of citizenship in a participatory democracy, democratic citizens are made, not born. Typically, democratic citizenship education in the schools focuses on four areas: content knowledge, skills, values, and participation. For teaching civic knowledge, the high schools usually require a separate, one-semester civics/government course, now most likely to be found at the twelfth grade. Probably about 75 percent of high school students have such a course and, if International Politics is added, more than 80 percent have such government courses.

The purpose of the civics/government course is to understand how our government functions at all levels—local, state, federal, international—and how students acquire the skills to participate in the civic arena. *These goals are an important first step.* Content is necessary if students are to become informed, effective, and responsible citizens. This also concurs with the first recommendation of *The Civic Mission of Schools.* However, the traditional civics course has focused on describing the structure and functions of government, particularly at the federal level. Civics classes typically rely heavily on textbooks. But more teachers and students may find a wealth of information from government web sites; see the end of the chapter for a few of the many rich possibilities.

The project "We the People: The Citizen and the Constitution," funded by the Center for Civic Education (www.civiced.org), continues to give free professional development to middle and high school educators, as well as a set of textbooks and other materials for their classrooms. It has been estimated that more than 80,000 teachers have received training by the Center for Civic Education, and surveys show that student alumni are more likely than their peers to vote, pay attention to public affairs, and participate in politics. The fact that teachers who choose to attend the professional training are self-selective may help to explain some of these positive results.

Often, little attention is given to the study of how our economic, legal, and social systems (habits of the heart, community) underpin the reality of the multi-disciplinary nature of civic life. Making decisions is an important civic skill, and critical thinking, analysis, media literacy, and the like are needed. The practice of these skills is influenced by one's own values and understanding of history and global interdependence.

Many states have requirements, although many are vague, for the schools to foster civic development throughout all of the grades. Because course requirements are often not outlined, the teaching of civics generally takes an integrated approach, with the exception of the one high school civics course. In the elementary grades, civic education usually starts with a focus on holidays: Independence Day, Veterans Day, and Martin Luther King, Jr.'s birthday. Then civic education moves into including the heroes and heroines of the past as exemplars of civic character. By the middle and high schools, most of the civics standards are presented in history courses, as students study the American Revolution, the Constitution, the Bill of Rights, struggles for voting suffrage, and the civil rights movement. In world history, students encounter the origins of modern democracy. Along with content learning, there is in civic education a strong value component, a belief that students should have a clear sense of their rights and responsibilities for the common good.

Civics Standards

The National Standards for Civics and Government (1994) were produced by the Center for Civic Education in California. This is an important nonprofit organization that has produced and continues to create civics projects and curricular materials. They are probably best known for their popular *We the People . . . The Citizen and the Constitution,* a study of the Constitution and the Bill of Rights that has been implemented in all fifty states. *We the People . . . Project Citizen* is their popular middle school project that promotes participation in state and local government. For each program there is a textbook set, professional development resources for teachers, and state and national competitions.

The civics standards were organized into three main chronological blocks: K–4, 5–8, and 9–12 standards. The middle school and senior high school standards were organized into the following five important questions:

1. What are civic life, politics, and government?
2. What are the foundations of the American political system?
3. How does the government established by the Constitution embody the purposes, values, and principles of American democracy?
4. What is the relationship of the United States to other nations and to world affairs?
5. What are the roles of the citizen in American democracy?

From these broad questions, subordinate questions can be derived, such as the following:

- What are the purposes of rules and laws and how can you evaluate them?
- Why is it important to limit the power of government?
- Why do conflicts among fundamental values such as liberty and equality or individual rights and the common good arise and how might those conflicts be resolved?
- What are the rights of citizens and how should the scope and limits of those rights be determined?
- What are the personal and civic responsibilities of citizens in American constitutional democracy and when and why might tensions arise between them? (Branson, 2001)

Note that the civics standards were organized by questions, not topics. They stress a knowledge of democratic principles, values, and political issues. In general, the civics standards reflect mainstream ideas of citizens' rights and freedom and were accepted without major controversy. However, a few critics thought they were too conservative for not stressing more political participation and responsibility to the public good. Although the document was 179 pages long, it was well organized in an outline format.

When it came time for the states to produce their own standards, most found that the civics standards were easier to work with than the geography or economics standards. Therefore, in most cases, the national civics standards were readily incorporated into most state standards. Perhaps the civics standards were also more familiar and better understood by legislators and the public. In addition, the civics standards served as the basis of the NAEP 1998 Civics Report Card and the GED (General Education Diploma) examination.

■ NAEP 1998 CIVICS REPORT CARD

Results: What Students Know

The National Assessment of Educational Progress (NAEP) released the results of the *NAEP 1998 Civics Report Card for the Nation* in 1999. Most educators felt that the results were dismal and disheartening. Thirty percent of eighth graders and 35 percent of twelfth graders, or about one-third of all students, lacked even the most basic knowledge of the system in which as citizens they are supposed to participate. Only about one-quarter scored at or above the proficient level. Educators and other commentators came to many conclusions. All agree that improvement is needed. Some believe the results show there is a widespread lack of adequate state curriculum requirements, teacher preparation, and instruction in civics and government.

The Center for Civic Education claimed that in civic education there is an emphasis on the structure of institutions and current events without providing a framework of democratic values and principles. In addition, the Center for Civic Education commented that there is a lack of sequential development of the subject, with use of inadequate methods. Others believe that too many teachers have been seduced into thinking that teaching history "can do it all" and that history will somehow inform our students' civic literacy and inspire their civic involvement. Still others believe there should be *more* instruction on citizens' responsibilities as well as their rights.

The civics results showed that non-minority students had higher average scores than their Asian/Pacific Islander peers, followed by African Americans and their Hispanic counterparts. Higher levels of parents' education, along with frequency of discussion of schoolwork at home, were also associated with higher test scores. This reinforces the view that citizenship education does not take place only in the schools. Family influences, the media, students' characteristics such as gender and ethnic or racial background, and the local community all play a role in civic development.

Teacher Methods

According to the NAEP civics report, the highest percentage of students were taught on a weekly basis through "traditional" instructional activities such as using the textbook, completing worksheets, and hearing a teacher's lecture. Only 34 percent in the eighth grade participated in group activities or projects on at least a weekly basis. When small group activities were employed more often, even if only once or twice a month, the students who had group experiences outscored students who never or hardly ever participated in small group activities. Students who were in classes using the Internet once or twice a month also achieved higher average scores than students who never used the Internet. These results support calls for the increased use of small group activities and the Internet. Teachers should avoid teaching only rote facts about dry procedures, a strategy that is unlikely to benefit students and could actually alienate them from politics.

IEA Civic Knowledge and Engagement at Age 14

Scores released by the International Association for the Evaluation of Educational Achievement (IEA) in 2001 showed that U.S. students scored high on a "knowledge of civics" test taken by 14-year-olds in twenty-eight democratic countries, well above the average (Torney-Purta, Lehmann, Oswald, & Schulz, 2001). In addition, U.S. students scored high on their expected participation in political activities (voting). The survey also showed that U.S. teens were more likely than those in most other nations to trust their government and newspapers, express positive attitudes toward immigrants, and support women's political rights.

Promising also was that 85 percent of ninth-grade students reported being encouraged by teachers to make up their own minds about issues, and about two-thirds reported being encouraged by teachers to discuss political or social issues about which people have different opinions (Baldi, Perie, Skidmore, & Greenberg, 2001, p. 34). This one survey raises some hope about the status of civic education among U.S. youth. Discouraging was the continued gap on higher achievement between non-minority and Asian American students compared to Hispanic and African American students.

Some organizations and individuals, however, remain concerned that the health of our democratic system is in jeopardy and have mounted campaigns to promote civic education. To help students become more involved, some social studies teachers have their senior classes participate in **First Vote,** a Close Up Foundation project that registers voters and informs citizens about the importance of voting. Some political scientists examining the previous NAEP civics results indicate there is not a decline in knowledge: It simply has been low for years. They found wide variations in knowledge about specific topics. Twelfth graders do have a good understanding of criminal and civil justice and the general rights of citizens, perhaps partly due to television (Niemi & Junn, 1998). Students also have a good grasp of federalism, at least in terms of the ability to connect the correct level of government with various administrative responsibilities. Weaknesses, however, were that students knew much less about political parties and lobbying and, in terms of skills, found it difficult to interpret short excerpts or data in charts and graphs.

What is new and alarming, however, is that, compared to a previous generation, today's youth express more cynicism about the political process (see Sample Classroom Episode). They are less likely to be engaged in voting and related political activities such as helping in a political campaign or writing letters to government officials. On the positive side, young people are now more heavily involved in community service. Recommendations to improve civic education abound and are the focus of the next sections.

SAMPLE CLASSROOM EPISODE

COMBATING CYNICISM

1. While walking down the hall, Mia Gomez, the assistant principal, overhears Julian Muller, the social studies teacher, say to his class, "It doesn't do any good to try to change city hall." Mia wonders if she should speak to Julian about this remark. Should his remark go unchallenged? Doesn't it make students think that their civic efforts are in vain? Or would she be interfering in academic freedom? What do you think Mia should do?

2. In Owen Gordon's class, Jack, a student, says, "It doesn't do any good to become involved in politics. Nobody listens to the average person." Should Owen as a teacher try to combat this cynicism? If so, what examples could he use? Should teachers try to promote trust and interest in the political process? Or should students remain unchallenged about their views on the political process?

These two exercises indicate that teaching is a value-laden enterprise. One way to combat cynicism is to examine it. Students can investigate how many young voters vote. How serious is the problem of voter turnout in the United States? In other nations?

SMALL GROUP WORK	WHY DO YOU THINK THE NAEP CIVICS SCORES WERE LOW?
8.2	*Why should the NAEP civics scores be a source of concern? In light of the increased cynicism about government, how can teachers promote more positive images of our government? Or will students as young adults become even more disillusioned later when exposed to the real political scene?*

■ IMPROVING CIVIC EDUCATION IN THE CLASSROOM AND SCHOOL

Classroom Citizenship: Creating a Cooperative, Engaged Classroom

It is important to know how students behave, feel, and think. To encourage democratic dispositions, thinking, and engagement in students, all teachers have to consider the climate and activities of their classrooms. In particular, attention needs to be given to **engagement:** the attention, interest, and effort that students expend in the work of learning. *Engagement* is students' involvement with the class. To measure engagement, studies have had students answer the following questions for a given class: How often do you try as hard as you can? How often do you complete your assignments for this class? How often do you pay attention in this class? How often do you feel bored in this class? In more sophisticated studies, students have been supplied with beepers and, when paged, reported what was on their minds, how well they were concentrating, and the like.

Unfortunately, although students may sit quietly in class, many are actually thinking about themselves, other school activities, and external issues such as their family life, jobs, and social lives. Lack of or limited engagement in class adversely affects student achievement and may lead to dysfunctional behavior. Studies show that Hispanic, African American, and at-risk students are particularly likely to be disengaged. Lack of student engagement not only affects the students but also wears down teachers, who become demoralized. In particular, the subjects of social studies and English have been found to have more students disengaged than mathematics, foreign languages, and science (Yair, 2000). More active, group-based instruction in these classes attracted and maintained student attention, whereas teacher-centered activities decreased engagement, with students alienated from instruction almost half of the time. The highest engagement for students occurs when they work in labs and in groups. Higher-achieving students and Asian and non-minority students were also more likely to be engaged. What do these findings mean for civic education?

The disengagement of social studies students is a serious, pervasive problem, particularly in the U.S. high school (Newmann, 1992), but it may vary with different classes. Teachers frequently talk about their "best" and "worst" class. Within a given class there is undoubtedly variety in the degree of student engagement. Even though most of the class may be bored, a few students can be interested and involved. Conversely, the majority of the class can be engaged while just a few students are disengaged. Disengagement occurs when students perceive the classroom to be unchallenging, irrelevant, or too academically demanding. Newmann (1992) believes that the main sources of student disengagement are meaningless, low-level schoolwork and poor interpersonal relationships between teachers and students.

What suggestions have been made to break the pattern of student disengagement and promote a better climate and learning in the classroom? Let us look at the following recommendations. Some of these suggestions are broad enough to apply to all social studies classes, whereas others are targeted specifically at the teaching of civics. A few involve some simple psychological ideas.

Let Students Get to Know One Another

Almost as serious as the teacher not knowing the names of all of the students at the end of a semester is when students do not know the names of their fellow classmates. Of course, there are variations within classes on this matter. In some honors and AP classes or where tracking takes place, students more or less know one another from other classes. It also depends on the size of the school, with smaller schools more likely to be friendlier. Check the first day or so to see whether students can name five to seven different students in the class. If the students do not know one another, small group work is an important start for them to get to know some of their fellow students. Team-building activities, which at first may involve a nonacademic task such as naming their favorite sports, films, or music, may help to make each group feel comfortable in working together (Chapter 4). The group may develop their own team logo or identification.

When debriefing students about what their small groups have discussed, also be sure to use the names of the groups' reporters (and change this assignment for every task) so that gradually students can identify names and faces of members of other groups. This means the teacher must learn the names of students as quickly as possible. Greeting them daily, plus using any other aids such as photos with the name below, is helpful for quickly learning the names of all the students in your class. Teachers can use their cameras with good results by taking pictures of small groups and labeling them with the names of the students.

Basic Rules and Their Rationale

From the first day on, discuss in clear terms your basic rules for the classroom and why you have these rules. Typically these are broad, such as, "Both the students and the teacher will be treated with respect," and "No one is to interfere with the learning of others." Usually these rules are written out on a syllabus, and you will need to reinforce them during the semester. It is especially important that the rules for respect be observed in discussing controversial issues and during small group work when students disagree or are not compatible. To be fully engaged, students need to feel secure.

Recommended Practices

The Civic Mission of Schools recommends that teachers incorporate discussion of current local, national, and international issues and events into the classroom, particularly those that young people view as important to their lives. In these discussions, students should feel comfortable about speaking from a variety of perspectives. This points to the importance of having a cooperative, engaged classroom, as discussed in the previous section. In addition, teachers should use high-quality news media to inform and address current issues.

A focus on key **concepts** such as individual rights is appropriate, rather than presenting a mass of information. **Case studies,** especially of legal disputes (law-focused education), are valuable for enabling students to examine key concepts such as what rights citizens have to bear arms or exercise freedom of speech in a given situation. In a similar manner, the use of **literature,** especially works that show how individuals exemplify civic virtues in difficult situations, can bring civic education to life. **Cooperative learning** can also foster skills of working together with others, an essential participatory civic skill. More specific programs for the development of decision-making skills and active learning in civic education are as follows.

Issues-Centered Civic Education

Advocates of issues-centered education see value in focusing on current political issues. This approach is appropriate for teaching civics, with its emphasis on the development of decision-making skills. Oliver and Shaver's (1966) jurisprudential inquiry model centers on the deliberation of controversial public issues. This model presumes that in our society individuals differ in their views and that democratic values often are in conflict in political, social, or economic cases. For example, asking whether the Internet or music should be censored indicates a conflict between freedom of speech versus the community standards, between minority rights and majority rule. Asking whether we should have charter schools or all-male or all-female schools puts many different values in conflict: individual choice versus access to public education, and the segregation of students versus choice.

To study these values, Oliver and Shaver (1966) and Newmann (1970) encouraged students to carefully and rationally follow the series of steps that are outlined in Figure 8.1. Often students find that there is not clearly a "right" answer, partly because some members of the class have different values.

FIGURE 8.1 The Values/Issues Center Approach

1. Identify the problem or issue.

2. Clarify the values question(s).

3. Gather and evaluate the facts about the problem.

4. Suggest several solutions to the problem. Deliberate on the good and bad consequences of each solution. Think in terms of both short-term and long-term consequences. What are the possible positive and negative consequences of the proposed policies?

5. Decide the best solution among the solutions proposed.

Again, to resolve these differences, it is necessary for students to negotiate their differences through open discussion on important political issues (Hess, 2000). Students need the skills to be able to participate in such discussions or deliberations. At the same time, this approach presumes that U.S. students share basic values (the "American creed"), an important requirement for successful discussion. These basic values cement the nation together and include, among other things, due process of the law, respect for others, free access to information, and respect for the value of rational thought (Shaver, 1985). These key values are usually taught in the study of the Declaration of Independence, the Constitution, and key judicial landmark decisions.

Our basic values mean that, for effective deliberation, students must share or learn to share certain values and procedures that must be respected as students try to clarify and resolve the public issues through discussion. They must respect the differences of other viewpoints and treat one another with civility. These shared values are critical to the survival of U.S. society. Teacher skill in a variety of methods—debates, small group discussions, mock elections, role plays, and leading discussions—is vital (Chapters 3 and 4) in enabling the class and the teacher to go through the various steps in value or issues analysis.

What Issues Should Be Studied?

What issues should be used for deliberation? Ideally, the issue should be of high interest to students without being too abstract, involve some tension between democratic values, and point to good current curriculum resources such as newspapers, web sites (see web sites at the end of the chapter), or court cases. The issue also should be controversial and invite student engagement. In many cases, it will be multidisciplinary, combining history, the social sciences, and the humanities.

For a start, a teacher may want to use a prepared issue from the National Issues Forums (www.nifi.org). National Issues Forums is a nonpartisan organization that identifies critical issues ranging from health care to racial and ethnic tensions. Each of their issue booklets asks readers to consider different options for acting on an issue. This organization's booklets on various issues outline necessary background material plus a clear statement of the issue or problem, what should be done (several choices), why this course of action, and what critics say. The current issues booklets can be downloaded at no charge. A related video is inexpensive.

Some teachers use issues from magazines such as *Newsweek* or *Time*. Persistent topics include environment and population, national and international security, technology and society, the global economy, and human rights. More specific issues could be capital punishment, genetically modified food, gun control, and affirmative action.

In other cases, the issue could be a school-based problem, such as, What can be done to make the lunchtime experience more pleasant for everyone? Local community problems also can be worthwhile. For data on these problems, the Internet offers many resources on public issues such as the Current Events section of the Awesome Library site (www.awesomelibrary.org/Classroom/Social_Studies/Current_Events/Current_Events.html). The Policy.com web site is also good (http://policy.com/). Examining web sites gives students the opportunity to evaluate and use the very diverse sources of information as well as the information from the many government institutions such as Congress and various agencies.

But who really gets to engage in controversial issues? Along with NAEP's *Civics Report Card* is IEA's civic education study. Research indicates that the content in civics textbooks is about the same throughout the United States. Nevertheless, students in urban schools serving low-income families were less likely to experience varied instructional strategies and a democratic school climate compared to schools with students from more affluent families. This can result in students in different school environments ending up with different ideas about democracy, national identity, and diversity (Hahn & Torney-Purta, 1999).

Value of Issues Approach in Civic Education

Teachers should be encouraged to use controversial public issues in the civic education classroom. In this approach, content and skills are tightly interwoven. Reviewing the limited research on issues-centered instruction, Hahn (1996) felt that students who discussed controversial issues and considered multiple viewpoints within an open classroom climate were more likely to become interested in the political arena, to develop a greater sense of political efficacy and confidence, and to become more knowledgeable. Teaching controversial issues can both reinforce commitment to the basic values and help students learn that in civic life often you have to choose between values.

However, there are concerns about this approach. Leming (1998) and others believe that we are overselling the possible benefits of issues analysis and feel that more modest approaches are needed to avoid frustration of both students and their teachers. Too often students with varied reading levels do not have the basic skills to interpret material such as political cartoons or editorials and thus do not have sufficient background to understand an issue now or in later life.

Teaching Controversial Issues

Perhaps one reason for not putting more emphasis on the deliberation of public issues and current events is that some social studies teachers may be concerned about how students and the community will react to the teaching of a controversial issue. In particular, will they be accused of advocating or indoctrinating one point of view or position? Or have they made a negative comment about a student's beliefs? Five teachers in New Mexico were suspended or disciplined for expressing antiwar views on Iraq. Two of these teachers faced dismissal for refusing to remove antiwar signs from their classrooms. The district said that its policy requires teachers to present a balance of viewpoints and to store material used to advocate one side of an issue once the lesson is completed.

This fear can be a real headache because in many schools it is not always clear to social studies teachers or the public what academic freedom teachers have to teach controversial issues. Often a school does not have a written policy, although national organizations such as the National Council for the Social Studies and the American Library Association have issued policy statements on the teaching of controversial issues. It is important to find out if your school or district has a policy protecting a teacher's right to present controversial issues.

Another factor is the teacher's own value system. More traditional social studies teachers may give little attention to either controversial issues or current events, believing that their main purpose is to cover the basic curriculum. They feel a need for coverage and do not want to take time away from what they regard as the essentials. Many others, while agreeing that controversial issues are important, also believe that their role is to be the "neutral" or "balance" facilitator. These teachers aim to ensure that various positions get a fair hearing. They, as teachers, should not indicate their own point of view as they guide their students in discussing controversial issues. These teachers believe that far more students will be willing to freely examine the issues if the teacher does not appear to be espousing a particular point of view. To avoid closing down discussion, some teachers state their position only at the end of the discussion. Critics of this neutral position comment that observant students usually can detect the teacher's position based on how she or he responds to certain student comments, and further comment that this type of teacher may not be a good role model if she or he is seen as being unwilling to publicly give his or her point of view on a given issue.

In turn, those who state their own position on a controversial issue can be arranged along a spectrum that ranges from making their position known but allowing other positions to be discussed, to indoctrinating and even cutting off discussion of other points of view. The teacher must indicate that her or his stand is *only one* opinion and that other viewpoints exist. Using a variety of sources usually addresses this problem of keeping a balance. Students and parents are justifiably upset with indoctrination, especially if the teacher adopts a "preaching," absolutist teaching style. Disputes can get carried to the principal or even the school board if other points of view were not on the table. These guidelines for allowing a variety of opinions in the classroom also apply to inviting speakers or using literature from organizations.

However, the net result of these concerns is that some social studies teachers hesitate to set up political issues to be studied, although this is what students will need to do as citizens. In small school districts, some tenured teachers and the department chair may even tell new teachers to get tenure before dealing too much with controversial issues. A few schools may also tend to discourage students from participating in political campaigns and issues because the school wants to project an image of being nonpartisan.

Teaching of Religion

One extremely controversial area for teachers is the teaching of religion. Yet religion has played an important role in the history of the United States, as it still does today, and this is true for other nations as well. The following are general recommendations for respecting beliefs in a neutral manner in the inclusive classroom, in which more of our increasingly diverse student population has a wide range of beliefs.

- Be academic, not devotional.
- Strive for student awareness of religions, but do not press for student acceptance of any religion.
- Expose students to the diversity of religious views, but do not impose any particular view.

In addition, avoid simulation or role playing of religious ceremonies, beliefs, or practices. In particular, teachers should be careful not to indoctrinate students into their own religious beliefs or nonbeliefs. Although cartoons are often quite engaging and students need to learn to interpret them, be judicious in the use of cartoons of different religions. For more information, go to the U.S. Department of Education guidelines on religious expression in public schools (www.ed.gov/inits/religion).

SMALL GROUP WORK	SHOULD YOU ADVOCATE YOUR POSITION?
8.3	*In discussing current events and controversial issues, should you give your point of view? Why or why not? How important do you think it is to incorporate controversial issues into the social studies curriculum?*

Simulations

The use of simulations for teaching civic education was highly recommended by *The Civic Mission of Schools*. In particular, simulations in which students must work in groups are encouraged so that they can experience different perspectives on what should be done and what action the group should take. Examples of such simulations are the Model UN format, in which small groups represent given nations such as Turkey or Indonesia. Here students can practice the skills of diplomacy. More common have been simulations of legislative deliberation, such as the Constitutional Convention or the actions of diplomats in the summer of 1914. In some classes, each student in a six-week simulation unit on Congress has to present a bill and try to get it passed through Congress, which is organized into committees. As a result of this simulation, students can better understand how Congress really works.

Civic Education Is the Responsibility of the Whole School

This broad citizenship goal is not limited to social studies classes, because citizenship education is also learned from daily life both inside and outside of the school. Students need opportunities to apply civic behavior. It is the responsibility of the whole school to teach students how to participate effectively in a democratic society. In physical education classes and team sports, good citizenship is shown when students play fairly. In all classes, good citizenship is displayed when students respect the opinions of those with whom they may not agree. Good citizenship can be demonstrated by the behavior of students in the halls or during lunchtime when they show civility for one another instead of making hurtful racist, sexist, or homophobic comments or other put-downs toward others.

Student Council and Other School Organizations

In many schools, the student council functions mainly as a popularity contest with its main focus on elections. But giving students as much opportunity as possible to make decisions and to see the consequences of their actions promotes civic behavior and helps to improve the school climate. Some student councils have worked successfully to create peer courts or other judicial bodies (see Sample Classroom

Episode). Other school organizations, from the computer club to service organizations, can also give students opportunities to practice decision making, one of the most important skills in civic behavior.

SAMPLE CLASSROOM EPISODE

TEEN COURTS FOR YOUTH

Juvenile courts were established to mitigate the harshness when youth were formerly tried as adults. One of the differences of a juvenile court was the lack of a trial by jury; instead, a presiding judge acted in the best interest of the juvenile. Today juvenile courts are changing. From the public there is growing demand to treat juvenile offenders, especially in violent cases, as adults. Experiments include having a juvenile court judge leave his or her courtroom to go to a local high school and preside over teen court. This is an alternative for young people charged for the first time with a minor offense. The judge presides and the defendant(s) tells his or her story to a jury, which is a random pool of volunteer high school students from the same school. In other communities, the volunteer high school jurors go to the courthouse to hear cases and to get credit for their community service requirement.

Some middle school and high schools also have a trial by jury format, in some cases staffed by members of the student council. In the following scenario, the defendant is an eighth-grade girl, Charlene, who slapped another girl, Samantha, in the face.

Student prosecutor attorney: Did you slap Samantha in the face on October 10?

Charlene: Yes, I did, but it was because she was telling lies about me.

Student prosecutor attorney: Don't you know it is against the school rules to hit any student?

Charlene: I know, but I got angry. I just did it.

Student prosecutor attorney: Have you ever hit anyone else at school?

Charlene: No. Never.

Student prosecutor attorney: What do you think should happen about your hitting Samantha?

Charlene: Maybe I should say I am sorry.

Final Result: The jury, after hearing from witnesses who saw the slapping incident, decided that Charlene should apologize to Samantha and as a penalty have ten hours of cleanup work around the school.

Feedback: This was a relatively easy case to decide. More troublesome are cases in which the evidence is not clear. For example, a student denies doing something. In what circumstances do student courts work best? What might students learn from such experiences? Do you think teen jurors would be too hard or soft on their own peers?

The Civic Mission of Schools also encourages student participation in school governance. Students do understand that ultimate educational authority rests with teachers, administrators, and school boards. However, students can be provided the opportunities to discuss school policies, be heard respectfully, and work with others to address school problems. Along with addressing specific issues, they can serve as representatives on committees and school boards and enact school constitutions. Journalism is also recommended, as well as an athletic program that promotes confidence, fair play, and teamwork over competition.

■ THE COMMUNITY: LOCAL GOVERNMENT AND SERVICE LEARNING

Local Government Emphasis

Moving beyond the classroom and the school, we reach the community. One important recommendation for high school teachers is to give far more attention to local government—to avoid duplicating the dull factual description of the three main branches of government covered in the standard government textbook. The rationale for this approach is that local government is close and concrete and is less abstract than considering what is happening in the federal or state government. As adult citizens, students will be more likely to participate at the local level. Most students also are more oriented to the "here and now" than to the far away. In addition, local speakers from governmental agencies and political groups are more readily available. Students can also more easily visit courtrooms and other government offices as well as talk to and interview residents and their own parents.

With a local government emphasis, students can approach real issues that impinge on their lives. Students can realize that concerns in their neighborhood can be addressed and action can be taken to improve the situation. Students have successfully investigated everything at the local level from homelessness to traffic problems. Students have become far more involved in political issues as well as gained knowledge and skills. Other topics with local impact include recreation, the economy, crime and safety, the environment, diversity, and human relations education.

This local approach to teaching government requires a teacher who is familiar with the issues and problems of the local community. This approach puts more responsibility on the teacher to use up-to-date local resources as the class moves away from the textbook. It helps when a teacher lives in the same community as the students. Often the teacher who focuses on local government is interested in local politics and can use this personal strength to the best advantage.

Service Learning

In recent years, to improve civic behavior, states and local districts have called for and in some cases made student requirements for **service** or **community service**. The increasing popularity of schools' sponsoring service or community service reflects the grave concern that more has to be done to teach youth to participate in a democratic society. More than half of all high schools use service learning in their curriculum. More than 200 teacher

Do you think a "Get Out to Vote" campaign will help students? What additional steps could students take?

education programs use service learning in their courses. In addition, policymakers such as those behind *The Civic Mission of Schools* view service learning as a means of engaging today's youth with both academic and civic values. According to *The Civic Mission of Schools,* service learning should have the following characteristics:

- Improve academic achievement
- Meet academic content standards
- Meet *real* community needs as defined by the community
- Pursue political responses to serious public issues
- Improve self-esteem

Students need to have an active role in choosing and designing projects. Students also should have opportunities to reflect on the service work. Other advocates use the four *R*s—respect, reciprocity, relevance, and reflection—as the basis of service learning.

Some advocates stress different aspects of service learning. According to Wade and Saxe (1996), a reflective, thoughtful seminar and enough time spent in the service activity are critical. Furthermore, according to Wade and Saxe, service learning should be focused through a social action perspective. Students should question the status quo and revitalize our democratic society while at the same time responding compassionately to those presently in need. In other words, a thoughtfully organized community service experience enhances what teachers have chosen as the objectives and curriculum in their classrooms. In more practical terms, Niemi and Chapman (1998) state that service learning occurs when a student gives an oral report to the class, writes a report, or receives a grade or portion of a grade for the service learning—in other words, when in some manner the service learning is incorporated into the classroom.

In contrast, *community service* is a broader term, meaning to help those in need. Sometimes it is called volunteer service. Focusing on helping others, community service is not necessarily tied to what is going on in a particular classroom. It has very broad appeal, with every recent president and other officials having advocated that all Americans, including students, do community or volunteer service. Service learning focuses on increasing civic skills, but the goal of community service is social responsibility or personal or character development.

The Constitutional Rights Foundation and Close Up Foundation have developed the following helpful framework for service learning:

1. Defining and Assessing Your Community: What is your community?
2. Choosing and Researching a Problem: What is the problem?
3. Examining Policy: What is policy? Who makes it? Does the policy work? Students look at government, business, media, and nonprofits.
4. Exploring Options: What can you do?
5. Taking Action: What will you do?

You can see the possibilities of achieving real learning following such an approach.

Implementation of Service Learning

In actual practice, however, because of the wide diversity of theories and activities that are found under the umbrella of service learning and community service, it is often difficult to see the distinction between service learning and community service. The most common requirement is that each student has to devote a certain number of hours to a service learning or community project. Often a student has a choice of what project he or she wishes to pursue, but in other cases, the whole class focuses on one problem such as the environment. Activities range from tutoring, working with senior citizens, helping to improve the environment, and working on health projects. Eco-restoration projects have been popular. In the health area, some students have created public awareness campaigns on the importance of child immunization or worked with a local hospital to put on a health fair with free blood pressure checks and pointing out other health issues facing the community. Classes have designed a web site for a nonprofit organization and kept it current. Other classes have made videos that nonprofit agencies can use for publicity. For this project, the nonprofit organization has to agree on the worthwhileness of the project, as well as blur the faces of clients appearing on the tape to protect their privacy. The quality of the service learning experience probably varies enormously from one class to another and from one person to another, even within the same class.

Unless there is a coordinator for service learning, most social studies teachers are responsibile for implementing the service learning requirement, although service learning is not limited to social studies teachers. However, often the service learning requirement occurs in a civics/government course. If a choice is given, teachers provide their students with a list of possible alternatives, or the class discusses what project the whole class will focus on. If the student is not responsible for making the contacts with the community organizations or government agencies, the teacher makes these contacts and supervises the field experience, even if an honor system about reporting hours is usually observed. If only one agency is involved, such as a nursing home or a soup kitchen, the teacher still needs time to foster communication, negotiation, and mutual respect between the school and the agency.

The school schedule is usually not flexible enough to allow students time away from their regular classes for service learning. In effect, service learning becomes an activity performed by the students after school hours. Because many high school students are working and their schedules are tight, students and their parents have complained that service learning can be, in fact, unpaid peon labor unless it is carefully structured. Volunteer service is not really voluntary when it is mandated for graduation.

In many schools, students who finish "their hours" give a brief report on their service experiences when they complete their projects, regardless of what unit the class is studying. Almost all students express satisfaction with their service learning or community participation. You can hope they genuinely liked their service experience, but it is not always clear if they were more interested in getting a good grade. However, satisfaction appears especially obvious when students perform a concrete service, perhaps a one-shot environmental project such as cleaning up the local creek or sorting clothes or distributing canned goods for an annual Thanksgiving food drive.

Teachers like these oral service reports because they encourage laggard students to do the service learning. Often all students who give an oral report get a high grade. A rubric is not used to carefully evaluate the experience. Other students who did not complete the project in time, or did not hand in reflective written reports on their service experiences, receive below-average grades for their service experience.

Using data from a national survey, Niemi and Chapman (1998) looked at the relationship between ninth- through twelfth-grade students' participation in community service and their civic development. They concluded that community service activity was associated with greater political knowledge, more frequent conversation with parents about the news, greater perceived participation skills, and a higher sense of internal political efficacy. But community service in general did not seem to promote several other factors associated with good citizenship, such as tolerance of diversity. Niemi and Chapman suggested that the *type* of community service might be a factor in ascribing benefits or lack of benefits of community service toward civic development.

Niemi and Chapman (1998) also pointed out the importance of the *amount* of time given to community service by the students. Those who had performed thirty-five or more hours of work had the most positive relationships between service learning and civic development. This may mean that smaller amounts of service have little relationship to civic development. This makes sense; the more hours spent may make a difference. However, the requirement of a substantial number of hours does not seem prevalent in most schools, partly because too many hours of community service does not appeal to students or their parents. Discouraging was the fact that when service learning was incorporated into the curriculum, it did *not* noticeably improve students' civic development.

Teachers need to be very careful, when planning service or community learning, to ensure that it increases civic behaviors. This raises the question of how much choice students should have in doing service or community learning. Teachers also should not oversell what service learning and community service can do so that there is not a backlash against it as being ineffective. In particular, service learning appears to have promoted much goodwill among those doing the actual service learning, but it has been more difficult to provide evidence that it has helped the recipients. Measuring the perceived results of service learning has been difficult. Service learning is a promising practice, but it does not guarantee that students will become better citizens.

SMALL GROUP WORK	**DECISIONS ABOUT SERVICE LEARNING**
8.4	*Would you use service learning in your classroom? Why or why not? Should students have a choice as to what type of service or community service they want to perform? In some credential education classes, a community or service learning experience is required, often in a different ethnic or racial setting than that of the prospective teacher. Is this a good idea?*

■ GLOBAL EDUCATION AND MULTICULTURAL/ DIVERSITY EDUCATION

Moving further away from the classroom, the school, and the local community, we come to the global focus. Social studies teachers and teachers in other subject areas have tried to teach democratic values, knowledge, and skills so that students will have the capacity and the will to become effective, participating U.S. citizens. As noted before, U.S. social studies teachers teaching civic education vary in terms of how much they stress cultural transmission or reform ideals to improve the gap between our ideals and reality. Thus there are disagreements about the kind of civic behavior that is most desirable in students.

But along with being citizens of the United States, we are all citizens of the world. This is often called *multidimensional citizenship, universal citizenship,* or *multicultural citizenship,* for citizenship can no longer be confined within national boundaries. An important issue is teaching a balance between national and global identification, and teachers differ on how much attention they give to global education.

First, let us clarify terms. **Global education** is about the cultures and people of other lands. Viewing problems from a global perspective involves the following philosophy:

1. As global citizens, we share a responsibility to solve the world's complex global problems.
2. We are all interdependent members of the family of humankind and therefore need to understand and appreciate people of cultures different from our own.
3. We are all stewards of our planet, our home.

Other definitions of global education emphasize cross-cultural awareness, the commonalities in cultures that transcend diversity, the world as an interconnected system, shared human values and choices, knowledge of global systems, and a need for analytical skills and participation strategies (Merryfield & Remy, 1995; Merryfield & White, 1996). Other definitions emphasize an appreciation of other cultures, understanding today's global issues and conditions, and an awareness of human choices to actively engage in social participation and action in global issues. These global viewpoints point out that young people need to be willing to address global problems and have an ability to work with others. Another way is to look at global issues and problems in global education, as shown in Figure 8.2. Along with learning content objectives and understanding origins and past patterns of worldwide issues, students in global education also have to recognize concepts such as stereotyping, overgeneralization, and recognizing different points of view.

Multicultural/Diversity Education

Notice the parallels between a global perspective and **multicultural education.** Global education looks at the multiple worldviews and cultures beyond the United States. Multicultural education highlights the racial and ethnic diversity within the United States. Multiculturalism has many definitions. Some stress cultural pluralism, social justice empowerment, and the incorporation of multiple perspectives in the curriculum. In addition, multicultural education can be grouped into four clusters: (1) curriculum reform, with the incorporation of multiple perspectives in the curriculum; (2) equity pedagogy, stressing that *all* students can learn; (3) a reduction of racial and cultural prejudice; and (4) the belief that societal change is necessary (Bennett, 2001).

In addition to race and ethnicity, the definition of **diversity** includes gender, sexual orientation, physical differences, religion, and socioeconomic status. The emphasis on diversity partly reflects the concern that multicultural education has typically engaged race and ethnicity more energetically and sympathetically than gender, culture, or class. Feminists especially have been aware that one-half of the U.S. and world population has been neglected or put on the margins in the social studies curriculum (Asher & Crocco, 2001).

FIGURE 8.2 Theme Issues in Global Education

Peace and Security
War, peacekeeping

Development/Economic Issues
Poverty, population

Environmental Issues
Pollution, extinction

Human Rights
Refugees, persecution

Now multicultural definitions include the elements of *diversity,* the broader term. More definitions of multicultural education now also stress the need to foster worldwide cultural pluralism (Banks, 1994; Bennett, 1995). This is because the core values of both global and multicultural perspectives include respect for human dignity for all people, acceptance and appreciation of cultural diversity, and a commitment to people in one's own community and the world community. Both have a vision of people living in greater harmony with one another and the Earth by combating racism, sexism, and other problems.

SMALL GROUP WORK	MULTICULTURAL EDUCATION
8.5	*You probably already have had a multicultural course. What role do you think you will play in teaching multicultural education?*

The Place of Global Education

Global education, unlike history, is usually not a separate course. Instead, it needs to be infused into the social studies curriculum. Almost all agree that U.S. students' knowledge of other countries, cultures, and languages needs to be improved, both for our nation's economic prosperity and for national security. Global education or *international education,* can occur in practically any social studies course. It can also be integrated with other courses such as science when the topic is population or biodiversity.

Global education is becoming more important because of **globalization,** the process of interaction and integration among people, companies, and governments of different nations. Globalization is a process driven by international trade and investment and is aided by information technology. Although globalization is not new, today globalization is rapidly transforming the whole planet. The volume of world trade has increased dramatically along with economic ties and political links. World trade includes cultural exports and imports such as movies, music, books, dress styles, and fads. There is more business and tourist travel, as well as millions of people migrating, than ever before. Telephone calls and transfers of money across borders have greatly increased. Globalization, however, is also deeply controversial, with resistance at both a popular level, as evidenced by demonstrations, and at the governmental level, sometimes through foreign policy. Some feel that the world is being "Americanized," whereas others believe that we as a nation are being "globalized" through more non-U.S. companies, stores, and products. Another big issue is globalization as a threat to the environment.

What are the most common courses in which global education could occur? The civics course is one candidate, as almost every "domestic" issue, such as interest rates in the United States, also has an impact beyond the nation. Recent world history and U.S. history also offer many possibilities. The study of ancient civilizations brings up topics such as conflict between nations, human rights, and the use of their environment. In addition, students normally need to see the historical content and global connections of problems such as immigration, agriculture and world hunger, energy, environmental issues, and the growth of the world's population. It is important to show different views on historical and contemporary events, as when European explorers encountered other cultures, or differing views on immigration.

Some teachers take global perspective on topics close to their students' lives, such as jobs, standard of living, and how their personal choices affect the lives of others around the world. Some of these topics have emphasized ways in which many of the products we use, such as food and clothing, have a global dimension. Other choices could include developments in their own community. What recent immigrants live in the community and why did they settle here? Were any of them refugees?

Teaching a global perspective offers many challenges. For example, how much of the harsh reality of world hunger should be emphasized? Or, how much of the world resources do the highly developed, industrialized nations such as the United States consume? How can students overcome feelings of despair or guilt? Feeling guilty without taking action is usually not productive. If they are merely made aware of problems, students may become pessimistic about finding any solutions for tough problems. But a personal local response can lead to empowerment through various levels of citizenship action. This could be on the individual level (recyling) or on a group level (joining an organization at the local, state, national, or international level).

To solve problems and create a more humane nation and world means taking action. In some schools, the focus has been on hunger, child labor, children's rights, war, refugees, and the like. Action can be as simple as sending an e-mail to a political leader, or students can "think globally, act locally."

A great wealth of resources is now available on the Internet. Besides the more traditional and popular use of international guests in the classroom, it is now possible for students to interact with others throughout the world through e-mail and other forms of communication. Multiple web sites on almost any global topic are available, ranging from the United Nations to Amnesty International and the Universal Human Rights. Teaching Tolerance (www.teachingtolerance.org) offers links to hundreds of organizations working against hate and intolerance. Looking at what other nations' newspapers (translated into English) think about certain issues can be valuable. But students do need to learn to evaluate data from the web sites because most groups are advocating their own policies.

SMALL GROUP WORK	**GLOBALIZATION**
8.6	*Globalization is a complex and controversial topic. Would you as a teacher address any globalization issues such as cultural exports and imports? Why or why not? In what units or lesson plans will globalization be emphasized? How should students be prepared to live in a world with increasing globalization?*

Stages in Teacher Development

Here again teachers differ on how much emphasis they give to global education or teaching a global perspective. The different viewpoints of teachers are also similar to how teachers view and implement multicultural education. Experts in the field of multicultural education and global education believe that teachers and students are at various developmental stages with regard to both global and multicultural awareness (Figure 8.3). The first stage is self-identification—who you are, your gender, language, social class, racial and ethnic identity—then moving out to national and global identity.

Because they are in different stages of self-identity and have diverse perspectives on global education and multicultural education, some teachers are only ready to teach the contributions of different groups and their holidays, heroines, and heros. Others are ready to explore tough global issues such as peacekeeping in troubled lands. Some teachers stress the importance of multicultural education as a struggle against institutional racism, going beyond an appreciation of diversity (Banks, 1996; Gay, 2000; Sleeter, 2001). Social studies teachers may be categorized as traditionalists, straddlers, or multiculturalists (Danker, 2001). Traditionalists see themselves as transmitters of the dominant culture. Straddlers define themselves as transmitters of the dominant culture, but they are open to change to improve teaching. Multiculturalists see themselves as agents of change. However, some teachers may not be very aware of the perspectives of global and multicultural education or may be unsure how to proceed with a topic that has both knowledge and strong value factors. It is helpful for teachers to broaden their understanding of other cultures, especially about their students' cultural backgrounds.

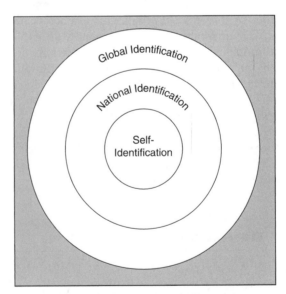

FIGURE 8.3 Developmental Stages of Identification

SMALL GROUP WORK	**STEREOTYPING**
8.7	*Should students be taught about stereotyping and other related biases that have negative effects on racial/ethnic, sexist, and anti-gay/lesbian relations? Or does bringing up the topic merely reinforce stereotypes?*

LARGE CLASS DISCUSSION	**CONTROVERSIAL ISSUE**
	What is the proper balance between nationalism and global education? Multicultural education and unity?

■ SUMMARY

Civic education is an important goal for both social studies teachers and the whole school. *The Civic Mission of Schools* listed six promising approaches to civic education. Yet the NAEP 1988 civics report card indicated that about one-third of all students lacked a basic knowledge of our government. Many ways to improve civic education in the classroom are available. Local government and service learning or community service were examined for their possible contributions to civic learning. Last, global and multicultural perspectives were considered in viewing citizenship.

■ REFERENCES ■

Asher, N., & Crocco, M. S. (2001). (En)gendering multicultural identities and representations in education. *Theory & Research in Social Education, 29*(1), 129–151.

Baldi, S., Perie, M., Skidmore, D., & Greenberg, E. (2001). *What democracy means to ninth graders: U.S. results from the International IEA Civic Education Study* (NCES Report 2001–096). Washington, DC: U.S. Department of Education, National Center for Education Statistics.

Banks, J. (1994). *Multiethnic education: Theory and practice.* Boston: Allyn and Bacon.

Banks, J. (Ed.). (1996). *Multicultural education, transformative knowledge and action: Historical and contemporary perspectives.* New York: Teachers College Press.

Bennett, C. I. (1995). *Comprehensive multicultural education: Theory and practice* (3rd ed.). Boston: Allyn and Bacon.

Bennett, C. I. (2001). Genres of research in multicultural education. *Review of Educational Research, 71,* 171–217.

Branson, M. S. (200l, March). *Content that counts: Educating for informed, effective, and responsible citizenship*. Paper presented at the Annual Meeting of the California Council for the Social Studies, Oakland.

Carnegie Corp. & CIRCLE. (2003). *The civic mission of schools*. New York: Carnegie Corporation of New York & CIRCLE/College Park, MD: The Center for Information and Research on Civic Learning and Engagement, the University of Maryland.

Center for Civic Education. (1994). *The national standards for civics and government*. Calabasa, CA: Author.

Danker, A. C. (2001). Keepers of tradition, agents of change: Social studies teachers and multicultural education. *The International Social Studies Forum, 1,* 45–62.

Gay, G. (1997). The relationship between multicultural and democratic education. *The Social Studies, 88*(1), 5–10.

Gay, G. (2000). *Culturally responsive teaching: Theory, research and practice*. New York: Teachers College Press.

Gross, R. E., & Dynneson, T. L. (Eds). (1991). *Social science perspectives on citizenship education*. New York: Teachers College Press.

Hahn, C. L. (1996). Research on issues-centered social studies. In R. W. Evans & D. W. Saxe (Eds.), *Handbook on teaching social issues*. Bulletin #93. Washington, DC: National Council for the Social Studies.

Hahn, C. L., & Torney-Purta, J. (1999). The IEA civic education project: National and international perspectives. *Social Education, 63*(7), 425–431.

Hess, D. (2000). Developing strong voters through democratic deliberation. *Social Education, 64*(5), 293–296.

Kaltsounis, T. (1997). Multicultural education and citizenship education at a crossroads: Searching for common ground. *The Social Studies, 88*(1), 18–22.

Leming, J. S. (1998). Some critical thoughts about the teaching of critical thinking. *The Social Studies, 89*(2), 61–66.

Merryfield, M. M., & Remy, R. C. (Eds.). (1995). *Teaching about international conflict and peace*. Albany: State University of New York Press.

Merryfield, M. M., & White, C. W. (1996). Issues-centered global education. In R. W. Evans & D. W. Saxe (Eds), *Handbook on teaching social issues: Theory and practice* (pp. 177–187). Washington, DC: National Council for the Social Studies.

National Assessment of Educational Progress. (1999). *NAEP 1998 civics report card for the nation*. Washington, DC: U.S. Department of Education, National Center for Education Statistics. NCES 2000–457.

Newmann, F. M. (with D. W. Oliver). (1970). *Clarifying public controversy: An approach to teaching social studies*. Boston: Little, Brown.

Newmann, F. M. (1989). Reflective civic participation. *Social Education, 53*(6), 357–366.

Newmann, F. M. (Ed.). (1992). *Student engagement and achievement in American secondary schools*. New York: Teachers College Press.

Niemi, R., & Chapman, C. (1998). *The civic development of 9th through 12th grade students in the United States, 1996* (NCES Report 1999–31). Washington, DC: U.S. Department of Education, National Center for Education Statistics.

Niemi, R., & Junn, J. (1998). *Civic education: What makes students learn*. New Haven, CT: Yale University Press.

Oliver, D. W., & Shaver, J. P. (1966). *Teaching public issues in the high school*. Boston: Houghton Mifflin.

Parker, W. C. (1997). Navigating the unity/diversity tension in education for democracy. *The Social Studies, 88*(1), 12–17.

Shaver, J. (1985). Commitment to values and the study of social problems in citizenship education. *Social Education, 49,* 194–197.

Sleeter, C. (2001). *Culture, difference, and power*. New York: Teachers College Press.

Torney-Purta, J., Lehmann, R., Oswald, H., & Schulz, W. (2001). *Citzenship and education in twenty-eight countries: Civic knowledge and engagement at age fourteen*. Amsterdam: IEA Secretariat.

Van Sledright, B. A., & Grant, S. G. (1991). Surviving its own rhetoric: Building a conversational community within the social studies. *Theory and Research in Social Education, 19,* 283–305.

Wade, R. C., & Saxe, D. W. (1996). Community service-learning in the social studies: Historical roots, empirical evidence, critical issues. *Theory and Research in Social Education, 24*(4), 331–359.

Westheimer, J., & Kahne, J. (2002). *Educating the "good" citizen: The politics of school-based civic education programs*. Paper presented at the Annual Meeting of the American Political Science Association, Boston.

Yair, G. (2000). Educational battlefields in America: The tug-of-war over students' engagement with instruction. *Sociology of Education, 73*(4), 247–269.

■ WEB SITES ■

General Civics Education Web Sites
American Forum for Global Education
www.globaled.org
Organization promoting global education.

The American Promise
www.americanpromise.com
Free teacher's guide plus newsletter.

Center for Civic Education
www.civiced.org
Free newsletter, standards, and curriculum materials.

Close Up Foundation
www.closeup.org
Curriculum materials and other activities such as field trips to Washington, D.C., for a "close up" experience in the governmental process.

Constitutional Rights Foundation
www.crf-usa.org
Free newsletter, and curriculum materials.

Global Education Web Sites
Center for Teaching International Relations (CTIR)
www.du.edu/ctir/
Materials to increase global awareness.

ISN International Relations and Security Networks
www.isn.ethz.ch
Information service in the fields of international relations and security.

Population Reference Bureau
www.prb.org
Information on U.S. and international population trends.

The United Nations Cyberschoolbus
www.un.org/cyberschoolbus
Promotes education on international issues and the UN. Curriculum materials for all grade levels.

United States Information Agency (USIA)
http://usinfo.state.gov/
Explains U.S. foreign policy by the State Department.

United States Institute of Peace
www.usip.org
Nonpartisan federal institution to promote peaceful resolution of international conflict.

World Resources Institute
www.wri.org/
Environmental materials and other resources.

Government Web Sites
GovSpot
www.govspot.com
A collection of top government and civic resources; simplifies the search for the best government web sites and documents.

U.S. House of Representatives
www.house.gov

U.S. Senate
www.senate.gov

U.S. Congress
http://thomas.loc.gov

CongressLink
www.congresslink.org
Lesson plans using Bloom's taxonomy, information.

Current Events
ABC News
www.abcnews.go.com

Newsweek
http://school.newsweek.com/

New York Times Learning Network
www.nytimes.com/learning
Daily lesson plans for grades 3–12; access to top news events.

USA Today
www.usatoday.com

US News & World Report
www.usnews.com/usnews/home.htm

Chapter 9

Technology and Professional Growth

In this chapter, we look at how technology can change what happens in social studies classrooms, and then consider the need for professional growth for all social studies teachers. Topics covered include:

- Technology Issues and Challenges
- Student Computer Standards/Media Literacy
- The Computer as a Productivity Tool: Word Processing
- Using the Internet: E-Mail and the World Wide Web
- Locating and Evaluating Resources
- Other Uses of Computers
- Professional Growth

■ TECHNOLOGY ISSUES AND CHALLENGES

Support for Technology

When we speak of technology in education, the term is now associated with the use of computers. **Technology** is a euphemism for computers. On the other hand, technology broadly considered refers to the many technologies used in the classroom such as television, VCRs, overhead projectors, and CD players, all of which should be used as creatively as possible. However, in this discussion, we use the definition of **computer technology** when referring to computers and access to the Internet.

Today most students have positive attitudes toward technology. A majority of children (four-fifths) have access to the Internet at home. Teenagers use cell phones, watch videos, and use the Internet for e-mail and instant messaging (See Sample Classroom Episode), and some write blogs. Young people may use digital cameras and a variety of software. Nevertheless, there is still a "digital divide," with some students lacking access to computers and the Internet. In addition, "failing" schools have more teachers classified as technology novices (25 percent) versus 18 percent of

SAMPLE CLASSROOM EPISODE

BAN INSTANT MESSAGING IN THE CLASSROOM?

The Lincoln High School faculty is debating the value of instant messaging during classroom time. Students are using laptop computers or handheld devices in more classes. Those against instant messaging believe that teenagers will chat at every opportunity they can get. According to this argument, students' highest interest is in their own personal social world of who is going out with whom and what everyone is going to do Friday night. The temptation to chat is just too high for many students. The students know that the teacher cannot monitor what each and every student is doing all of the time. Cheating on tests is also facilitated by instant messaging.

On the other side, teachers in favor of instant messaging believe it can encourage sharing of information on group projects and that students can help one another with assignments. Shy students feel more comfortable asking questions of the teacher through instant messaging, posing questions they would not ask in front of the class. By these questions, teachers can recognize students' strengths and weaknesses and guide them. Instant messaging can motivate more students, and it is the wave of the future.

Should instant messaging be banned in the classroom? Or is it a good communication tool?

---

teachers in all schools. This means that these teachers in failing schools are less likely to use technology.

Unfortunately, technology has a disappointing record in schools. Perhaps expectations for computer use in schools were unrealistic compared to the enormous impact that computers made on business and industry. Too often, teachers simply applied technology to existing ways of teaching and learning, with marginal results. The research in computer learning also was not as helpful as desired. Initially, education research focused on the question, Is the technology method better than a nontechnology-based one? The issue of how technology could improve or enhance existing methods was neglected. By itself, technology cannot improve learning. It has to be combined with curriculum and instructional strategies.

However, data regarding the benefits of computer technology for academic achievement are conflicting. Some studies report a positive relationship between the use of education technology and student achievement (Mann, Shakeshaft, Becker, & Kottkamp, 1999). Wenglinsky (1998) examined NAEP data on mathematics and found that academic achievement using educational technology was negligible for fourth graders but substantial for eighth graders. When used properly, computers can serve as important tools for improving student achievement in mathematics and enhancing the overall learning environment of the school. Others report marginal to negligible effects of technology on achievement (Becker, 1990; Clark, 1994). Very little research in the social studies has examined whether technology benefits student learning in K–12 levels.

Critics see technology as devouring school budgets. Some teachers would rather spend the money on other resources, such as library books. But computer technology is not a mere fad in the schools. It is here to stay and hopefully will become more user-friendly and therefore more widely used in social studies classes. The success of technology will be its integration into effective lesson plans. Such an approach can foster more student-centered learning, possibilities for individualizing student assignments, and increased emphasis on independent student work. Now the focus is on integration of technology into the curriculum or exploiting the advantages of technology for learning.

Handheld Computers and Tablet PCs

Wireless technology is getting more attention. Note-taking, answering questions, calculating, graphing data, and viewing are a few of the applications of **handheld computers** or **personal digital assistants (PDAs)**. For example, using PDAs students can locate consumer debt or the unemployment rate to examine data in their local area. On the whole, however, social studies classes so far have not used handheld computers extensively, primarily because they have not frequently used database or spreadsheet software to access or input data to be analyzed. PDAs are used more in social studies classrooms to send e-mail or search the Web.

Tablet PCs can be especially useful for teachers. Using a stylus on a screen, a teacher can write directly on documents, PowerPoint presentations, and student work. With the tablet and electronic access, the teacher can circle errors and offer suggestions. After marking a document for one class, the teacher can return to the original material without erasing. This is convenient if the teacher wants to use the document for more than one class. Currently, however, tablet PCs are more expensive than laptop computers, and some of the screens can be difficult to see under certain light.

Problems with Using Computers and the Internet in the Schools

Cyber security issues have been receiving more attention. Although computers have the potential to improve teaching and learning, they also can cause distraction and disruption. Computer viruses coming in over the Internet have been a major concern. Even more serious is **malware.** Malware is software that can spy on any data or use of computers and report the observations to outside parties. Malware slows down computer usage and can obstruct their instructional use. Furthermore, a teacher or a student can unknowingly introduce havoc into the entire school's or even the whole district's computer network by using unauthorized software or equipment or by visiting unauthorized Internet sites. Much more awareness by all users in the school is necessary to reduce the effect of viruses and malware.

Staff Development and Credential Requirements

Another problem is that staff development for teachers in computer technology has always lagged behind the acquisition of computer systems in the schools. Obtaining hardware has been the first priority of the schools. But unless teachers feel comfortable using computer technology, it will gather dust in the classroom. The first step for usage in the classroom is for the teacher to be familiar, comfortable, and proficient with the computer in his or her own home. For example, unless you are using e-mail at home, you are not likely to use it in your classroom. Teachers typically master steps such as finding information on the Internet first at home before they try to access the Internet in the classroom. Teachers have had to try using different search engines themselves before sending students to find information.

Typically there are a few teachers—about 5 percent (Cuban, 2001)—who are enthusiastic and heavy users of computers in their classroom, *heavy user* defined as use at least one or more times a week. Through the title of one of his articles, "Computers Meet Classroom: Classroom Wins," Cuban describes the difficulties of changing the traditional classroom. Teachers also vary on the number of hours of technology training they have received; a higher number of hours is related to increased classroom use. The different levels of teacher skills in using computer technology make it more difficult to design opportunities for teachers to learn to use computer technology in their classrooms. Unfortunately, the training or workshops often do not have a follow-up to critique problems or report the good experiences that supported learning opportunities.

More states now have technology requirements for teacher certification. You, with your computer courses during your credential program, may well be ahead in computer skills, confidence, and a favorable attitude toward computers of many experienced teachers. Yet it takes time to implement lessons using a computer (See Sample Classroom Episode). But these courses will not be sufficient for the entirety of your teaching career, because technology changes. You, too, will need additional workshops and rich experiences in order to use technology effectively in the classroom. Virtual

SAMPLE CLASSROOM EPISODE

A COMPUTER-USING TEACHER?

Olivia, a novice teacher, wonders if she should politely challenge her administrator for preliminarily marking her down for not being "a computer-using teacher." True, the administrator has never seen any of Olivia's students or Olivia herself using computers when the administrator has visited Olivia's classroom. But that ignores the many student handouts Olivia generates every week using a computer. As a new teacher, Olivia is constantly spending time on preparation. She often uses the computer to find new lesson plans and ideas. In addition, she uses a computer to record her student grades as well as to create tests and quizzes. Olivia is also using e-mail for professional purposes—notes to other teachers in her school and to students' parents. Does being a computer-using teacher mean that computer use has to be evident during the class period? Doesn't out-of-class time count too?

From this description, do you think that Olivia is a computer-using teacher? Does the label only apply when students use computers in the classroom and create products with computers, or when the teacher explicitly uses computers for instruction?

learning, wireless networking, collaboration tools, video, digital handheld devices, optical networking, and videoconferencing all offer promise for innovative teaching if one learns how to use them. Promising is NetOp School (Cross Tec Corporation), through which teachers can control the display on each student's screen from one desktop location. Teachers can then lead students through a desktop demonstration (e.g., how to graph economic data), observe the screen activity, or assist students individually from their own computer as well as send files to all students.

SMALL GROUP WORK	**IS TECHNOLOGY BEING USED?**
9.1	*Think about the last school you visited or the one to which you are presently assigned. How much and what type of technology is being used by social studies teachers? What factors appear to be contributing to usage? Nonusage?*

Even with exposure to new hardware and software, busy teachers averaging a forty-seven-hour work week with preparation and grading feel they lack the time to design lesson plans that incorporate computer technology into their teaching. It may take hours to preview web sites and to locate photos. It also takes time to attend computer courses and workshops to upgrade skills. In addition, there may be no technical support to help teachers, a real barrier to computer use. Too frequently teachers run into maintenance problems and get "stuck" without having any assistance available. A technology coordinator is often not easily available. This is frustrating and discouraging. All teachers need to have an alternative lesson plan for when unreliable computer(s) are not working. This sound piece of advice also holds true if using a video or any other piece of equipment that may malfunction.

We should also remember that how computer technology is used in each classroom is unique. It is not really computer technology itself that makes a difference but *how it is used*. Its implementation depends on a teacher's choice of methods and students' backgrounds, particularly on the confidence with computers that an increasing number of students have. On the other hand, this points out that those fewer students without home computer experiences require far more attention to help them develop computer literacy.

Gender Differences and Home Usage

Of concern is the fact that middle and high school males express greater confidence than females in using computers, even perceiving computers as a male domain (Young, 2000). Currently, girls are just as likely as boys to use computers at school and at home. However, computer camps and after-school computer clubs attract more males. When it comes to formal knowledge, boys have a big advantage. In the Advanced Placement exam for computer science in 2002, 86 percent of the students who took the exam were male. On average, males scored higher than females on the test. These data indicate that women are less likely to have careers in computer science and related science/engineering fields.

How can mentoring help students
with technology?

Student home computer usage statistics have shown that most school-age students, regardless of gender, use their computers primarily for recreational activities,
including gaming, chatting on the Internet, and general "surfing." The amount of
time spent on computers is not as important as how it is spent. Students with home
access to a computer do feel more confident about computers. They have mastered
skills such as how to open and close programs and files. But they often cannot
demonstrate the ability to carry out a computer-related task in school without direct
instruction or supervision. They raise their hands to ask questions of the teacher
rather than attempt to use available help menus.

Often students just tinker with software in a seemingly disinterested way, with
little response to feedback from the computer. Parent roles appear to be important
here because they can set a positive example for their children—as when children
see computer use being a work-related task. If parents use the computer only for
games, it is no surprise when their children use computers in the same way. Furthermore, how students interpret the value of the content and skills associated with
computer technology also depends on their parents, community, and educational
experiences.

Enhancing Technology in the Curriculum

Millions of dollars are spent each year on computer technology in the schools. In fact, it is estimated that approximately $80 billion has been invested in the last decade to bring Internet access to every school and almost every classroom. But computer technology does not benefit anyone unless it is used. At the same time, technology should not be used just because it is there. Technology also has to be used appropriately. This means that lesson and unit planning should focus *first* on content and strategies. Then look for ways that technology can improve the lesson. Let us examine some common activities in social studies to see how using technology might benefit students.

Teachers

- **Teacher Lecture.** Use computer presentation programs (such as PowerPoint) and videoclips. Computer presentations are easier for students to follow and to take notes on. Videoclips can add visual and auditory components to a lecture that aid students with different learning styles. The disadvantage is the teacher time needed to make PowerPoint presentations and to locate videoclips. In addition, some teachers have reported that turning off the lights for PowerPoint presentations encourages napping and other inattentive behavior in their students.

- **Illustrate Concepts.** Use scanners to incorporate illustrations of concepts found in print. Textbooks other than the one students in your class are using are a good source. Use suggested activities available from the web sites of textbook publishers such as Glencoe, Harcourt, and Macmillan/McGraw-Hill. Visual representation will appeal to the different learning styles of students. Students can also use scanners to present a wide variety of printed material. Use word processing to enlarge print to help ELLs and other students with learning or physical disabilities.

- **Manager.** Collect and interpret assessment data to meet individual needs.

Student Experiences

- **Timelines.** Use *Timeliner* or other software to create timelines. They are easy to use and help to reinforce dates and information in history.

- **Videotape.** Presentations, skits, debates, and projects can be videotaped for students to evaluate their performance and to share later with parents or others. These presentations could be shared on the Internet with the permission of the students.

- **Student Research.** Students use online sources for up-to-date information. Use CD-ROM encyclopedias as well as e-mail to primary sources. Notes can be copied and pasted into a rough draft.

- **Student Writing.** Use word processing as well as spelling and grammar checkers. Add illustrations or graphics to help clarify content.

What skills are needed to do a successful multimedia presentation?

Benefits and Costs

Teachers always need to ask not only what are the potential benefits of computer technology but also what are the trade-offs. In particular, technology can help students with different learning styles and address the needs of ELLs. Computers could promote individualization and personal tutoring, formerly available only to a few students. Nevertheless, social studies teachers, on the whole, have been reluctant to move away from traditional methods to use computer technology (Berson, 1996; Ehman & Glenn, 1991; Martorella, 1997).

■ STUDENT COMPUTER STANDARDS/MEDIA LITERACY

Recommendations

As with social studies standards, many states have set up recommended technology standards for students to acquire by certain grade levels. The three main computer literacy standards can be summarized as follows:

1. Basic skills or operations
   Use word processing, use e-mail, and find pertinent reliable data and information. Also operate equipment such as a VCR, audiotape player, and the like.
2. Critical thinking skills
   Select and evaluate information resources.

3. Presentation skills

Use a variety of media and formats to communicate information and ideas effectively; prepare publications.

Some information literacy standards also emphasize social responsibility, practicing ethical behavior with regard to information. In other formats, technology standards may be organized into research, analysis, and communication. *National Educational Technology Standards (NETS) for Students* by the International Society for Technology in Education (www.iste.org) uses six broad categories: basic operations and concepts; social, ethical, and human issues; technology productivity tools; technology communication tools; technology research tools; and technology problem-solving and decision-making tools.

Notice that these computer literacy standards are not divorced from the core literacy standards. If you cannot read, you cannot effectively use the Internet, which is basically a reading and writing medium. Students using the Internet normally need at least a sixth-grade reading level to be able to comprehend the text material. Otherwise, they just look at the visuals. In addition, to find information and do research, critical thinking skills are needed. One can argue that rather than the Internet *fostering* critical thinking skills, users *require* such skills. In addition, motivation to use the Internet is important. Beyond reading ability there also has to be enough familiarity with social studies content and skills to find information. It is difficult to conduct or to understand a computer search if you do not understand the content and do not know how to find information. And, obviously, it helps to know how to type or use a keyboard.

These student computer literacy standards presume that the teacher has already mastered these basic computer literacy skills so they can be taught or reinforced in social studies classes. Early in each course, teachers should survey students to see who has a computer and Internet access at home. Then get a self-assessment from students as to how they view their own computer competencies. Some students may be more knowledgeable about computer technology than the teacher. These students are valuable resources for helping other students. These tech-savvy students can also help their teachers, because there can be a "digital disconnect" between these tech-competent students and their teachers.

Not all students have developed the recommended and appropriate computer literacy skills as outlined by school librarians and professional organizations. Student computer literacy may depend on how much these skills were taught in the previous grades or learned at home. In fact, more students use computers and the Internet outside the classroom than in the classroom, but home usage concentrates on recreational gaming, chatrooms, and general surfing, which may not translate into computer skills for the classroom.

■ THE COMPUTER AS A PRODUCTIVITY TOOL: WORD PROCESSING

The most frequent school use of computers by both teachers and students is for word processing. Teachers use word processing as they design their lesson plans, tests, letters, handouts, and charts. The convenience of word processing is beyond argument, as it helps personal productivity. In particular, teachers with ELLs may find that using a larger font can make it easier for their students to read English. Reading a teacher's handwriting, even the best handwriting, is always harder than reading uniform, printed text. It is especially important in typing to avoid errors in addresses for web sites and similar exact material. In addition to word processing, more teachers use software to keep track of students' grades.

Word processing is used in many of the assignments given to students—writing up the results of an Internet search, writing an editorial, writing a summary of what the small group agreed on, or writing a reaction to a learning experience. In addition, more homework and reports are handed in by students who have access to word processing and appreciate its convenience. This means that these students have some typing skills. Most teachers encourage the use of student word processing because it is easier to read and has fewer spelling and grammar errors. However, word processing makes it more difficult to prove that a given student actually did the work.

■ USING THE INTERNET: E-MAIL AND THE WORLD WIDE WEB

E-Mail: Teachers

After word processing, the second most frequent teacher and student use of computers is e-mail. The use of e-mail continues to grow by leaps and bounds among teachers. Chatrooms, listservs, and news groups for teachers are abundant and growing. **Videoconferences,** however, are typically used only for special occasions because of costs. Costs are expected to fall, and distant classrooms could communicate effectively through videoconferences. Moreover, in the future more professional development courses using a variety of technologies, including videoconferencing, will offer possibilities for continuous professional growth.

Using e-mail, teachers can ask for help in designing lesson plans or answering questions they may have. Many teachers find communicating with colleagues to be very supportive to their teaching. To a lesser degree, teachers also communicate with parents and students, as well as post homework/assignments. This aspect of e-mail will be a growing trend. Some teachers report that they face a daily deluge of e-mail from parents. There are both pros and cons of growing parent contact.

E-Mail for Students

For students, the whole world becomes available due to the ease of telecommunication with computers. KeyPals are available from all over the world (www.teaching.com/keypals). However, permission slips signed by parents are needed for these exchanges.

An advantage of e-mail is that it can allow students who do not enter class discussions to participate more, especially if the teacher gives an assigned number of e-mails for each student to post. As usual, students with higher verbal skills are probably more easily able to express themselves than those with more limited skills. But even the many students who do not like to write may find online communication more rewarding than the traditional social studies writing assignments.

In particular, computer technology can build and support **learning communities** beyond the classroom. Computer technology can be used to support collaborative learning activities, as when students from different schools report local data on an issue—the environment, drugs, violence, and the like. Thus, students can work in teams outside of their classroom and interact with more people and ideas. They can work together to combine into a new paper the different individual drafts on a topic and have online debates with other students. There is the potential for social and political action and an awareness of the local situation and the world outside with its many different perspectives (Cogan, Grossman, & Lei, 2000). Students can extract information from a huge number of sources.

Weblogs or **blogs** have generally been considered a personal online journal to which outside users can comment through their own postings. Most of the blogs posted on the Internet are individual blogs. Because of privacy concerns, most schools have been reluctant to encourage individual blogs by their students. However, classroom blogs have been used. For example, students read a controversial article. They then rotate or use a sign-up schedule to post their reactions to the article or to respond to other students' comments. Ideally, students can politely challenge one another to higher levels of thinking. Classroom blogs differ from electronic discussion groups (discussed later) in which the teacher uses prompts to encourage discussion.

World Wide Web: Primary Source Material

The availability of online primary sources has the potential to drastically change the teaching of history, the most common subject of the social studies (Chapter 6). The best history sources are generally maintained by government agencies (the Smithsonian, the Library of Congress, and the like), universities, historical associations, and museums. Notable historical web sites are the University of Virginia's *Valley of the Shadow,* the University of North Carolina's *Documenting the American South,* the *New Deal Network,* the *National Security Archive,* the *Oyez Project,* the *Avalon Project,* and the History Channel. Online sources can address the problem of underrepresentation of different groups. For example, textbooks, already thick with many pages, simply cannot cover with sufficient detail the history of the many diverse backgrounds of students in social studies classes. The material from the Internet can help provide balance with respect to perspectives on individuals, groups, issues, problems, and topics, as well as material on ordinary people and everyday life.

Teachers often identify the primary sources themselves, evaluate the material, and then download the documents that are useful. Then they ask the students to evaluate the primary source, analyze the material from multiple perspectives, and compare how their interpretation meshes with other documents and their textbook. In other cases, teachers bookmark the web site. To keep students on task, teachers ask them to submit a brief summary of their work at the end of the class.

You are aware of the problem that limited reading skills present for students using primary sources. Older source documents with their archaic language may create additional hurdles for students. To avoid this, many teachers extract a few sentences or paragraphs for students to read, thus adapting the material to their classroom (Chapter 6). Using art, photographs, and the increasing number of videos on the Internet may help mitigate the reading problem.

More common than using primary sources is having students in social studies classes use searches to find information. This presumes that students know how to use various search engines. Some social studies teachers do not ask their students to search for web sites during class time. They are concerned that students may run into web sites that sound all right but that feature pornography or hate groups, as well as encounter frustrating, fruitless searches. In light of these concerns to protect their children, most parents support the use of blocking software to control access to certain web sites. However, no blocking system is completely secure.

Evaluating Web Sites

Too often too many students have blind faith in the information they find on the Internet. Web sites must always be evaluated for their purpose or aim, what individuals or groups develop or maintain them, how current they are, and whether they are suitable and appropriate for your class. This includes looking at their reliability and accuracy. What is the authoritativeness of the web site? You can have more confidence in an article from the *New York Times* than in one from an unknown author or institution. Information from commercial sites or special interest groups may need especially careful scrutiny as well as a look at how much agreement there is with authoritative resources.

Here are five criteria that can be used for evaluating web sites:

- Authority
- Accuracy
- Objectivity
- Currency
- Coverage

Another alternative is to ask students to evaluate the web site by filling out a form that asks about accuracy and what lifestyles, values, and points of view are represented, and to save the specific pages related to their topic. In addition, students could be asked what is missing from the web site.

However, compared to elementary teachers, secondary school teachers are more likely to assign computer projects **outside** of the classroom. They presume that students already know the different search engines (which give different results) and know how to identify and evaluate appropriate resources. A computer search may be for an individual or group project (Chapters 3 and 4).

The Librarians' Index to the Internet (www.lii.org) is a helpful site. This subject directory contains over 10,000 Internet resources, including the major categories of people and government. Before the Librarians' Index lists a site, staff librarians review it at least twice. Also useful is Library Spot (www.libraryspot.com), which offers links to reference materials such as encyclopedias, dictionaries, periodicals, and quotations. To do a better search, teach students to start with a narrow focus and to use the special features of search engines such as Google. If possible, use an exact phrase such as "Manifest

Destiny" rather than "the westward movement." Or try "Manifest Destiny *and* Texas." Otherwise, students may be overwhelmed by the vast amount of information.

SMALL GROUP WORK	WILL YOUR STUDENTS USE INTERNET SEARCHES?
9.2	*What are three projects that you think would be worthwhile for middle and high school students to research using the Internet?*

■ LOCATING AND EVALUATING RESOURCES

Using Social Studies Software

As they design their lesson plans, teachers can consider using social studies software. This presumes that the teacher has access to such software. The best source of worthwhile social studies software is the annual *Educational Software Preview Guide* published by the International Society for Technology in Education (iste) at the University of Oregon (www.iste.org). Their guide is organized into such categories as social studies, multicultural, problem solving/logic, and reference library. It is invaluable for learning what software has been favorably reviewed at sites by computer-using educators. Useful social studies software programs include CD-ROMs, simulations (creating a world on the screen where realistic conditions apply), and problem-solving programs as well as references.

CD-ROMs

CD-ROMs for the social studies can be classified into the following three categories: reference, simulation, and documentary-style.

Reference

In social studies classrooms, **reference** materials are probably the most common type of software because librarians and schools purchase the relatively less expensive CD-ROM encyclopedias, atlases, and current event resources rather than traditional printed reference books. The multimedia encyclopedias are especially valuable, with their visuals, a relatively easy search-by-keyword feature, and support materials for the teacher. However, because software publishers do not want the viewer to see pages and pages of "dull" text, electronic encyclopedias, dictionaries, and thesauri usually contain less material on a given subject or word than the traditional printed format.

Often the electronic reference materials are a good starting point for research projects or a quick way to find out simple facts. There are still advantages to also using the traditional printed reference materials found on the shelves of the library, and students need to be aware of this benefit. Nevertheless, the less expensive CD-ROMs do allow an individual classroom and home users to have reference material that normally would be found only in the library.

Simulations

The classic social studies simulation is *The Oregon Trail* (Learning Company) with its many modifications of different U.S. pioneer trails as well as many trails in other nations or regions (*Mayaquest*, Learning Company). Also popular are the more than one dozen *Decisions, Decisions* simulations (Tom Snyder Productions, www.teachsp.com), where in a simulation format students build a new nation or run for president of the United States using problem-solving skills. These CD-ROM simulations focus on making decisions, which makes them very attractive.

Barriers to the use of social studies software such as simulations appear to be the initial cost of the software and the time needed for the teacher to become familiar with using the software before students can use it effectively. First the teacher can teach one or a few students to use the software, and these students in turn teach other members of the class to use the software successfully. Remember the necessity of debriefing after a simulation. After a few students have used the simulation, arrange them into a group to debrief their experience. Whole class simulations, such as students being legislators, often can be more powerful than having each student work individually on a simulation.

Documentary-Style CD-ROMs

These CD-ROMs use videoclips, narrated slides, maps, and other features and are similar to watching a filmed documentary. An example is *FDR: A Legend in His Own Time* (Forest Technologies), in which students explore the life and leadership of Franklin Delano Roosevelt, tour his family homes, watch footage, and hear some of his speeches. These CD-ROMs and other software are expensive for publishers to produce. For this reason, publishers often want a general audience to buy the products, especially those in the historical documentary-style format. The result is that often the content on famous individuals (including political, military, science, business, and cultural leaders) and movements (such as the women's movement or the civil rights movement in the United States) may be too general, with a focus on home entertainment and not enough challenge for classroom use. In some cases, only part of the CD-ROM may be of educational value. Often a presentation in front of the class showing a portion of the CD-ROM is appropriate. Some CD-ROMs concentrate on primary sources.

Ideally the software enables students to think about content in ways they would otherwise find difficult, and the content exploits the special capabilities of the software such as word search and hypertext. In all cases, preview the software before purchasing it. Some county offices provide this opportunity. Previewing at vendors' booths is also available at social studies conferences.

■ OTHER USES OF COMPUTERS

Electronic Discussion Groups and Distance Learning

Electronic discussions groups (EDGs) or threaded discussion groups have been shown to be successful as a technique for extending classroom content and perhaps for discussing sensitive public issues (Merryfield, 2000). EDGs may also promote greater candor and cause readers to consider the merit of an idea instead of considering the status of the contributor. EDGs are not intended to replace face-to-face discussions, but they can be helpful for discussing a topic that requires more investigation than class time allows. An EDG often starts with an instructor's prompt to a reading or a topic, followed by asynchronous electronic discussions or posts by students.

Like e-mail, an advantage of electronic discussion groups is that some quiet students, often girls, who rarely talk in class may participate more. On the other hand, an electronic discussion group is not a guarantee of participation, because some students still will not write extensively or to the point. In electronic discussions, students may also make declarations of their opinions rather than respond to classmates' comments, especially when they disagree. Why get a classmate annoyed with you? (This behavior of avoiding controversy also applies to face-to-face classroom discussions.) Some students regard electronic discussion groups as extra homework that takes too much of their time outside class. Make sure that every student has access to a computer if the threaded discussion is homework. Threaded discussions are also more difficult for ELLs because the activity moves from listening to writing skills. Therefore, a combination of face-to-face discussions and threaded discussions makes sense for most classes.

Electronic discussion groups, along with **distance learning** and **online mentoring**, will probably become more popular as entire classes gain access to computers. Distance learning in the social studies may be used more for elective classes such as sociology or human geography, when there are not enough students to justify a class or the school does not have the staff available to teach such courses. Or students may want to get college credit for a U.S. history course. Schools may also use videos as a telecourse for distant learners.

For small high schools that are using online courses, students' and teachers' roles change. More responsibility now falls on students to learn the content and achieve objectives. Teachers in the online courses cannot spend as much time in teaching students how to learn. Additional support such as a help line is therefore crucial. An adequate technological infrastructure is also essential for success in an online course. But the rewards can be great because students can encounter content and curriculum they normally would not have the opportunity to learn.

Virtual High School, a collaborative of over 200 high schools, has more than 150 full semester courses in all areas of the curriculum. Many of these courses are Advanced Placement. In addition, the Virtual High School Consortium includes member schools in other countries and offers the opportunity to gain an international perspective as students are involved in online discussions with students around the world.

These presentations have ranged from studying certain monuments and historic sites in the local community to researching how the ancient Egyptians mummified their dead. In evaluating student presentations, emphasis should always be on the content presented. Having a rubric to emphasize the content is very important. Otherwise, there is a tendency in evaluation to focus on the graphics and sounds rather than the content. In addition, students should be able to understand the meaning of their project. Too often, the cut-and-paste operations featuring beautiful pictures and graphs from web sites substitute for student comprehension.

Electronic or Virtual Field Trips

High school teachers have generally been constrained in taking their students on field trips. Even with a block schedule and other teachers' permissions, it has been difficult and expensive to arrange for a bus or other means of transportation for students to visit and observe different places. However, electronic or virtual field trips to a museum, a historical site, or anywhere in the world can now be easily brought to the students. Students can learn about people, customs, sights, sounds, and lifestyles of a given place by joining teams of researchers exploring distant regions such as a rain forest or Antarctica. These electronic field trips can range from a tour of the White House (www.whitehouse.gov/history/whtour/) to world-class museums such as the Louvre (www.louvre.fr) as well as various parts of the world (Virtual Field Trips: www.ibiblio.org/cisco/trips.html).

To be successful in using electronic field trips, the teacher visits the web site(s) before assigning it to students. The teacher then can provide students with a purpose for viewing the web site(s). In addition, the teacher must specify how students are going to show what they have gained from the field trip. This could range from answering questions to producing a product such as a travel brochure or a presentation to the class on what they have found. The challenge is to provide questions that lead students to explore a site thoroughly, analyze the information, and show what they have learned.

WebQuests

A WebQuest is an inquiry-oriented activity in which most or all of the information for learners is drawn from the Internet. In this manner, students do not waste time finding information but can think at higher levels of learning. The focus is a question that, in order to be answered, needs analysis. Good WebQuests, like other controversial issues in the social studies, expose students to opposing viewpoints. WebQuests can be done individually or more often by teams using cooperative learning.

Bernie Dodge has been a leader in the development of WebQuests, and his web site lists the best of WebQuests by subject area and grade level (http//webquest .sdsu.edu). Within a given WebQuest, a variety of tasks or activities are usually focused around the question. Examples are "Nicaragua Quest," in which students engage in the politics, history, and culture of Nicaragua through role playing and discussion, or "Easter Island," in which students explore the history of Easter Island and see the interactions between culture and environment; then students explore the validity of using Easter Island as a model of the impact of human population/culture on the global environment.

WebQuests are useful because they have already done some of the teacher's work. However, before introducing a particular WebQuest, make sure that the URLs are current and available. Some of these WebQuests are several years old. In addition, some WebQuests are interesting but not directly related to the curriculum being studied. Nevertheless, they can be used for enrichment for students who are already competent in certain subject areas. Of course, teachers can design their own

WebQuests around controversial issues such as globalization and immigration. But again, first check to be sure that URLs are available. Otherwise, your good idea cannot be implemented.

■ PROFESSIONAL GROWTH

As we have seen, the use of technology involves integration into the curriculum. This requires constant learning and relearning. The use of technology illustrates the necessity for a teacher to continue to grow professionally and to keep up with this rapidly changing sector.

Professional growth is essential for teachers. The most important thing teachers can do to improve the quality of their instruction is to continually educate themselves. No teacher education credential program can do the whole job of teaching the knowledge and skills needed by a teacher, or pinpoint exactly where the new emphases in methods and materials will be.

In addition, more states are requiring beginning teachers (after two years) to demonstrate and document their effectiveness. This may include a portfolio, live observation, or a videotape of instruction. Beginning teachers and all teachers without life credentials also may have to document their professional growth for renewal of their credentials. This will be a continual process during their teaching careers. You will need to keep track of documents supporting your professional growth. Photos of class activities can often clarify your teaching skills to an outside audience.

Just as other professionals need to keep current in their field, one's own growth is central to teaching. Some commentators like the term *renewal and responsibility* to describe what teachers need to do (Goodlad, 1994). Try to become the best teacher you can. It is vital to be committed to continual learning and professional development. In addition, social studies teachers need to keep abreast of current issues and events. Read newspapers, magazines, and other sources about occurring events—from the local to the global. What is going on at the present time can be relevant to the teaching of your content.

What guidelines should be used to set up growth experiences to become a more effective teacher? The most useful professional development is closely aligned with the specific content and skills your students are expected to learn. Your own needs as a novice teacher may also order your priorities. The list of needs of novice teachers is long and varied: managing the classroom effectively, motivating students, providing for individual differences, assessing student work, generating new ideas for instruction, and locating and evaluating resources. These needs emphasize that it is important for all novice teachers—indeed, for all teachers—to hold high expectations for student success. Often teachers lower their expectations for students the longer they teach.

Professional growth can be categorized into three areas:

1. Continuously updating your knowledge of history and the social sciences
   - Learning new information and viewpoints of other cultures
   - Taking academic courses
   - Reading books and journals

- Joining a professional organization
- Attending workshops sponsored by the academic disciplines such as economic and geography organizations
- Traveling

2. Keeping up with the methods to improve student learning
    - Joining NCSS or similar organizations
    - Attending national, state, and local conferences on the teaching of social studies
    - Attending workshops and classes
    - Working with professional development centers
    - Checking areas of the humanities for possible integration

3. Locating resources such as historical narratives and primary sources, media such as videos, art, music, literature, and other materials for use in the social studies
    - Reviewing new textbooks and looking at social studies catalogs
    - Using county libraries and other sources
    - Using the Internet

If professional memberships are too costly, having your library or department subscribe to journals is an alternative.

Yet all these activities for professional growth must also fit in to what is happening at your particular school. Most likely it includes *collaborative* efforts and reflective practice with other teachers. This could include looking at students' work so that challenging curricular changes can take place. Consensus is needed and collaborative work is essential to improving the school. Working alone to effect changes is not as promising as a group or team effort.

However, some teachers find private journal writing helpful for stress reduction and gaining perspective. Venting feelings can be necessary. But effective teachers do more than just vent—they think about ways to improve student learning.

Long-Range and Short-Range Planning

Long-range and short-term plans are both necessary for a teacher to remain fresh, creative, and motivated. A long-range plan of more than a few years might be to travel abroad and in the United States to places that you teach about. Or you can work for National Board certification in Social Studies–History or a master's degree, policies encouraged by school district's salary schedules. National Board certification takes over hundreds of hours and has a 50 percent failure rate for first-time applicants. However, these elite teachers generally receive bonuses or higher salaries than those who do not succeed or do not apply. Other plans such as the American Board for Certification of Teacher Excellence are putting more emphasis on classroom results. The net result may be that the teaching profession will evolve in something more like law and medicine, with more emphasis on passing tough examinations.

A short-term goal might be to learn how to use one new piece of software every year, or attend a short summer or school-year institute, workshop, or conference in your state. Plan also to read in depth in one of the social sciences or history each year.

Part of your willingness to see teaching as a career in which you are constantly learning depends on your student population and your department culture. If your department and your school have a strong commitment to ensuring that all students learn, you are more likely to try new practices that can help all students reach high standards. However, if you are isolated and run into roadblocks, you are more prone to frustration and burnout. Being part of a professional learning community can pay off in big dividends for you and your students. Teacher reflection is especially important in realizing the need to change teacher practices.

Many teachers will be needed in the future, perhaps over two million, as teachers retire and others leave the profession. School budgets also influence how many new teachers are hired. There will be wide variations among the states; in a few states it is actually predicted that there will be a decline in the number of teachers. The fact that many new teachers are entering the profession highlights the need for all schools to provide resources for teachers' professional growth. Hopefully, school districts will work with teachers and offer opportunities for professional growth that will be on-going and current. Mentor programs assisting new teachers can be valuable. For unless teachers can reflect on and improve their practice, they may be overwhelmed as they encounter the many challenges teachers face. These teachers are then the most likely to leave the classroom; teacher retention is a serious problem. Many have felt "lost at sea" without adequate textbooks, teaching guides, and materials. Designing curriculum and planning daily lesson plans has eaten up hours of time. These novice teachers have felt frustrated at their school sites.

LARGE CLASS DISCUSSION	**CONTROVERSIAL ISSUE**

Novice teachers often are overwhelmed by the demands of designing and planning daily lessons. Their physical and psychological health has been impaired. Why do you think this occurs? How does this affect the introduction of technology into classrooms?

■ SUMMARY

Computer technology has the potential to improve student learning, although there are barriers to teachers' use of computer technology. Teachers have to be concerned about gender differences and socioeconomic equity issues involving the classroom use of computer technology. Currently, the most popular application for both teachers and students is word processing. Other popular applications for teachers are e-mail and keeping track of students' grades. High school social studies students also do computer searches for information. Applications such as multimedia presentations and virtual field trips are used less frequently. Travel, advanced study, conferencing, and wide reading that is closely aligned with the content and skills your students are expected to learn are critical for your professional growth. Become the best social studies teacher you can be. The students need you and the rewards are great.

■ REFERENCES ■

Becker, H. J. (1990). *Effects of computer use on mathematics achievement. Findings from a national field experiment in grades five to eight. Classes: Rationale, study design, and aggregate effect sizes* (Report No. 51). Baltimore: Center for Research on Elementary and Middle Schools.

Berson, M. J. (1996). Effectiveness of computer technology in social studies: A review of the literature. *Journal of Research on Computing in Education 28*(4), 486–499.

Clark, R. W. (1994). Media will never influence learning. *Educational Technology Research and Development, 42*(2), 21–29.

Cogan, J. J., Grossman, D., & Lei, M. (2000). Citizenship: The democratic imagination in a global context. *Social Education, 64*(1), 48–52.

Cuban, L. (2001). *Oversold and underused: Computers in the classroom.* Cambridge: Harvard University Press.

Ehman, L. H., & Glenn, A. D. (1991). Interactive technology in the social studies. In J. P. Shaver (Ed.), *Handbook of research on social studies teaching and learning* (pp. 513–522). New York: Macmillan.

Goodlad, J. I. (1994). *Educational renewal: Better teachers, better schools.* San Francisco: Jossey-Bass.

Mann, D., Shakeshaft, C., Becker, J., & Kottkamp, R. (1999). *West Virginia story: Achievement gains from a statewide comprehensive instructional technology program.* Santa Monica, CA: Milken Exchange on Education Technology.

Martorella, P. H. (1997). Technology and social studies—Or which way to the sleeping giant? *Theory and Research in Social Education, 25*(4), 511–514.

Merryfield, M. M. (2000). Using electronic technologies to promote equity and cultural diversity in social studies education. *Theory and Research in Social Education, 28*(4), 502–526.

Wenglinsky, H. (1998). *Does it compute? The relationship between educational technology and student achievement in mathematics* (Policy Information Report). Princeton: Educational Testing Service.

Young, B. J. (2000). Gender differences in student attitudes toward computers. *Journal of Research on Computing in Education, 33*(2), 204–213.

■ WEB SITES ■

Classwell (formerly Globalearn)
www.classwell.com
Expeditions to various places. Fee for teacher material.

National Board for Professional Teaching Standards
www.nbpts.org
Information on their certification.

PBS Teachersource
www.pbs.org/teachersource
Lesson plans based on PBS programs such as *The American Experience.*

■ JOURNALS ■

Learning & Leading with Technology. The International Society for Technology in Education, Eugene, OR.

Meridian: A Middle School Computer Technologies Journal. Online journal. State University, Raleigh, NC. www.ncsu.edu/meridian/.

Index

Photo Credits

DAT